MW01626156

PRAISE FOR MTV FAMOUS

"When I first met Pete he was opening for me at Nissan Pavillion in Virginia. I'm always interested and supportive of local music. I watched for two days as his band shot a music video, I had not seen anyone with his work ethic and passion for what he was doing in a long time. When the time came for me to change music directors I gave Pete a shot, and here we are 20 years later touring arenas and amphitheaters all over the world, recording hit songs and having a blast. His creativity, passion, and work ethic are just as they were 20 years ago and through it all he has become one of my very best friends."

~Bret Michaels, Rock Icon – Reality TV Star

"Pete's the real deal! I first met him in '91 when he was 18 and opening for my solo band, and he went on to be the musical director for Bret Michaels for 20 years and counting. I had a great time working with him in the studio, and he has certainly carried the rock and roll torch way up high!"

~Ace Frehley, co-founder and lead guitarist of *Kiss*

"Beyond being a great person and musician, Pete is also a passionate rock fan, something I can always relate to being one myself. I always look forward to swapping stories about our favorite groups whenever I get the chance to see him."

~Eddie Trunk, terrestrial and satellite radio DJ and podcast personality

"Pete Evick is a journeyman rocker who has helped keep some timeless music alive and kicking for decades. Bottom line? Pete ROCKS!"

~Dee Snider, lead singer of *Twisted Sister*

Pete Evick

with Steve Olivas

JRNYman Publishing
Nashville, Tennessee

Published by JRNYman Publishing, Nashville, TN

First Edition
Printed in the United States

Interior book design and layout by Darren Kirby
Cover layout by Darren Kirby
www.darrenkirby.com

Cover art by Christopher Carroll

Photo on back cover courtesy Pete Evick

Hardcover ISBN: 978-1-956577-07-5
Paperback ISBN: 978-1-956577-08-2
Ebook ISBN: 978-1-956577-06-8

TABLE OF CONTENTS

FOREWORD

The first time I met Pete Evick was, fittingly, backstage at a Poison show – Jones Beach, New York, 2003. We instantly hit it off. We're both from the Northeast. We both grew up in the suburbs. We were both raised on Kiss and Van Halen and FM radio and pyro-filled arena concerts and MTV. We both have an intense love for and ridiculous obsession with guitars. We've both played "Every Rose Has Its Thorn" onstage with Bret Michaels. I think I did it first... though he has done it approximately 10,000 times more.

That day at Jones Beach was early in Pete's time with Bret. And this was a Poison gig anyway, so he was off-duty, so to speak. He had just entered what guys like us – who came of age during the larger-than-life, spectacle era of hard rock – would have considered the big time, and he came off as humble, respectful and supremely grateful to be there.

Twenty years on, having traveled the world, written, recorded and produced hit songs, collaborated with some of the biggest names in rock, experienced his own MTV fame, and played god-only-knows how many shows year in and year out, he still comes off just as humble, respectful and supremely grateful to be where he is.

It's my belief that most people who know Pete – and Pete's a friendly guy, so a lot of people know Pete – would say the same. And since Pete's also a busy guy, we don't see each other too often in person. But when we do, it's like no time has passed. We still talk about music (mostly Van Halen, admittedly) and guitars. But also about life and careers and creating. However long we spend catching it up, it's never long enough. So that said, there's a lot I know about Pete, and also a lot I don't. But one of the main things I know is what is made abundantly clear in this book: He loves what he does, and he works his ass off in order to do it.

Sure, he plays with Bret, and Bret's a giant star. Some people might say that's a lucky break. And it is a break. But it's not luck. Pete put in his 10,000 hours. Played every dingy bar and club on the east coast. Got record deals and lost record deals. Experienced being a big fish in a small pond and a guppy in the ocean. (Kinda, sorta) auditioned for Poison (kinda, sorta) and lost the gig to Richie

Kotzen. As for where he ended up? It's where he probably could have never imagined he would be, but probably always knew he should be. Or, at the very least, believed that if he were given a shot at being there, he would absolutely kick the ever-loving shit out of the opportunity.

Is he a rock star? That depends on your definition of the phrase. He's certainly had plenty of rock star moments, and lived out plenty of rock-star dreams. But maybe more importantly, he's an honest-to-god working musician. Still grinding, still grateful. And throughout the good and the bad, the ugly and the beautiful, the triumphant and the tragic, he's always had a knack for extracting a life lesson out of the experience. To me, his generosity in sharing those lessons has always been one of the most special parts of our friendship (that, and letting me take the lead guitar on "Nothin' But a Good Time"). The beauty of this book is in his doing the same with you, the reader.

So that said, enjoy *MTV Famous*, but don't try this at home.

Actually, screw it. Try it. Just make sure, like Pete, you give it everything you've got.

—Richard Bienstock

PROLOGUE

"Let's you and me take a walk."

I didn't have to turn around. I knew the voice.

"Yeah, of course," I agreed.

On the outside, I was as cool as the crisp Spring-time air filling my lungs. On the inside, my anxiety revved into a cacophony of excited (*What does he want to talk about!!!*) and nervous (*What does he want to talk about???*) energy.

I stood and joined him as we strode around the hotel. We were near a busy street, so his voice was accompanied by the distant symphony of cars and trucks pushing up and down the boulevard.

"You doing okay, Pete?"

"Yeah man…I'm great."

I was able to match his stride as our walk got underway. I'm a bit shorter than him, but his stature in my mind makes him larger than life to me.

In my Pantheon of rock and roll demigods, there aren't many inductees. Eddie Van Halen has a special statue toward the front. Probably his own wing, too. Jon Bon Jovi has a spot. Sammy Hagar has a spot. Every guy who has ever played in KISS (well, almost every guy) is definitely in there. These guys are consummate "rock stars." They belong to the last great generation of true musical Superheroes. And they share their rareified air with the man who I've played guitar with for the past twenty years.

Bret Michaels.

I'd played in his band for about a year by this time, so I had outgrown any tendencies toward feeling giddy when we hung out. But he was still my boss, my mentor, and a man I looked up to when it came to gleaning advice or wisdom.

And now he said to me, "We need to talk."

I stuffed my hands in my pockets. It wasn't a cold evening, but I have spent my entire life trying to cover up for feeling awkward. I knew all the tricks.

"How is your family doing?"

"Umm…they're great, thanks."

Frankly, I was just happy to be here. Bret's solo career was entering its fourth year, and he had hired an entirely new backing band for each of the first three years. I was a part of that third group. The fact that I was re-hired for a *second* year was fantastic.

He drew a breath, "Listen, if we're really going to be a band, let's you and I go over some things—"

All of a sudden it clicked. My nervous energy transformed into elation.

Are we really "a band"?

That singular moment feels like the nexus of my adulthood.

We spent the next two or three hours wandering around the hotel grounds, chatting about everything from music to business to family to life. I felt like a young Skywalker in the presence of Master Yoda, but to the casual onlooker, we were just two dudes killing time before bus call.

And we had some time to kill. Being the conscientious person that I am, I always arrive well ahead of time when I have an important appointment. If you're on time, you're late in my book. Bret likes everyone to be in the night before; he leaves nothing to chance. So when bus call is at 10 o'clock on a Wednesday morning in Nashville, you arrive Tuesday night.

The things he told me that day addressed one of the main issues I had been struggling with as a musician: What separates the people who make it from the people who don't? I'd had a record deal well before the time I was hired into Bret's band. I had recorded. I had toured. I had worked my ass off to make sure every T was crossed and every I was dotted…but I didn't have gold records or a marquee name.

It was maddening, considering that lawyers, record execs, DJs, and everyone in the industry seemed to believe we had "IT".

Bret's talk with me unfolded like when you watch that television commercial for an allergy medication. I don't remember which medicine exactly. They all run together in my head. But it's the commercial where you think you're seeing everything clearly, and then a film gets peeled back (presumably from in front of your screen), and suddenly you see the contrast—you recognize how clear things are compared to how they used to be.

That's how I felt. Bret pulled the smoky film from my eyes—and what had been almost opaque was now pulsating in brilliant color. It changed my life, man.

He changed my life.

Reflecting back on that talk, I felt the inspiration to write this book. When I wrote my first book, *The Moments that Make Us*, I felt the need to share a simple concept with everyone. That our lives are shaped by a series of individual moments—significant peaks and valleys in the sine wave of our time on this planet. Much of what we do is mundane. But there are people, places, and events that strike like boulders hitting the placid lake of our existence.

Heck, most of our lives are completely non-memorable. I know mine is. Most everything I have experienced acts like little pebbles nudging me gently in one direction or another. But then there are the boulders, splashing down in ways that ripple throughout the rest of my life.

I am so very proud of *The Moments That Make Us*. But when it came out in 2015, it felt incomplete. Like, those moments of impact don't stop just because you hit the magic age of 18. Remembering my walk with Bret reminded me that those moments continue to happen throughout the lifespan.

Hence, this book.

I thought about whether to write stories from my adulthood or stories from my time in the music industry. And then it occurred to me: I cannot separate the two. In fact, as I sat down to catalog the stories, I noticed that most of the jarring moments—the triumphs and the tragedies— happened during my tenure as a working musician. Hell, the nexus of the storm seemed to congeal in February of 1998.

Most of the stories are great. They'll hold the attention of a room full of people. But I'm not gonna lie, some of these stories were tough to think about. There has been some pain along the way. I'm as emotional of a person as you'll ever meet, so panic and anxiety are constant companions. Inside my head, there is almost always a hurricane swirling. When there isn't, a cyclone takes its place.

Those moments, man—those singular grains of sand through the hourglass of life. Some are like the smell of freshly cut grass in June. They fill your lungs with satisfaction and send your spirit soaring. Some moments are like a withering tree in December. Cold and lifeless, they punctuate the despair that covers your internal landscape.

Through sharing some of the most impactful moments of my time in the music industry, I hope to cause you to reflect back on your own life—to organize and catalog some of those pivotal moments that you will never forget. Those flashbulb memories that are tied to so much punch, you will never forget any detail of the experience. I want you to think about the people, places, and events that pulled the layer of hazy film from in front of your eyes and made you the person you are today.

Later in this book, I'll finish telling you what Bret said to me that day in Nashville. In the meantime, I will walk you through some more of the watershed moments from my career. Within each story lies a lesson, a takeaway that has made me a better or more resilient person. The details of my stories will be different from your stories, but the concepts remain universal.

* * *

One final thought before we begin.

In this book, The Term "MTV famous" is used over and over again. First and foremost, I think it's funny—but it also explains a lot about the era I come from. For the purposes of this book, "MTV famous" is my way of saying that what I wanted wasn't the MONEY or the GLAMOUR. In fact, I wrote a song called "Big Rock Guitars," and one of the lyrics is:

I never did it for the wine the woman the money or fancy cars,
from the moment that I heard that sound I fell in love,
with those big rock guitars.

To me, "MTV famous" meant that I wrote or helped to write a song that resonated so much with people, that it was played on

MTV. What I wanted was to be part of something special, emotional, and powerful; I wanted to make people happy. I wanted to help make everyone's day better…just like MTV did for me. No matter where I was and no matter what I was doing, I knew that in the summer of 1984 (at 4pm) the "Panama" video was going to play and I had to be there to see it. Back then, they played new videos on a schedule that you could easily figure out and plan to be there. Although I don't know that it was ever a spoken rule, we just all figured it out.

Anyway, that's what "MTV famous" means in this book. I wanted to make someone feel the way I felt when I rushed home to see the "Mama Weer All Crazee Now" video, or the "Panama" video, or the "Wanted Dead or Alive" or "Fallen Angel" video.

After all, why else would anyone make such great music?

PART 1:

MY LIFE...PRE-BRET MICHAELS BAND

CHAPTER 1:
EVICKEAN GENESIS

I was born in 1972. When MTV launched on August 1, 1981, I was a mere 8 years old. Actually, my birthday is on August 10, so I was probably already telling people I was 9. But be that as it may, I had no awareness of the genesis of the video era in music.

Not that it didn't have a huge impact on me.

By the time I rolled into middle school and music had shoved its handprints into the wet cement of my developing brain, I was hooked on the pageantry, debauchery, and beauty of marrying music to mini-movies. The musicians I heard on the radio were tossed onto the television screen, performing for my entertainment. Mark Goodman, Alan Hunter, Martha Quinn, Nina Blackwood, and JJ Jackson became trusted friends.

I remember when Michael Jackson's "Thriller" video became a national spectacle. I remember naming off the singers in the "We are the World" video. I remember Saturday night concerts. I remember Music News, the moon-landing promo, and the MTV theme music.

I remember the labels at the beginning and end of every video. Through them, I learned the names of every song, the album they came off, and that I didn't give a shit about the record label the album was on.

I remember it all.

And I watched it all…in awe.

But here's the thing: MTV did something to my generation of budding musicians that was very subtle. It affected us in ways that were monumental and extraordinary (don't get me wrong), but it also planted a tiny seed that blossomed into a bigger problem for us down the road.

It changed how we defined "success."

Here's what I mean. Take John Cougar Mellencamp, for example. I have vivid memories of watching his early video for "Jack & Diane." By today's standards, it isn't anything spectacular; photos and 8mm clips spliced in with a shot of hands clapping in time with the music and John singing the lyrics. Technology was what it was back in 1982/83.

I always thought the song was good. Not my favorite Mellencamp song—and I'm a giant Mellencamp fan. However, I knew all the words. *Everyone* knew all the words. To this day, everyone knows all the words.

That song made a deep impact on the collective psyche of everyone glued to the television set, watching MTV in the early 80s. The single itself went to #1 and sold over a million copies. The album it was on, *American Fool*, went 5x platinum. John Cougar had two other videos, "Hurts So Good" and "Hand to Hold Onto" off that album in heavy rotation on MTV.

So, when I watched the "Jack & Diane" video, it would have never occurred to me that John Cougar was anything other than a superstar—*ever*. I would have never guessed he might have struggled as a singer/songwriter. I would have never known *American Fool* was actually his fifth studio album, and that almost nobody had ever heard of his first two. And hard-pressed, I would have been way off if I were to guess his age in that video. He looked *cool*, man—too cool to be anything but a young man with a bit of a pompadour.

John was actually in his 30s when that album came out. Pretty wild.

Furthermore, both the song and the video for "Pink Houses" (1983) had an enormous impact on me and are part of my live performances to this day. The picture he painted about a part of America I had never seen (being raised in the DC area) is so succinctly called the *heart*land. I found it fascinating.

Let's be clear that while I used to think "Jack and Diane" was good, I've since come to realize that it's GREAT. I totally get what is great about it. John Mellencamp is in fact one of my favorite songwriters of all time. Not just for "Pink Houses," but everything he's done since. In fact, the *Human Wheels* album is something I can never get enough of.

To my middle-school brain, John Mellencamp was a big star,

has always been a big star, and will always be a big star. He had "made it" in music because he was on MTV, selling out arenas and moving millions of albums.

That was how a new generation began to define "success."

When I got hot and heavy into playing guitar, I would play in front of a mirror sometimes, planning out how I would be featured in my future videos on MTV. No sense leaving anything to chance—I didn't want to disappoint my legion of future fans. I didn't have the chiseled good looks of Eddie Van Halen, but I figured they would fill in as I moved through puberty.

I'm still waiting.

Come hell or high water, I was going to make it onto MTV. It became my quest; my Vision Quest…my Quest for Fire. Anything less would not only be a letdown, but it would spell abject failure. MTV gave me that warped perspective. I have no doubt that it also gave the exact same warped perspective to thousands of other kids just like me.

I didn't know John Mellencamp had a back story. I hadn't yet learned of how hard the guys in Van Halen worked to get noticed in Los Angeles. I figured there were only two categories of musicians: Those on MTV, and the poor guys with nothing to show for their efforts.

Nothing could be further from the truth. The struggle is real, people.

So, let's begin at the beginning. When it all began.

* * *

In the beginning God created the heavens and the earth. And the earth was without form, and void; and darkness was upon the face of the deep…

Okay, hold up. While I would love for my book to sell as many copies as the King James Version of the Bible, I think my origin story is steeped in much more humble beginnings. To that point, I will skip the conception (not immaculate) and live birth. I will also zoom past the first five years. Not that any of that stuff was boring, but more because I want to keep this book focused on music and my career.

This story will begin when I was five years old. My mother (not God—but plays Him in this saga) started everything by separating darkness from light. She was the first person to put a guitar in my hands.

* * *

A word about my mother. She was as big a fan of music as me when I was growing up. In fact, she was a *huge* fan of Elvis Presley. I honestly don't know for certain if she ever met him; she took a lot of secrets to her grave…but rumor has it she had met him. She definitely went to a lot of his shows from the moment his musical career began, all the way through the time he was The King. Obviously, Elvis didn't spend a lot of time "playing in clubs" before he blew up to international fame, but my mom was there every step of the way.

In fact, there is a famous photograph of Elvis playing at the Tupelo (MS) Fairgrounds on September 26, 1956. In the photo, Elvis is leaning forward and reaching out to the fans in the first couple rows. He is wearing a nondescript dark shirt and dark pants—a far cry from the flamboyant figure he would eventually become. Elvis wasn't yet The King, but this photo demonstrates the charisma he had and the way he commanded a crowd. In fact, by this point, Elvis had only released one album (titled *Elvis Presley*), which became the first rock and roll album to ever hit #1 on the *Billboard* Top Pop Album chart.

Interesting side note: that album didn't even contain the song, "Heartbreak Hotel," which had already been released as a single and went all the way to #1 on the *Billboard* Hot 100, staying there for seven consecutive weeks.

But that photograph…it captured Elvis on the precipice of becoming the man who ushered in a new musical landscape called rock and roll. The girls in the front rows are going crazy and reaching back at him. I'd seen that picture my whole life but hadn't seen it blown up to the point of being able to make out faces in the crowd. My mother used to always tell me that she was at that show.

Let's zip forward in the timeline for a moment. The Bret Michaels Band opened a new concert venue at Graceland a few years ago, called The Soundstage. We were the first act to perform there, which is quite a feather in my career cap. When you walk into the catering room, one entire wall is covered by a mural-sized version of that photograph.

I gazed at the photo. It was nice—a cool stroll down memory lane for me. But like a sign from God, my eye was drawn to one particular face in the crowd.

It was my mother.

This was proof that all the stories mom used to tell me were true. I had no reason to doubt her, but you know how people tend to stretch a story over time. Along those lines, I had also been around the rock and roll lifestyle for well over two decades by that point. In a flash, I wondered *just how well* my mother might have known Elvis.

You go, mom. She had been dead for twenty years by that point. She'll get no judgment from me.

* * *

My mom loved Elvis and loved rock and roll. She likewise wanted me to carry her love of music. So, as I mentioned earlier, she put a guitar in my hands when I was five years old.

My mom was a little bit clairvoyant back then. I remember her always telling me that she wanted me to make it and become a successful musician, which I tried to do. And although I reached a rather modest level of success, to my mom, it would have been *huge.* She passed away before I reached the peak of my career, but she would surely have felt it was all she ever envisioned for me.

Having said that, she would add that she never wanted me to be as famous as Elvis because "…he could never live his own life."

By the way, she never even asked me if I *wanted* to be in the music business. In that sense, I suppose she wrote a script and put it in my head. I have followed it ever since.

Not that it was an easy ride for either of us at first. At five years old, I owned a guitar but did not care one iota about it. I had no interest in playing it. I was sick of hearing about Elvis. I was sick of hearing about Johnny Cash. I was sick of hearing about Hank Williams. I was five years old and wanted to play with my *Star Wars* toys.

My mom let it go and we put the guitar in a closet—where it sat until 1978. I was six years old by then; primed, rugged, and almost a man.

Ha! Like I'm even that at age 50.

But back then, I remember seeing a television commercial for an upcoming Kiss concert. Promoters would run TV ads in those days to hype their shows and sell some extra tickets. That Kiss commercial blew my tiny six-year-old mind. I don't know what it was exactly, but it felt like someone hot-wired my brain and started it up. Like you see in movies—Paul Stanley and Ace Frehley touched those two wires together and made sparks fly…until the engine roared to life, and I was hooked.

Within that *second*, everything changed. I was going to be a rock star. Seriously—one minute I did not give a single fuck about music, and the next minute I was going to devote the rest of my life to living the rock and roll dream.

I ran back to my room and yanked the guitar out of my closet. Unfortunately, it was an acoustic guitar. I was no expert, but this piece of junk certainly didn't look like the awesome weapons being wielded by those superheroes on television.

That became a problem for me. Fortunately, Paul Stanley offered a solution.

The commercial I saw highlighted some of the more dazzling moments from Kiss's stage show. At one point, Paul smashed his guitar. For those of you old enough to remember, that was a trend for a while. I think Pete Townshend of The Who was the first guy to do it—but then it was seen as "totally rock and roll" to destroy your equipment on stage.

Needless to say, I saw this as a win-win scenario. I could be "totally rock and roll," while at the same time ridding myself of this candy-ass toy. So around nine minutes after deciding I was going to make a career out of being a musician, I went out back and smashed the ever-loving shit out of my acoustic guitar.

I can't say mom was pleased. Nor can I say that I was given a replacement guitar. But I will say that my love and fascination with Kiss grew over time. Not to mention, every kid in my neighborhood was deep into Kiss as well.

I'm not sure if I should be embarrassed to tell this story, but I used to get together with my friends, Mike, Charlie, and John, and pretend we *were* Kiss. We'd play their albums and lip sync to them, all the while "playing" our instruments (a tennis racket, in my case) and doing our best impressions of the foursome. We put on fake concerts. It was great.

My dad, God love him, saw how into it I was. He knew we put on these concerts, and how a fire burned in me to actually *be* Ace Frehley. So, he took a jigsaw and cut a guitar shape out of a piece of plywood for me. Then he put screws in the neck and strung some fishing line to represent the strings. In essence, he made me a guitar that looked a whole lot more authentic than a tennis racket.

It was a cool little stage prop.

However, my rock and roll warrior soul could not be contained. I used to climb up onto our picnic table like it was a drum riser—and then jump off and smash the shit out of my prop guitar. And then I would walk into the garage and calmly ask my dad to make me another one.

It took about five repetitions of this scene for my dad to finally get irritated. But instead of punishing me, he pulled a move that I *still* consider to be divinely inspired. He said, "I bet if I bought your ass a real guitar, you wouldn't smash it."

And with that, away we went. My dad took me to Harmony Hut—a record-store-slash-music-store in the mall—and he bought me a Les Paul.

Let that soak in for a minute. *He bought me a Les Paul.* I was eight years old. I'd had a history of jumping off the picnic table and smashing the shit out of my guitars. I didn't know how to play a single note on the thing—but he bought me a Les Paul.

Now I'm an adult and have two children of my own. As a parent, I cannot for the life of me figure out what my dad was thinking. He must have reached a point of absolute desperation. Or else he was an evil genius. Because it worked.

One of my buddies in the neighborhood had a little crappy acoustic guitar that was completely unplayable—and remarkably uninspiring. Me, I had a real electric guitar. And not only that, I had the exact same real electric guitar that Ace Frehley played.

Talk about inspiration.

My dad's crazy idea is what launched me into all-out guitar mode. A lot of teachers recommend getting a little starter guitar for kids who show interest in the instrument. Fuck that—I say get them something that will make them want to play like the superheroes they see on TV. It worked for me. I wanted to pick up that Les Paul every single day.

And life went on for a while. Ace Frehley was The Guy. Kiss was my people. And that Les Paul was my weapon of choice. My friend group consisted of other burgeoning music aficionados—particularly those well-schooled in the fine offerings of Ace, Paul, Gene, and Peter.

Life was good. Until my mind was blown again—and a new superhero rose from another spinning black disc.

* * *

My buddies and I wore out our copy of Kiss's *Love Gun* album. I was eight years old and worked hard to master the staccato opening riff to the title song, "Love Gun." And I was pretty sure I'd nailed the proper technique for my eventual interview on MTV.

And then one stormy afternoon…

I was at my buddy John's house. We were in his living room, doing our thing and basking in the glory of Ace Frehley's solo album. In 1978, all four members of Kiss put out solo records as a stunt, and probably to scratch an artistic itch. All four albums came with a poster of the individual artist—and all four posters linked together like a giant, four-piece puzzle you could hang on your wall. It was glorious.

I liked (and still do like) Ace's album the best. So naturally, it was what John and I were listening to in his living room.

As "Rip it Out" or "Snow Blind" played in the background, John's older brother, Brad burst in.

"Turn that shit off. Here's what's real."

He pulled Ace from the turntable and replaced it with *Van Halen*, the self-titled debut of a new band from Pasadena, California. We blinked, confused. Mere days prior to this, Brad loved Kiss as much as we did. What could account for this act of flagrant blasphemy?

The speakers filled John's living room with the lead track, "Runnin' with the Devil." My knees grew weak. I had to sit down. My body was having a physical reaction to the sound of Van Halen. When that track bled into "Eruption" and then "You Really Got Me," I didn't know what to do with myself. My eight-year-old ears couldn't process the sounds they were hearing.

I am being totally sincere when I tell you this moment was life-altering for me. I wasn't just hearing a cool new song. I was hearing a new *language*.

I don't know how I made it home that night. I walked around my block in a daze. Although I lived only four houses down from John, the journey felt like I was running the endless mile.

When I walked through our front door, I immediately went to my mother and announced, "Mom…I need a guitar teacher."

Up until that moment, I was basically self-taught. I would pick up tips here and there from people who knew how to play, but I was able to figure out most of the chords to Kiss tunes, and then did my best to mimic some of the lead riffs from Ace Frehley.

But this Van Halen shit…whoa. This was above my eight-year-old pay grade.

So my mom did me a proper. She signed me up for lessons with a man named Alan Webb. Alan was cool, but he was old school with regard to his teaching methods. For example, he wanted to start me off by using the Mel Bay *Modern Guitar Method* book. The book might have been called *Guitar Method: Grade 1*. It was originally published in 1948—long before the blistering taps and wailing notes of Eddie Van Halen ever graced the airwaves.

Mr. Webb wasn't wrong in his approach; Mel Bay's books were (and still are) commonly used for beginners to learn the basics. The problem was, I wasn't a beginner. I was eight years old and damn close to being interviewed on MTV.

So I did what any almost-rock-star would do. I declared, "I want to learn Van Halen."

Poor Mr. Webb. I still remember the look on his face. It was a look that said, *Kid...the guitar is bigger than you. I don't think we're going to be able to do this right away*.

But to his credit, he struck a deal with me. We see-sawed back and forth during our lessons. During one session, he would teach me the basics. That part, from a foundational point of view, was absolutely necessary. I needed to practice correctly, and that meant learning the names of the notes and how they hung together to form chords. I needed to learn proper fingering techniques so I could move smoothly from one to the other. Mel Bay was good for this part —but not all that inspiring.

To keep my interest, every other session was spent breaking down popular songs. Not Van Halen at first—I needed to polish my skills before we could tackle anything Eddie was doing on the fret board. But he would teach me popular songs so I could play something relatable…something *fun*.

For example, he taught me how to play the theme from *M*A*S*H*. I was a huge fan of the TV show, so it was super cool to be able to play the exact same thing I heard on television each week. He also went over the *Star Wars* theme (which was as important to me as Van Halen) and simple classics like "We Wish You a Merry Christmas."

Alan Webb was such an intuitive teacher, he worked magic with me. He lured me in and taught me the compulsories by reinforcing me with recognizable songs I could play for my friends and family. It was the perfect storm. I stuck with Mr. Webb for several years and owe him a debt of gratitude.

The most amazing thing he ever did for me happened when I was in fourth grade.

* * *

Every year, my grade school would put on a talent show. Parents (mostly moms, to be honest) would pack the school cafeteria and watch their kids fumble through "Mary Had a Little Lamb" on the recorder or maybe the piano. Then they would all clap like Tchaikovsky just left the stage.

Back then, it all seemed corny as Hell. Now that I'm a parent myself, I totally get it.

But when I announced to Mr. Webb that I was entering the talent show as a guitarist, he gave me another classic "Mr. Webb look." It was a look that said, *Geez kid...you're really not very good yet.*

To his point, I couldn't even tune my own guitar yet. Mr. Webb, in an act of unimaginable selflessness, actually came to my grade school to tune my guitar before I walked out on stage for the talent show.

Anyway, he and I hatched a plan. I don't know if this plan was dastardly or diabolical per se, but it was sure better than anything Snidely Whiplash could have pulled off. We decided that I was going to play "Rip it Out," off Ace Frehley's solo album.

And over the course of the next few weeks, I learned that song.

Now here's the deal. I am 50 years old as I sit here writing this book. To this day, I have a bad rhythm problem. I can literally play any lick from Steve Vai or Yngwie Malmsteen or Eddie Van Halen—but if I don't have a metronome or a drummer playing with me, my sense of timing is a disaster of Biblical proportions. Maybe it's because I'm missing a gene that allows me to tap my foot in a consistent manner.

I don't know what "it" is—but whatever it is, I ain't got it. It's awful. And I was first introduced to this problem on the day of the talent show rehearsal.

There was a kid in my neighborhood named TJ Nokes. He was a third grader, but he played the drums and was (somewhat fortuitously) also signed up to play in the talent show. TJ's dad found out I was going to play a Kiss song and tried to get us to play together. TJ came from more of an R&B setting, but I think his dad was excited to get two young kids to play together.

I had never played with a drummer before. Outside of Alan Webb, I had done the vast majority of my guitar work sitting alone in my room. And I played Kiss songs—so obviously I was a superstar and light years ahead of this TJ Nokes kid.

Poor TJ. We played "Rip it Out" together a couple times—but could not get on the same page with regard to tempo. I knew the song backward and forward, and what I heard in my head was *not* what we were playing. In his defense, he had never heard the song before; his dad was just instructing him to play a simple beat.

Being a Kiss expert, and a cocky little bastard at the time, I knew it was his fault. Being a drummer and having worked with a metronome for a few years, he knew it was my fault.

So I fired his ass.

But not exactly.

In all honesty, his dad decided it wasn't going to work. And I was fine with that. No sense getting dragged down by some eight-year-old with a rhythm problem and a bad tendency to blame me for his mistakes.

Anyway, I went up there and played "Rip it Out" like a boss. And it was a sold-out show—every seat was packed in our little cafeteria that day. From a musical point of view, I can't imagine it was all that great to the moms who sat perfectly still and listened politely. But in my mind, I had just played Carnegie Hall and there wasn't a dry eye in the house.

And I'm only half kidding. I am not an egotistical person in real life. In fact, I have pretty serious social anxiety in almost every situation that involves me interacting with the outside world. But I have never been short on confidence when it comes to playing in front of an audience. I get more nervous standing in line at the grocery store than I do walking on stage in front of 50,000 people. It's weird.

I can honestly say that I have never experienced stage fright. Like, never once. Not even in the fourth grade, playing a pretty complicated (for a kid) Ace Frehley song.

The applause as I left the stage that evening hooked me for life. What a great, dizzying feeling. This is exactly what I was going to do for the rest of my life. And that sentiment carried over from elementary school to middle school.

* * *

By the time I entered the sixth grade in 1983, a lot had changed. I had been taking lessons from Alan Webb at the Music and Arts Center, which was a cooperate run, family-friendly establishment. I had also eventually found Music City, a mom-and-pop music store run by *rock and rollers*. The owner (Steve) looked as cool as Eddie Van Halen and David Lee Roth put together. Along these same lines, they had teachers (Mike and Dan Himmel) who LOVED Van Halen. While I hated to leave Alan because I get very emotionally attached to my mentors, it was time for me to get into the other scene. It turned out the Himmel brothers were part of the local rock scene and considered rock gods. Both were completely amazing players, but Mike had more of a star quality and drive than his brother. I took lessons from both; I learned everything there was to learn with these guys, from Van Halen and Judas Priest to Kiss and Quiet Riot. But I was also learning how to be *rock and roll*.

Similar to my elementary school, the middle school also held a talent show every year. By now I was advancing rapidly in my development as a guitar player. So I took the leap, and played "Eruption."

Eddie Van Halen was the Rachmaninoff of guitar. And "Eruption" was his *Sonata no. 2 in B flat minor*. It remains impossible for some, unfathomable for most…but a cakewalk for a budding virtuoso like me.

So I stepped before another sold out crowd (the janitor may have had to set up additional folding chairs in the back of the cafeteria). I was fearless and brimming with the knowledge that this experience would border on religious for the fortunate moms who were able to attend. When I struck the first note, I swear a collective gasp rang out from the audience.

Either that, or one of the lunch ladies slammed an oven door —but no matter.

My fingers tapped and danced along the fret board like barefooted angels. I picked and strummed like I was channeling the soul of Hendrix. My face contorted; my body bent and swayed as it became one with the music.

And I nailed it, man. I mean, if I was playing the devil in a Charlie Daniels Band song, I would have walked away with a Gibson made of gold.

...or...

It might have been fucking brutal. I'm sure it sounded like someone vacuuming a cat out from under the sofa, but I didn't care. I *was* Eddie Van Halen for 1 minute and 42 seconds.

The talent show coincided with a project we were doing in English class. The entire class was assigned to produce a 30-minute news program, just like the ones we watched while eating dinner at home. Each class member was assigned to different roles. As for me, I played a rock star getting interviewed for a segment.

If you've never seen the Van Halen music video for the song, "Hot for Teacher," go watch it real quick on YouTube. The guitar solo features Eddie, in the school library, filmed from a low POV while playing and walking down a long table.

With a "camera crew" (holding a school camera someone checked out of the A/V closet), we put together some folding tables and I recreated Eddie's walk. Except I was playing "Locked In" by Judas Priest instead of "Hot for Teacher." I can't remember why exactly, but it was probably because I didn't quite know the "Hot for Teacher" solo yet, plus I was really getting into Judas Priest at the time.

And did I mention, I was also a cocky little bastard?

It's funny...but I was *way* more arrogant back then than I could ever come close to today. In sixth grade, I was convinced that I was the greatest guitar player who ever lived. That was probably annoying to those around me back then, but perhaps the blind ignorance of youth was my saving grace. It propelled me forward fearlessly. I was able to keep learning and keep performing without a hint of indecision or reticence.

Throughout middle school, nothing else mattered to me except music. I was engulfed and consumed—every nook and cranny of my brain was filled with morsels ranging from nonsense music knowledge (I could beat Ken Jennings in an "80's Music Trivia" challenge on Jeopardy), to a yearning to learn more and more, to a burning itch to keep getting in front of people and performing.

Hmm. "Burning itch" sounded way better in my head than it did when I read it back to myself. I may go back and rewrite it later.

As evidence of my immersion, every school report was about music in some form or fashion. In history class (for example), we had to write a report on the most important people in history. Not any who are living—we were told to pick people who had passed away. Most kids wrote about George Washington or Abraham Lincoln or Martin Luther King, Jr.

I wrote about Randy Rhoads.

In another class (maybe Civics?) we were assigned to draw out (from an aerial view) our idea of a Utopian city. Most kids drew theirs with the streets forming a gridiron pattern, or maybe like spokes radiating out from a center point.

Mine was drawn in such a way that the streets were laid out as the Twisted Sister logo.

Nothing. Else. Mattered.

* * *

And throughout ALL of this, my mom was all-in and fully on board. My mom fed and nurtured my addiction like a guy in a trench coat behind the 7-11. She *never* discouraged me, no matter what. Hell, I remember being a little kid when my parents had company over. I would walk around the house singing Kiss songs at the top of my lungs and *nobody stopped me.*

Now I look back in horror. What must it have been like for adults to be visiting my house, and hearing a seven-year-old kid relentlessly belting out the lyrics to "Christine Sixteen" or "Calling Dr. Love" or "Plaster Caster"?

If my parents had dinner guests, I would spend the mealtime educating everyone about different aspects of Kiss.

I'm not talking about once in a while—I did that shit all day long.

Geez…here's a random memory. We had a kind neighbor named Margaret Birch. She and my mom were super close. She was also married to my dad's best friend, George Birch…and they led a quiet existence. I mean that in every sense of the word—Margaret kept a *quiet* home. She was a teacher, and one of the nicest human beings I have ever met.

My house? Well, it wasn't quite so quiet. My mom had a huge temper problem that I inherited…and she could get LOUD. For example, one day I came home from school and the cops were at my house. My mom had gotten into a huge fight with my sister and threw our living room stereo at her. Naturally, my sister called the cops. As I was walking to the house, I'll never forget how wonderful Margaret Birch swooped in out of nowhere and ushered me into her house to protect me from (seemingly) seeing my mom get hauled off to jail.

Just an amazing woman.

Anyway, Margaret used to walk her dog around our neighborhood for exercise. I liked her a lot and would join her on many of these walks. Somehow—and there is no scale that can possibly measure the amount of patience this poor woman must have had—she would tolerate me talking about Kiss throughout the entire walk. She would ask about me about school and my grades and such—but then the conversation would invariably make an abrupt turn to things like the inside fold of the Kiss *Alive II* album cover. Then I would excitedly educate her on the number of drums in Peter Criss's drum kit, or how many speakers flanked their enormous stage.

Oh my gosh—these memories are all coming back now. I remember she was babysitting me one day and we went to the mall. Somehow—and I think this got her into Heaven no matter what she did afterwards—I convinced her to buy me the Kiss *Double Platinum* album. I probably lied to her and said my parents would pay her back or some such shit, but she went ahead and got it for me.

Then (this is so embarrassing), we went back to her house—where I played the fuck out of that album as if I was playing it in my house. I cranked the volume and sang at the top of my lungs for three or four straight hours.

Dear reader, I have no idea how she was able to persevere through that auditory assault. I think the only way she was able to make it through was to join me on some of the lyrics. I have a vivid memory of her singing the high parts of the Kiss song "100,000 Years" off their self-titled debut album. The song features a funky-ass bass groove playing beneath Paul singing the melody. Anyway, there is one part in the chorus where Paul goes high. He sings, "100,000 yee-HEEERS."

Ms. Birch would join in and sing the, "Yee-HEEERS" part.

Yes, I was completely clueless as a kid. My relationship with Margaret Birch started early and then continued into middle school. By then I was too cool to walk around the block with my neighbor and her dog. But let's leave this thread and I'll get back on point.

My mom was all-in and fully on board. She had to be; someone had to step in and take up for me when school people started to question my mental health. All the way into middle school when I was drawing a Utopian Society road map as the Twisted Sister logo, teachers and administrators wondered if I was losing my mind. It started early.

I remember when Crayola used to have the BIG box of crayons. The box had a built-in crayon sharpener because we were a technologically advanced society by then. Inside that box were SIXTY-FOUR color choices, including sparkly cool silver and gold crayons. I wish I was exaggerating, but I spent an entire week doing nothing but drawing Gene Simmons in gold crayon.

This must have been around Halloween because we had to make masks in art class. Of course, I made a Gene Simmons mask because…well, I really had no choice. The teacher never said a word to me about this fascination or about how she was growing concerned about me. Instead, she spoke to the principal.

Yup. She ratted me out to the principal, Miss McKay. Who in turn ratted me out to my mother.

The teacher sent me to Miss McKay's office. When I arrived, I found my mother sitting there, waiting for me. On the desk between them were all of my gold Gene Simmons pictures, fanned out like evidence in a capital murder trial.

I sat next to my mom, terrified. Miss McKay then opened a conversation with my mom like I wasn't even sitting there.

"I think we have a problem."

My mom listened politely.

Miss McKay continued, "This is a member of a Satanic rock band. Whatever your child does at home is great…but here in school, we cannot have this kind of behavior."

I was then sent home for the remainder of the day.

Instead of punishing me, I think my mom took me shopping

with her and spent the day with me. It was like nothing happened. She had my back, maybe even more than I was ever aware. This continued into middle school, when she always took up for me if the school called with "a few questions..."

God bless my mom. She was my guardian angel. And my dad was no slouch either. He was more level-headed than my mom, but he subtly (and not so subtly) encouraged me too.

Like when my father made me a metal mask, exactly like the one on Quiet Riot's *Metal Health* album cover. I was into Quiet Riot by then, as they joined the ranks of Kiss, Van Halen, and Judas Priest in my personal Pantheon of the Gods.

My dad was a mechanic by trade, but he was a skilled craftsman in many areas. He could fabricate all sorts of things using metal, so I asked if he would make me a mask like the on the album.

Check out the album art if you can't picture it in your mind. A lot of people think it's lead singer, Kevin DuBrow, in the photo. But it's not. It's actually the guy who came up with the concept: photographer, Stan Watts. Watts made the mask and then wore Frankie Banali's (Quiet Riot's drummer) red motorcycle jacket backwards to look like a strait jacket. Fucking genius.

Anyway, my dad looked it over and agreed.

He fashioned it out of aluminum, and fucking *nailed* it.

I loved it. And then wore it to middle school.

My homeroom teacher in sixth grade was Mrs. Kerns. My God...that poor woman. Mrs. Kerns took roll call as always. She went down the list, calling our names, and listened for a beat while the students responded with "here" or "yeah."

When she got to my name, she must have noticed that my voice was oddly muffled. I don't think she could have anticipated that the muffle was normal for a kid who was wearing an aluminum asylum mask to school, but I'm sure she didn't sweat those details back then.

She would after this day, to be sure.

Mrs. Kerns said, "Evick?"

And I replied with a distorted, "Here."

I'll never forget the look on her face.

To my brain, this was just another Tuesday. To Mrs. Kerns, this might have been the day she decided to quit teaching.

She spoke slowly, in a calculated tone, “Pete…I’m going to need you to take that off.”

I ignored her.

This went on for several minutes, until the kid who sat next to me grew even more annoyed than Mrs. Kerns. Or maybe he wasn’t as annoyed as her, but he was 12 and had a lot more latitude with regard to what he could get away with.

He reached over, ripped the mask from my head, and stomped on it.

As I wrote about in my first book, I fought a lot in middle and high school. I had a short fuse and wasn’t going to take shit from anyone. But at this exact moment, I was still worried about getting in trouble at school. I had perfect attendance and got good grades. I wouldn’t start fighting until the next year.

I took the mask back from him and bent it back into shape, simple as that.

God bless my parents.

CHAPTER 2:
THE POWER OF THE GUITAR

As I entered high school, I started to *really* play guitar. Up to this point, I did what most kids did. I learned to play recognizable licks and riffs out of Van Halen and Kiss and Twisted Sister tunes. Now, I began to play complete songs…beginning to end.

Frankly, there hadn't been a reason to know entire songs. I wasn't in a band, so wouldn't have the occasion to perform a song—talent shows notwithstanding. That all changed at Stonewall Jackson High School. And the song that got the ball rolling was "In my Dreams" by Dokken.

* * *

Almost from the moment I set foot in high school, I wanted to start a band. It seemed to be the right time; I had a limited number of years to become MTV famous, so no time like the present to begin the journey.

I teamed up with two new friends, Shawn Key and Pete DeFranks. We agreed to form a band even though we really didn't have any idea how to do such a thing. But we did what we knew how to do. We got together for a "rehearsal" at Shawn's house.

I packed up my guitar and arrived, ready to take my career to the next level. Shawn was a normal upper-middle class Virginia kid who lived on the good side of town; unlike me, he (and Pete, for that matter) was a total "prep." His family didn't seem particularly rich per se. They were probably very well off at one time, but Shawn's dad had died awhile before I met them…and that might have (I'm speculating here) created some financial stress for the family. In any case, none of us were blessed with the opportunity for such accouterments like microphones, amps, or cables. However, Shawn *did* have a tiny orange Ludwig Sparkle drum set in the corner. And that was all we needed.

Not to be dissuaded, we set up and counted in the only song all three of us knew—"In My Dreams" by Dokken. Pete had to yell the vocals; his singing competing with the music because we didn't have a PA system.

Pete's vocals were cool. He sounded enough like Don Dokken to give me hope that high schoolers could sing like rock stars. But as a whole, I just wasn't feeling it.

In a word, we were…terrible. I can't even tell you what that band was called because we weren't together long enough to give ourselves a name. The complete life cycle of our Dokken-infused threesome was about two hours and eighteen minutes, all-in. It started that afternoon, and I ended it that afternoon.

We came, we played, we folded.

Veni. Vidi. Vici…Virginia style.

There is an old saying that when a door closes, a window opens. Change does not spell failure—rather, it means the time is ripe for an alternate opportunity. And that opportunity came on the back of a kid named Tom Bolton.

* * *

Tom showed up at Shawn's house on that fateful Dokken day. The kids who were into music all seemed to know each other and tended to run in similar circles. So, when Tom appeared in Shawn's bedroom, nobody thought it was unusual. I must admit, it was a bit odd for me at first. I was from the "other" side of town. But because of the way our high school was zoned, kids mixed in from all walks of life and economic backgrounds. I had my handful of buddies but was faced with having to meet all new people.

As it turned out, Tom was in the process of starting another band with a friend of his, a drummer named Ray Madonna. I also suspect Tom was at Shawn's house that day to scout me. My reputation around the school was pretty solid, and Tom needed a good guitar player.

To his credit, Tom waited until after our Dokken disaster to approach me. He pulled me aside and said, "Hey man…I'm starting a band too. You should come over and check it out."

So, I did. I lugged my gear to Ray's house. When I walked into his room, I was blown away. These guys were *metal*. Ray had Ozzy and Judas Priest posters on his wall. He also had a drum kit that looked exactly like the one Randy Castillo was playing in Ozzy's "Ultimate Sin" video. They had a PA system and were allowed to play LOUD.

It was everything I had dreamed of.

And before I go on, let me defend Shawn Key and Pete DeFranks. They were perfectly suitable musicians—but Shawn was pop, not metal. In fact, Shawn went on to become one of the finest drummers and most knowledgeable musicians I have ever known. We just didn't vibe together like Tom, Ray, and I vibed.

And we did. Tom was a stranger when we met at Shawn's house, but we were band mates by the time I got home that evening. During the brief time I was at Ray's house, we played "Crazy Train" (Ozzy), "Living After Midnight" (Judas Priest), and "The Trooper" (Iron Maiden). It was just what the doctor ordered.

It was 1986 and the perfect time to start a band. I call this period "The era before the Great Divide." From about 1982 until about 1986, rock and metal were fused into one giant ball of fucking awesome. 1986/87 spelled change. Poison released *Look What the Cat Dragged In*, and things started to change. Later that year, Europe released *The Final Countdown*, Cinderella released *Night Songs*, Ratt released *Dancing Undercover*, and Tesla released *Mechanical Resonance*.

All of those started to define a new genre of rock and roll. But nothing solidified the Great Divide like the album released in August of that year. Bon Jovi released *Slippery When Wet*, and rock music broke in two.

On one side of the divide was traditional rock and metal. Iron Maiden, Judas Priest, W.A.S.P., Motorhead, AC/DC, and Black Sabbath towed that line. On the other side, there was a burgeoning "Sunset Strip" metal genre, punctuated by the bands I have already mentioned, and joined soon thereafter by Warrant, Faster Pussycat, and LA Guns.

Those were just the Hollywood bands that were formed

before 1988. In 1989, the floodgates really opened, as it seemed every four-piece on the Sunset Strip got signed to a record deal.

And then there were the acts that seemed able to walk the line between the two sides. Acts like Ozzy, Night Ranger, The Scorpions, Van Halen, and Kiss drew fans from all facets of rock music.

It was a great time to be a high school fan of rock music. Hell, it was a great time to be *alive*. I was living the dream.

From my perspective, this band with Tom and Ray was going to be together forever. We were called Amethyst and were going to climb the ladder until we peaked at the same altitude as any one of those bands I just wrote about. Nothing could stop us.

Nothing that is, except for Queensrÿche.

* * *

My freshman year was filled with music and high spirits. Ray and I became fast friends. We used to drive around in his Volkswagen bug, blasting *Look What the Cat Dragged In* and picking up as many of our girl friends as we could cram into the VW's lunchbox-sized back seat. Maureen, Dawn, Stephanie, Bianca, Kim…great friends with whom Ray and I still talk to today. Then we would arrive at Ray's house and entertain the masses with our mad music skills.

It was *Say Anything* and *Better off Dead* and *Pretty in Pink* and *The Breakfast Club* all rolled into one fabulous run. Every John Hughes film ever made played out in Manassas, Virginia that year. And *Look What the Cat Dragged In* was the soundtrack.

It was all ideal. Ray and I loved Poison and loved that album. Tom even liked it, but not as much as he liked Queensrÿche. As I recall, he went with me to purchase Poison's second album, *Open Up and Say…Ahh!* when it first came out. I remember we bought a 7-11 pizza on our way back to my house and ate it as we put on the record. I fell even MORE in love with this new band from Mechanicsburg, Pennsylvania, than I had already been.

But then along came Queensrÿche, and their watershed album, *Operation Mindcrime*.

Don't get me wrong, I have respect for Queensrÿche as a

band. But their lyrics tend to be heavy. In fact, the songs on that album tell a complete story—that chronicles the difficult journey of a man who loses his mind after being tapped to kill a nun in order to begin a political revolution.

What the fuck, right?

I didn't want to get all enmeshed in angry political bullshit. I wanted to have fun and feel good, listen to feel-good lyrics while rocking the night away. I didn't want to go home and mull over a fucking revolution.

Truth be told, I'm a conspiracy theorist at heart, and the story of *Operation Mindcrime* might have been one of my favorite movies of all time—IF it was a movie. I just didn't want it in my rock and roll.

Unfortunately, Ray liked *Mindcrime*—and worse yet, Tom *loved* it.

So now we had a problem. I wanted to play Poison and they wanted to add Queensrÿche. That just didn't fit for me. A band's identity can't be like Poison *and* be like Queensrÿche. You just can't do it.

Let me be clear, they both liked Poison, and agreed to play the music. It was me that was the unnegotiable asshole. I did not want to play Queensrÿche.

In my little town, a second Great Divide began to emerge. On one side were the "party and have fun" bands (like Poison). On the other, were the thinking man's bands—like Queensrÿche, and later Fates Warning and Crimson Glory.

Not to mention, Ray was older and graduating—he had the choice to run off to L.A. anyway. I think you can see where this was headed. In short, I had to find a new band.

* * *

Ray and I were friends with a girl named Stephanie Staples. She told me about a kid she knew named Chuck, who worked at our local Burger King—and also happened to play drums. I didn't know anything about him because he went to the other high school in town, but I was eager to get another band going. So, I went out to meet him.

This was 1988, and when I stepped through the glass door at Burger King, I met another lifelong friend. Chuck Fanslau and I hit it off immediately. And he *still* plays with me, to this day. Along with Bret Michaels, he's one of my two best friends and go-to musical partners.

We chatted over burgers and shakes that afternoon. I learned that Chuck was already in a band, and that they played "Love on the Rocks" by Poison. Sounded cool to me. So, I made my move. In an act of supreme (an uncharacteristic) arrogance, I said, "I'm going to join your band."

I don't remember how Chuck took the news, but I do know that we ended up going over to his house to play "Love on the Rocks." We had an immediate synergy, so I made another bold proclamation.

"This is great and everything, but I have a different vision. Why don't you quit your band, and we will form our own band."

Again, I don't remember the details of how the conversation went after that. But I do know that Chuck did exactly what I suggested. He quit his band, and we grabbed a rhythm guitar and a bass player; a couple buddies of mine named Justin Raybuck and Eric Fenner. And with that, we went to start anew.

A lot of change was happening in our lives. Somewhere in between all this, I was in another band called "Sweet Talk" which was where I came to know "Bear" Paul Lyles, who later ended up with Chuck, Justin, and I. Sweet Talk had yet another drummer who left to run off to LA; an amazing guy who was ahead of his years in wisdom, named Von Pilkington. We also had a great guitar-player-turned-bass-player (who also went to LA), named Jess Peck.

* * *

We worked out three tight sets of cover tunes—and played a lot of Poison songs. Chuck and I agreed on everything we loved about rock and roll. I took the name Amethyst with me, so our new group was supposed to be an upgrade over my old group—except we could never seem to find a solid lead singer. Sometimes I would sing; sometimes Chuck would sing. We played with several guys who were good but not great…all in all, it was fine for what we were trying to accomplish at the moment.

My goal was to be a full-time, career musician. I think Chuck shared that vision, because late in my junior year in high school, that's what ended up happening. We were playing constantly—weeknights and weekends. We were just kids, but booking agents from all over the area were eager to throw us up onto their stages.

It was a grind, I'm not gonna lie. In Virginia, a cover band would play three sets of music and cover the time slot of 9:30pm-1:30am. One of our main gigs was at a club in Dumfries, Virginia, called Tiki Fala. They had music seven nights per week. Regional touring acts would fill the cherry time slots on weekends, and B or C bands would round out the Monday, Tuesday, and Wednesday nights. We drew *that* straw, but were delighted to have an actual, steady, and PAID gig.

But buddy, let me tell you: that club was a glorious and perfect fucking mess. It was a dingy pool hall and a dirty, dirty rock and roll club and Chinese restaurant. It sat very close to the Quantico Marine Base, so every night, Tiki Fala was packed—but the crowd would consist of two types of people. Half the crowd was made up of Marines, and the other half consisted of the grittiest, blue collar working types Virginia had to offer!

Those two elements do not mix very well. At least one fight broke out every night, sometime between eleven o'clock and midnight. You could set your watch to it. Literally.

Every. Fucking. Night.

We weren't even eighteen years old yet—so as far as we knew, this was all normal. It was the world we lived in, for sure. And there was a bouncer—I wish I could remember the guy's name—that stood at the front entrance and protected us every night. He was like Andre the Giant to me. Calm, cool, pleasant…he was Patrick Swayze's Dalton before Patrick Swayze was Dalton.

I say calm and cool, but he was *powerful*. When he would shove a drunken asshole away from the stage, it looked to me like the asshole would fly thirty feet before caroming off a wall. It was fantastic!

People thought my parents were nuts to let their kid do that every night, in that kind of place, and keep that kind of schedule. But it was what it was. In my brain, that was exactly what I had to do to achieve my long-term goals.

As a quick side note, nearly every high-level musician will tell you that they started young playing in bars and clubs. You have to cut your teeth early so you get a head start over every weekend-warrior band that starts up in college. Not to mention, each of us had a burning passion for music in our childhoods. It's like nothing can slow down that desire.

But (and this is a big but) in order to play like that during high school, you either need parents who are absent, checked out, or don't give a shit. Or, you have to have parents who are on board and supportive of your dreams.

I had the latter. My dad never stood in the way…he would have probably preferred that I go to college or get a nice union job as a tradesman, but he was completely behind anything I wanted to do that would earn a decent income. He provided money or gear when I needed it, and provided silent approval when I didn't.

My mom on the other hand, was delighted to help me out. Remember the story of the guitar when I was five years old? Extrapolate that notion into the rest of my development as a professional musician. She was happy to lift me into this wild ride.

I remember we used to have a calendar sitting on one of the end tables in our living room. My mom kept it there because it was next to the phone. When a booking agent would call, she would mark the date and venue on the calendar.

I'd like to add that the first agent to ever give my band a job was a woman named Diana Stagnato. She was a singer, a TV host, and an agent all rolled in one. To this day, she works her ass off booking bands. After Diana came my dear friend who still books my acoustic act today, Chip Seligman. Both of these people are forever etched into my heart; they gave a kid a chance…and I bugged the fuck out of both of them.

And listen, I will emphasize here that I was always a good kid (fight me) and an even better student. I got A's and B's all throughout school, and—not even kidding—had perfect attendance from kindergarten all the way through high school.

Hell, I would leave school in the afternoon and have to drive straight to the club—but I would bring my homework with me. I would sit in the corner (or a back room, because I was underage) and do my algebra worksheets while waiting for our start time. Many of these places doubled as restaurants (in Virginia, you had to serve food in order to serve alcohol), so I would always be able to scavenge something to eat.

By the way, the attendance thing was extremely important to me. It might have been OCD, or it might have become a goal as I came closer and closer to finishing it out, but at some point, I decided I would do it. It wasn't easy…every kid gets sick, or a family goes on vacation, or some grandparent dies in Phoenix so you've got to go to the funeral—but not me. I had my ass in my seat every single day. Things got a little dicey when we would play a club until one or two in the morning the night before. However, I made sure to walk through the school's front door at *some* point during the day so my name would be checked off as "HERE!"

There is a dirty little secret embedded in this story.

You can only wake up at the crack of noon—and then march into school in time to close out sixth period—for so long before the administration notices. Thus, I got called into the principal's office.

Mr. Campbell (the principal) was there, as was my guidance counselor. I sat down and prepared for the inquisition. They wore concerned looks on their faces as they addressed my quasi-truancy.

I stopped them by reframing the conversation.

"Look…this is what I want to do for a living. Truth be told, it's *already* what I am doing for a living. Can we consider this as my work-release program?"

The school actually had a provision to allow kids to leave school in order to work. So if a kid got an internship at a local bank or had a chance to apprentice in some sort of trade job (work with a mechanic in town or learn to frame houses), they would be granted leave from their classes. This seemed like an open and shut case for my situation.

I was earnest in my presentation. There was nothing sarcastic or rebellious about what I was doing. I honestly felt Truth in every word I spoke.

I must have made a pretty compelling argument, because it

worked. To their credit, the counselor and the principal agreed. They decided to let me slide. I was allowed to show up late and pursue my "trade" for as long as I was making it as a working musician. Truth be told I was also already working at Music City during my senior year. So, some days it would be school, music store, bar.

So far, so good, right?

Here is where the dirty little secret enters the story. I was given the white-glove treatment when it came to academics. Maybe it was my track record of being an A and B student; maybe it was my sparkling personality; maybe it was the street cred I brought the school when they bragged about having a local rock star in their student body. But all of a sudden, any poor grades I earned would magically turn into good grades.

I felt a little bit like a blue-chip athlete coming up through the ranks. In high school, they get the smart kids to do their homework for them. In college, professors are pressured by athletic directors and administrators to give passing grades regardless of work quantity or quality. That was how I ended my school career. I got good grades senior year, despite my sporadic presence in the school building.

I'm not proud of that deal, but it helped me limp through to graduation. The ends may not always justify the means but look at me now. I play next to one of the biggest rock stars in the world and I convinced you to pick up and read this book. Not bad for a kid from Manassas.

Honestly, the school personnel seemed to completely embrace the concept. Many of my teachers would come out and see us play. Mr. Campbell actually posed for a photo with me and my buddy, Dave Compton—a photo that sat on the credenza behind his desk for the rest of my tenure at Stonewall Jackson High school.

How many principals create photo-ops with their long-haired ne'er-do-well students? If any of them take pictures with students, it's usually with the valedictorian or the star quarterback—not with two kids wearing Poison and Metallica concert t-shirts.

They believed in me.

* * *

Out on the club circuit, we were a bunch of kids trying to scrape together a living. In the high school, we were kings.

Let me refer back to the John Hughes movies I mentioned a while ago. *The Breakfast Club* made a huge impact on me. I was a freshman when it came out and remember how much I was touched by the story line and by the mismatched characters that somehow gelled into a rag-tag group of friends at the end. To my mind, it was pure genius how John Hughes wove the tale by speaking The Truth about the nature of high school kids.

I wanted us to be in a real-life Breakfast Club…and pretty much accomplished it. Music was the great equalizer. It brought together every clique and broke down barriers that insecure teenagers built around themselves. The jocks, the nerds, the burnouts, the skaters, the outcasts—it didn't matter who they were, we were somehow able to bring them all together when we played music.

It started early. I was in choir when I was a freshman. Don't laugh—my sister was in choir years before me, so the teacher figured I was genetically destined to also be a naturally good singer.

She was wrong.

But one day she asked if I would bring my guitar to choir practice. She had accurately surmised that my singing wasn't enough to justify my presence, so maybe I could provide a musical accompaniment.

Anyway, a girl named Audra leaned over and asked if I could play Van Halen's song, "Panama."

Pfft. Can I play Panama!

I launched into the iconic riff. And the student body changed around me.

Word got out that I could play the guitar and that I was good. So, the students began to show up when I would play. Amethyst played for the skater punks at a half-pipe outside of town. When we practiced in my basement, students from every walk of life would show up to hang out and listen and mingle.

My mom, God she was a saint, loved it. She enjoyed playing house mom and encouraging her kid to live his best life. Instead of fearing or despising all the teenagers, she embraced them and welcomed them into her home.

So many teenagers would show up, their parked cars would sometimes come close to choking off my neighborhood. In fact, the cops would swing by to make sure everything was on the up and up. Heck, *they* would even stick around sometimes and listen to the band.

I loved the idea of being the guy who could break down barriers among the different students. It was important to me and made me feel good to see everyone get along. Think *The Breakfast Club*, right?

So as my outro from Stonewall Jackson High School, I decided to make a bold statement. My band always played the school talent shows. And in high school, we always played a Poison song. But this year we would also play something else. My idea for the senior talent show was to have representatives of every clique and cranny join us on stage and sing "Rock and Roll All Night" by Kiss. Everyone knew that phrasing in the Kiss song. It was an anthem and was pretty well universally known among high school kids in 1990.

I…wanna rock and roll all night…and party every day…

I meticulously planned the whole event. I went around and collaborated with representatives of every clique, who all agreed. It was going to be perfect—like my own personal valedictorian speech. It was going to be my opus; Judd Nelson's fist pump as the credits roll to end *The Breakfast Club*.

But something went wrong. I honestly cannot remember why we weren't allowed to do it, but the staff put the kibosh on the whole thing. Maybe they didn't want that many people on stage at one time. Maybe they were afraid the warring factions would grate on each other's nerves and erupt into a fist fight. Whatever the case, I was told at the eleventh hour that I was not to pull off my epic swan song.

Disappointed but not dissuaded, I still got up there and played a Poison song and the Kiss song. I would not be John Hughes or Martin Luther King today…but I was still a rocker at heart. And the students still liked to hear me play. And buddy, I still really *loved* to play. So, I did.

As I was walking off the stage, the king of the jocks, a guy named JB Childress approached me. He was going to have been the representative of the jocks in my nixed stage show, but that didn't mean he and I were friends.

In fact, let me start by saying that JB and I were actually enemies up until this point. He was the king of his crowd, and I was the king of my crowd—so whenever there was a scrap between our buddies, he and I would have to step in and resolve the issue like generals leading opposing armies.

Listen, I don't make the rules.

Anyway, he and I always had a tense respect for each other, but never anything close to a friendship. So when I saw him making his way through the crowd and toward the stage, my heart sank.

Ah, shit...what's this about? Are we going to have to fight?

But when he got to me, he grabbed my arm and said, "What happened? I thought we were all going to do this with you."

I met his eyes, "Yeah, I know...I thought you were going to too."

"Well, fuck." He let go of my arm and turned away, "Fuck."

That was a powerful moment for me. JB actually *wanted* to get up there and participate in my talent show bit. Even though it didn't happen, that three second exchange with fucking JB Childress was my Gandhi moment.

Quick sidenote: JB and I are really great friends now. He went on to join the military. I have a great respect for that and what he sacrificed for our country. Not to mention, he thinks what I do is pretty cool and...well...we both like whiskey. These days, seeing JB is one of the highlights of my travels. I can't explain how much I look forward to hanging out with him.

* * *

There was divisiveness around the school...but never around my guitar.

That was power, man. The power of the guitar.

I might add that while I had so many people always coming through my parents' doors to check out the band during those high school years, I had a core group of my friends...most of whom I still talk to on a regular basis. We went everywhere together. Concerts, beaches, my gigs, the mall, movies, amusement parks...Mike, John,

Justin, Dave, Chuck, James, Mark, Sherry, Kelly, Deana, Missy, and Vicky were there. We did it all together.

Life was so much simpler then, they were all I needed, and all I wanted. Everything was fine as long as we were fine.

CHAPTER 3:
THE FORCE IS STRONG IN THIS ONE

The single greatest movie ever committed to celluloid is *Star Wars*. In my mind, it's not even a debate. Notice I didn't say *One of the greatest movies...* or *Perhaps the greatest movie...*

No. In my mind, there is only room for one greatest movie of all time. And that is, was, and always will be *Star Wars* (all three trilogies and spin offs as one giant movie). Having said that, I feel like I'm about to commit some sort of cinematic blasphemy. But it's my book and I will besmirch at will.

I'm a little bit like Luke Skywalker.

Yeah, I said it. Hear me out.

Luke always had The Force. It was a part of him during his childhood and adolescence. Genetically, he was a Skywalker—and therefore had the potential of Darth Vader within him. However, without a wise mentor to teach him how to harness The Force (he grew up apart from his father), he neither recognized nor understood the true nature of his destiny.

That is, until Obi Wan Kenobi entered his life. Obi Wan taught Luke how to channel The Force and maximize its power. He even sent Luke away to study on Dagobah under the Jedi master, Yoda.

By the way, you knew Yoda was a badass because he didn't have a last name. He was just YODA. Like all the great ones (Madonna, Cher, Prince, Slash…Yanni), Yoda went by a single, Force-filled, badass name.

Anyway, here is how I am like Luke: as a child, I didn't realize I had The Force within me. I didn't have a mentor to help me channel and *feel* The Force. I had to learn it on my own. And it was a bumpy ride. It wasn't until the "power of the guitar" became apparent that I started to notice how it showed itself in everyday life.

Once I recognized it, I started to understand how awe-inspiring this power could be.

For example, it got me out of a vandalism arrest. Not even kidding.

* * *

Young women will sometimes talk about how they get out of speeding tickets by looking sexy or by crying. I don't have those options. My sexiest outfit is complete darkness. And if I broke down crying while talking to a cop, I'd probably be committed for a 72-hour observation and have my shoelaces taken away.

Anyway, right around the time I graduated from high school, I had a green, custom-made B.C. Rich guitar. It's exactly the same guitar C.C. DeVille plays in the "Nothing but a Good Time" video, minus the yellow CC lettering.

And before you give me shit for going out and getting the same guitar slung by the guitar player in my favorite band, bear in mind that I got the B.C. Rich before that song ever came out. My parents had it made for me back in my old BMX days.

BMX riders will color coordinate their bikes. The hand grips, mag wheels, and piping would all be decked out in the same bright, vibrant colors. Kids whose parents had a little money would also coordinate their helmet and racing outfit to match the color scheme on their bike.

When I went out to freestyle or ride the quarter pipes, my color scheme was bright green. I can't remember exactly how (or why) I came to the decision, but I did choose bright green as my thing. So my folks had a guitar made that matched Pete Evick's BMX branding.

I had that guitar and played it all around town. Apparently, everyone noticed.

One day, my buddy, Tom (the Queensrÿche fan) and I were up to no good. The neighborhood behind his house was in the process of being developed back then. Tom and I were prowling around the construction sites, probably throwing rocks or doing whatever other dumb redneck shit we could think of.

As you can imagine, the cops caught us.

And listen, if you read my first book, you know that I got into a lot of fights when I was a teenager. I even reference that tendency in this book. But I was seriously never a bad kid. I did some sneaky shit and I did some stupid shit, but I was never a delinquent type.

This may or may not surprise you, but I never drank and never did drugs throughout high school. And I will take it one step further—I didn't have my first *drop* of alcohol until I was 25 years old. I didn't even drink NyQuil as a kid because it had alcohol in it.

Not to mention, I didn't so much as smoke weed. Like, ever. I still don't/haven't done drugs. I think I had a pot cookie one time in my late 20's or early 30's, but that's it. Period, end of story. Not that I'm against it in any way. Just not my thing.

I might have tried to be a bad boy back then, but I never wanted to get into trouble. My parents were proud of me—and that was extremely important. I didn't want to do anything to tarnish how they looked at me.

So, when Tom and I were finally cornered by the police, I remember being afraid. On television, guys with spider-web tattoos on their neck will be angry and spiteful when they are arrested. Dude, I was fucking *terrified.*

I remember standing next to Tom, my hands in the air—and probably shaking like a politician on Judgment Day. One of the cops walked toward me. I couldn't blink. I remember thinking, *This is it. I'm going away to Sing Sing*.

Being a musician, the irony of that prison's name is not lost on me.

When the cop finally got to me, he looked down and paused…brow furrowed.

"Are you the kid with that green guitar?"

My mouth was so dry I couldn't speak. I just nodded like a dumbass.

The cop gave a half smile and said, "Keep on playing."

He paused. And then, "Get out of here."

He fucking let us go.

It was hard to run home with all the urine soaking into my

pants legs, but I very distinctly remember thinking, *Oh...so* *that's* *the power of rock and roll.*

The power of the guitar, man.

*I didn't really wet myself.

**As far as you know.

That same theme has played throughout my life. Whether you're local (like I was in high school) or international (like Bret Michaels has become), you get perks because you can play the guitar.

Believe me, the perks are mighty. I sometimes wonder if they come close to rivaling the perks of being the president. Obviously, the sitting president is restricted on what he can or cannot do. But if Bill Clinton or George W. Bush walked into a place wearing a ball cap and sweatpants, would they be as quickly catered to as if Gene Simmons or Sir Paul McCartney did the same thing? Pick any time in the history of rock and roll. Imagine Elvis Presley or Prince trying to pull off that shit. There was no way they would be able to live an incognito life on the downlow.

The force was strong with me, and I was just getting started.

* * *

Guys…remember that girl in high school that you admired from afar? Maybe some of you have no idea what I'm talking about. But I'll bet most guys can relate to what I'm saying.

With regard to dating, I was very lucky. But there was still one girl who seemed like she was on another level from me. Heck, if you would have asked Freshman Pete Evick about her, I would have said she was a different *species* from me.

Her name was Theresa Grimes, and she was really cool (*think Duckie's Andie/Molly Ringwald in *Pretty in Pink*). I wasn't a stalker type, but I sort of knew my place in the grand scheme of the high school food chain. I didn't think I would have a shot if I asked her out.

The power of the guitar changed all that. It not only changed my position on the high school food chain, but it also changed my perception of myself. I grew in confidence and self-awareness. I remember when we were asked to play at Manassas Park High School. None of us were even in their school district—and I remember thinking, *Holy cow—the other side of town heard about us! We made it!*

So, at the end of my sophomore year, I decided I was going to grow past my formerly anxious self and make an overture toward Theresa Grimes. I was going to sweep her off her feet and give her no choice but to run away with me and live happily ever after.

Ah, if only…

So here was the plan: Amethyst was about to play a gig that was going to be attended by kids from several high schools. Actually, it didn't matter how many people were going to attend—Theresa Grimes was going to be there, and that was all that mattered at the time.

My idea was to take a rose and position it such that the stem would be held by a couple strings in my headstock (the top of the guitar neck where the tuning pegs are found) and the head of the rose would stick out…and be obvious. I would then walk into the crowd during a love song and "present" the rose to Theresa Grimes. In a rush of pheromones and deep appreciation, she would pluck the rose from my guitar, embrace me on weakened knees, and kiss me as the music faded and the audience gave us a standing ovation.

It was foolproof.

And in retrospect, most of it went exactly as planned. At least, *my* part did.

I played a B.C. Rich Warlock for that show. The rose was placed gingerly in the headstock, flower protruding like a love-struck bullseye. During the predetermined love song—an original song we had written—I strolled into the audience, sidled up next to Theresa Grimes, and presented her with the headstock offering.

At this point, I started thinking that Rob Lowe or Andrew McCarthy would play me in the movie version of this moment. Naturally, John Hughes would direct. But that was for future Pete to worry about. Right now, I have a girl to woo.

I played and played. In my mind's eye, Theresa would see the rose, take the rose, and think I was the sweetest thing ever…except she didn't.

I remember standing there (mostly confused) and trying to wave the headstock in front of her so she would see the damn flower. *Except she never looked at the headstock.* She just kept looking at me.

One would think that would suffice. Had I maintained my wits, I would have seen she was clearly smitten with me that evening. Probably rendered speechless and immobile by her overwhelming feelings of love. But I couldn't figure out why my foolproof plan had been foiled.

The moment that should have sealed my fate as the love of Theresa Grimes's life ended up becoming one of the most awkward moments of *my* life.

I remember leaning in and thinking, *Take the rose! Take the rose!*

She never figured it out. She never took the rose.

And as it turns out, she was never enraptured by my radiance.

Weird.

In fairness—and Theresa is still a good friend to this day, so I HOPE she'll read this book—it was an incredibly awkward moment for both of us. It wasn't that she didn't want to take the rose—it was that she didn't see the rose. The aspect I did not take into account was that I was accustomed to being in the spotlight and the center of attention. It's what I did, night after night. But when every eye in the place turned toward Theresa Grimes, she got nervous. It had to be freaky to have everybody staring at her. And then it grew even more uncomfortable when I started hovering and wouldn't leave her alone. She couldn't figure out what I was doing and was too good of a person to shoo me away.

She was Molly Ringwald and I was Judd Nelson.

And like the odd couple in *The Breakfast Club*, Theresa and I became boyfriend and girlfriend for a brief spell in high school. She and I remain good friends.

* * *

As with young Luke Skywalker, The Force grew stronger and stronger within me. Actually, it didn't grow stronger per se. Rather, it was always very strong (as with Luke), but it took me a minute to fully realize its potential.

One such moment of clarity happened when I got a call about a club called The Bayou.

The call was from Mike Himmel, my former guitar teacher who had a huge band in the area called Mirror Mirror. He was calling to offer us the opening slot for their gig.

Located in Georgetown, The Bayou was a huge level up from anything a band like Amethyst had ever played before. *Real* bands played The Bayou. Van Halen had played there, as had Bryan Adams, Poison, Kix, The Dave Matthews Band, and Hootie and the Blowfish. For all intents and purposes, The Bayou was the DC/Virginia equivalent to the iconic Whisky a Go Go on West Hollywood Boulevard.

If you played The Bayou, you had a career.

When the phone rang, I was almost 200 miles away on Graduation Beach Week vacation with my friends. The call was poorly timed but taught me an important lesson about life as a working musician.

It was summer vacation following my senior year in high school. Back then, every graduate would celebrate their newfound adulthood by packing up and making the long trek to Ocean City, Maryland, for an event called "Beach Week." Picture a full week of absolute hedonism, complete with alcohol, bikinis, and all the stupid you could fit into one pair of flip flops.

Yeah, yeah…I know I DID NOT DRINK. But all the rest was great.

In fact, it was glorious.

I drove a bunch of my friends up there and prepared to lose my mind. There were five of us stuffed into my car. Maybe six—the details are a bit fuzzy.

Anyway, when we arrived, I called home to let mom know we got there safely. The drive to Ocean City is LONG, especially for a group of eighteen-year-olds.

When my mom picked up and heard it was me, she said, "I'm

glad you called. You need to call Mike Himmel."

I said, "Well…what is it?"

"Just call him."

So, I did…and found out I had an opportunity to play The Bayou.

This was an enormous break. Except the gig was on Friday.

Bear in mind two things: first, it was currently either Tuesday or Wednesday (again, fuzzy details…). And second, mine was the only vehicle supporting five or six people. If I left, everyone either had to leave with me, or figure out a way to transport themselves the 184 miles back to Manassas.

Frankly, I did the only sensible thing. I told everyone I was sorry, but that we had to turn around and go home. Their vacation might be cut short, but I had to hustle back and play that gig. As I drove back, I thought, *So this is what happens in rock and roll.*

That was the big lesson. Rock and roll doesn't adjust its schedule for you. You adjust your schedule for rock and roll. It runs you; you don't run it.

I was no longer in control. Music was a wave I wanted to ride. And just as Bodhi rode his final wave in the movie *Point Break*, rock and roll is the "50 Year Storm." It takes you and has its way with you—and you either love it and ride it…or stay the Hell away from the water.

Amethyst played the gig. It was good to see Mirror Mirror and to reconnect with Mike Himmel. Mike was more than my guitar teacher; he basically taught me how to rock. Not so much by the mechanics of playing the instrument—but more about how to move and how to dig into my strings. Being an MTV rock star requires more than just proficiency up and down the fret board—it also requires that you look the part and *feel* the part.

Also on the bill that night was a band called HAVOC, whose guitar player, Steve Senes, is one of the most amazing players you'll ever see. He's an ungodly talent, and for a brief time, a member of EVICK. Steve can be heard ripping it up on our song "Big Rock Guitars."

The cherry on the sundae happened when my dad showed up at the gig. As I have mentioned, he never said much, but supported my decision to play music for my career. I knew he was proud of me—even though he wasn't much of a talker.

Anyway, I was up on stage at The Bayou, looking out over the crowd that might as well have been Madison Square Garden. From out of the throng, my dad walked up to the stage and greeted me like a stranger.

I don't mean that he pretended he didn't know me. Quite the opposite, in fact. Rather, I mean he carried himself differently. He walked differently and interacted with me differently. It was like he wasn't even my dad. Like, somehow overnight I suddenly became another adult in his eyes. I was seeing him as he was in a previous life; before kids and a job and a mortgage and all the pressures of adulthood suppressed the spirit that once drew him and my mother together.

He reached up and shook my hand.

"Do good, son. Make me proud tonight."

I blinked. Shaking his hand, welling with pride, I thought, *Well, if this ends tonight, at least I know I made it.*

The guitar around my neck had such power; it somehow got a seventeen-year-old fool like me onto the same stage once played by Eddie Van Halen. It helped me earn the respect of my father. And it got my dad to show a rare glimpse of genuine pride and emotion.

How awesome is that?

Speaking of power, I have a story that demonstrates the literal power wielded by the man with the guitar. And it almost ended badly.

* * *

There was an all-originals club in town called Jaxx. The owner at the time was named Jay Nedry, and he was good to us. He made us a part of *the scene*. Jay believed in work ethic, and our band was nothing if not a bunch of hard workers. As a reward for our hustle and flow, Jay would book big name rock bands and then give us the opportunity to open for them. Along the way, we opened for Ratt, Danger Danger, Warrant, Cheap Trick, and Ace Frehley among others. I got to play with my heroes, man.

Doors started to open. We played The Bayou. We opened for Ratt. The guys in Danger Danger knew our names. We were on the rise.

Now we were a bigger deal around town. We left the name Amethyst behind and moved on to calling ourselves Lady Luck. Regardless of the moniker, the band was making a name for itself, which led to better gigs. Better gigs meant we had higher expectations to meet regarding the music and our stage show. Higher expectations meant pushing the envelope.

And just as Luke Skywalker had to learn to remain in control of The Force, I had to learn the limits of just how far I could push the power of the guitar. Because a petulant Luke Skywalker could be dangerous when using The Force…and yet, isn't that the nature of young men?

Yes, it is. And I must say, we learned our limits quickly.

There was a club in Woodbridge, Virginia, called Stingray's. The physical structure was nothing special. It was the kind of place that, at first glance, you'd look around and think, *How the fuck does this place stay open?*

But we grew to love Stingray's because they were the only club that allowed us to bring in our ridiculously big drum riser.

Which drum riser was that, you may ask?

Well, remember that Chuck and I both loved Kiss. Chuck was a drummer, so he was always partial to Peter Criss. And if you have ever opened up the centerfold of the Kiss *Alive II* album, you have seen the massive drum kit and spectacular drum riser Peter Criss had constructed for his kit.

Chuck had built a big drum riser. Then, our bass player's (Justin) dad got together with my dad and helped us built lights and steps into the drum riser, so it rivaled the one on that album cover. At least, the best one a couple families from Manassas could afford. But I will say this: it was so big, it took two pick-up trucks to haul it from gig to gig.

And therein lies the rub. When we built the fucking thing, we didn't take practicality into account. Simple questions like, "Hey… will this monstrosity fit through the doors?" Or, "Umm…will we be able to maneuver this beast through the narrow hallways and onto the stage at these clubs?"

You know…things that reasonable people think about ahead of time.

Instead of asking those type of questions, we just kept asking, "How do we make this BIGGER? How do we make this COOLER?"

And we did and we did. My dad wired in a bunch of lights onto the monstrosity so we could sync a light show with the music. It was fuckin' killer. Definitely worthy of a three-day engagement at the L.A. Forum.

The other issue with the riser was that we didn't have a road crew and an entire day to assemble the thing. It took Chuck and I 90 minutes to schlep the pieces from the pick-up trucks and put them together on the stage. Club owners didn't want us monopolizing their stage and/or their space like that—another strike against any place other than Stingray's.

In hindsight, we weren't touring venues like the L.A. Forum. We were playing the Tiki Fala on Tuesday nights.

Stingray's allowed us to haul and place our big-ass drum riser onto their stage, and for that we were grateful. To repay them—and in keeping with the whole Kiss *Alive II* theme—we decided to entertain their crowd with a total Kiss-esque stage show. It wasn't just about the music, buddy…it was about *the show*. And that is where things got a little dicey.

To add a little razzle dazzle to the show, I built my own flash pots. Simply put, a flash pot is a can filled with some sort of explosive/incendiary material. When you hit a button, an electric charge is sent into the material, igniting it and producing a small but intense fireball. The technical term is pyrotechnics, but we just called them flash pots.

Audiences love that shit. Explosions…fire…mayhem…all part of the fun.

By the way, this was still the era prior to the 2003 Station (a Rhode Island nightclub) fire. In case you've never heard of it, 100 people died and over 200 hundred were injured during a show by Great White—when their pyrotechnics basically set the club on fire. In hindsight, their pyro was set up incorrectly and caused the acoustic foam around the drum riser to go up in flames. The club was filled with black smoke, the ceiling tiles ignited, and the rest is an ugly footnote in the history of rock and roll.

*I have many, many friends now that were there that night. This story is meant with no disrespect to them or to the people we lost.

Since '03, there has been a lot more attention paid to the details surrounding everyone's pyrotechnics. I don't mean to be insensitive to anybody (the Station fire was a fucking worst-case-scenario nightmare tragedy), but this wasn't 2003 and I wanted our show to rival anything ever done by Kiss.

Before I tell this story, let me first defend myself by saying two things. First, we practiced with these flash pots, over and over, to make sure they were done safely and correctly. I might have been a dumb redneck teenager, but I wasn't dangerously reckless. I knew what we were dealing with. And second, the thing I'm about to tell you about was not my fault. I'm not being sarcastic here—and I have videotape evidence to back me up.

We set up at Stingray's that afternoon—amps, drum riser, kit, and flash pots. Everything was going to be great. As was typical back in those days, we wanted to video tape our show. Also common was hitting "record" about 30 minutes prior to taking the stage. That way, we wouldn't forget during the chaos of the pre-show activities.

We took the stage and started our show. The crowd was into it. We were feeling it. The music took over and we achieved lift off.

I hit the switch to set off the first set of flash pots—and the flames hit the fucking ceiling. I remember thinking, *What the fuck—that wasn't supposed to happen?!?*

Thank God it didn't set the tiles on fire. We only burned the tiles. More accurately, we singed them. Whatever the case, our pots stopped just short of full structural ignition. People would have died, no joke. As it stood, we scared the shit out of everyone.

The owner was rightfully pissed.

But I remained confused.

I might be a space cadet in some areas of my life, but I am as detail oriented as a NASA engineer when it comes to my music and my band. There was no way this flash pot could have behaved in a manner other than what I had set it up to do.

When I went back to watch the videotape, the answer materialized right before my very eyes. A member of the band had inadvertently sabotaged my pyro.

He didn't intend to sabotage it, he intended to make it bigger and stronger and brighter.

The video showed him sneaking up to the flash pot (before the show) and adding powder to it. I didn't know he was going to do this, but I do know that he and I had argued several times over how big to make the explosions. He always wanted them to be bigger. I always wanted to be as big as they could be…while still remaining safe for the venue.

My father was a black powder expert. In fact, he would make his own bullets, and actually taught me that skill when I was young. As a result, I had spent most of my life around gunpowder and had been educated on how much of the stuff to use and not use.

Regardless of the band member's good intentions, he had a mind of his own and it almost led to disaster.

I love the metaphoric power of the guitar. The literal power must be kept within safe limits. We would have probably gone to jail had things turned out differently. It could have been that bad.

Thinking about jail reminds me of one last story. This one doesn't exactly speak to the power of the guitar, but it's short and it relates to that night at Stingray's. I think it'll be a good one to end this chapter with.

* * *

Lady Luck's singer was a guy named Mike Vance. Remember how I said it was really tough to find a good lead singer? I wasn't kidding, man. We had to spread the net wide to reel in Mike.

Mike wasn't a teenager like us. Nor was he in his twenties. Mike Vance owned a fucking deli in town. Like, he was a fully functioning *adult*. I think he was somewhere around 30 years old. Close enough, anyway. Our drummer worked at the deli and would talk offhandedly to Mike about our band.

As it turned out, Mike was also in a band. He was the singer in a band called Armageddon, a reasonably successful Christian metal band. The guy could sing and he looked like Sammy Hagar. More importantly, he wanted to sing with us…and he was cool.

Now ask yourself: Why would a 30-year-old guy want to hang out with a bunch of teenagers and play in a rock band with them, particularly when he was already singing in a Christian rock band that had a record deal? Could this breed of cat be completely stable and have his shit together?

If your answer was "no," then you'd be correct. Not that we had any idea at the time. We were just happy to have him.

But one morning I was getting ready (for school, I guess?) when my mom came down to my room and said, "Pete…you have to come look at the TV."

I ran into the living room in time to see a police sketch of our singer, Michael Vance. Obviously, they didn't know his name at the time—but you couldn't mistake that mug for anyone else. It was Michael Vance.

He was wanted for armed robbery. And not just any kind of run-of-the-mill armed robbery, mind you. He was wanted for *double* bank robbery. He robbed TWO banks the previous day. At gunpoint.

In retrospect, we should have known something was amiss with that guy. For example, he used to show up for rehearsals and bring a bunch of gear with him. He gave me a wireless once. Blew me away. We always wondered how he kept getting all the great gear, but we were young. We figured the deli was doing gangbusters business.

Anyway, they caught him. Mike went to jail and the deli was sold. Our drummer had to find a new day job.

You can look all this up; the information is online. I actually communicated with him a few years ago. I can't remember why or how we crossed paths. But to this day, he maintains his innocence.

* * *

That wraps up my teen years. They might have been unorthodox by most standards, but they introduced me to my career and taught me about the power of the guitar. Now if I could only keep momentum and continue a steady rise toward MTV fame and fortune.

Incredulously, I hit a few bumps along the way. But there was never a dull moment. My twenties defined a decade of continued—albeit *painful*—growth. Not all of it was bad (obviously), but buddy, it got bad enough that I grew to fully know The Dark Side.

CHAPTER 4: GROWING PAINS

High school had come and gone. We entered the 90s, and I was still open-throttle rock and roll. College was never an option—I was well on my way toward becoming a full-time working musician. I was out playing local clubs five or six nights per week, I was working out cover songs and writing new material, and I was working in a local music store. I was doing everything in my power to make it big.

However, the next ten years saw me almost change careers, completely revamp myself as a musician, start a band that rose like a meteor…and then crashed to earth like a meteor. And finally, I formed the band that has currently survived almost three decades of wear and tear.

I'm going to divide this chapter into four discreet stories. These stories have parts that overlap—particularly regarding their position on the grand timelines of my life and career—but I am going to treat them as being separate from one another. That separation will make it easier for both you and I to keep straight.

The first story is going to be the longest of the four—mostly because it will set up the context from which all four stories will grow.

Story One

Working as a cover artist has its pros and cons. The pro was getting paid—I realized quickly that I could earn $500 per night if I played cover songs—but only got $50 a night (on a good night) by playing originals. Getting paid was extremely important to me. Not that I wanted to necessarily get rich—actually, yeah I did—but more because I was making a go at standing on my own two feet financially. Being a starving musician probably had its artistic appeal, but I wanted to maintain a reasonably civilized lifestyle.

The major drawback of being a cover musician was the constant need to learn new songs. I was always listening to the radio and picking up on trends in rock music. Then I would break down the popular songs and learn them by literally playing them over and over in my basement. Then the band would come together and rehearse over and over.

We developed a huge catalog of covers over time. But it was to the detriment of writing originals. I just didn't have the time or energy to completely devote myself to both.

It really came down to two options: staying true to my dream —or getting paid. It was a difficult balance to strike.

My day job was still working at Music City. As I wrote about in my first book, *The Moments that Make Us*, the owner, Steve Goula, and the manager, Kevin Blair, were like fathers to me. My own father was still alive and kicking, but we were never overly close. Steve and Kevin filled that void and mentored me throughout some very trying years. To say that Music City was a leg supporting my delicate psyche would be an understatement.

There were actually two Music City locations, one in Manassas and the other about twenty miles away in Woodbridge, Virginia. I worked in Woodbridge, and that will become important in a minute.

The early 90s saw a lot of change in the music industry. Grunge swept in and bumped rock and roll from the world stage. Along with that change came a seismic shift in the music economy. It was no longer quite as "cool" to play guitar.

So Steve did what a good business owner would do. He sold off part of his empire so that the remainder could stay afloat. As a result, the Woodbridge store was sold to a man named Larry.

Originally, Steve's wife Karen was the manager of this store and as much a parental figure to me as Steve and Kevin. I also worked there with an incredible guy named Dave Crigger. Dave left to join Foghat (true story), but when Larry bought the place, Dave and Karen were out.

I was old enough to understand the basic tenants of business. I understood Steve's decision. But Larry was no Steve. In fact, Larry was (in a word) a major douche bag to me at the time. Looking back, I'm sure it was all just as awkward to him. I'm not sure why people who buy a business assume they are getting the employees too. Clearly, I didn't want a new boss…so I'm sure I was a douche bag too.

In no time at all, I fell into a bit of a funk. Even though I pride myself on how well I adapt to (and invite) change, this one felt jarring because suddenly, the Woodbridge store didn't feel like "family" anymore. My two father figures were gone; replaced by a guy I didn't like as much…and certainly didn't know as well.

Concurrent to this fiasco, I broke up with my Manassas girlfriend. That meant I now had two major changes happening right on top of each other. I subsequently began dating a girl from Loudoun County, Virginia—a much wealthier area than my little neck of the woods.

All well and good—except that she existed in an entirely different universe than my Manassas people. Having a new girlfriend meant spending a lot of time with her…which meant cutting me off from my friends and core group back in lowly Manassas.

All the stress came to a head one afternoon. My brain broke, and I was forced to change along with the change. I had a temporary meltdown—which ended with me shaking and crying and anguished in the Manassas Music City store. I told Steve and Kevin that I couldn't take any more of Larry's shit, so I had to quit.

Steve and Kevin didn't have the option of hiring me back in Manassas. But my head was spinning, so I made the decision to take my talents elsewhere. Because my girlfriend lived in Loudoun County, I went out there and applied at a local music store called Melodee Music.

I was hired on the spot. As luck would have it, their main employee was leaving for college. It was like a divine rock and roll intervention.

Rock and roll cracked the musical door in my brain, but Melodee Music kicked it the rest of the way open. Music City had a business model that was anchored in guitars, drums, and a steady stream of pure rock and roll. Melodee Music was all-encompassing. It was much bigger and sold every instrument imaginable. Yes, they sold guitars and drums (they had a FAR more comprehensive selection, in fact) but they also sold violins and saxophones, and had programs to rent instruments to school kids taking band lessons.

In short, they were a *complete* music shop. And thankfully, they gave me a job on the spot. The totality of their breadth of music had such an impact on me, I actually took up the saxophone for a short while. Chuck Fanslau did *not* approve—but fuck that guy. I was a budding ar-TEEST.

(kidding, buddy)

I met more and more people. Hell, I outgrew my humble Manassas roots. I was now a man of *Northern* Virginia. Looking back, I should have probably worn an ascot and drank expensive bourbon.

Anyway, I met amazing musicians who excelled in all genres of music—some of which were genres I didn't know existed. I met acoustic guitar players and folk musicians and jazz musicians—that all blew my mind.

The world expanded. It was inspiring.

One of the employees at Melodee Music was a guy named Danny Blitz. Danny was a bit of an arrogant S.O.B., but he represented a new kind of rock and roll. I will stick to this point until the day I die: Danny was Green Day before Green Day was Green Day. Danny had the look and the sound—and he opened my mind to new ways of thinking outside of my musical box.

Danny ended up moving to Los Angeles and finding some success as a songwriter. He wrote the popular song, "If Ozzy Was My Dad," which was based on *The Osbournes* television show. But that's not why I bring him up in my story. I'm bringing him up because he started me on an entirely different path in music. A path that I thought might end up changing my career.

* * *

Danny owned an 8-track, reel-to-reel recording machine. I had used a four-track recorder in high school, so I was familiar with the process of using devices like this. However, I was fascinated by the possibility of making *real* sounding records—records that had the same feel as those I heard on the radio. Four tracks were fine for our little high school gig…but eight tracks would bring me into the big leagues.

So, when Danny decided to sell his recorder, I jumped all over it. Subsequently, I immediately began to record music with it.

**To close off this story, I will add that Danny has since passed away. May he rest in peace.

Recording became my passion and my obsession. This desire was fueled by my coworkers and customers at the music store. When they heard what I had recorded, they were extremely complimentary and encouraging. It seemed I had a knack for this sort of thing. So, I forged ahead.

With this in mind, I approached my dad with an idea. As I have mentioned, my dad and I weren't close in a traditional sense, but he was always steady in support of my musical ambitions. But this "ask" was going to be bigger.

I asked if I could gut half of our basement and turn it into a recording studio.

He agreed. To this day, I still cannot believe he said yes…but there you go.

He helped me with the construction, and we did it. We built walls and ran wires and made a pretty solid studio set up. It was by no means as professional or polished as anything a studio in New York or Los Angeles would have—but it was the best thing anyone would find in the greater Manassas metropolitan area. We had a makeshift drum room and a control room. It was cool.

And I caught the fever. The recording and engineering process became so exciting to me, that I bit into it hook, line, and sinker. Along with obsession comes repetition. And along with repetition comes mastery. I became really, really good at producing first-rate sounding recordings. In a short time, my reputation grew… and bands started hiring me to produce their records.

I don't know how or why my parents and their neighbors remained cool with this, but they never said a negative word about all the bands that started showing up at our house. It was an eclectic bunch—bands from every surrounding county started to appear on our doorstep. Bands with names like Powder Monkey, Naked Soul Brothers, and The Arctic Shepards. Mostly alternative rock, I was ensconced into the grungy scene. And looking back, some of the bands were as good (or better) than mainstream bands like Pearl Jam.

Throughout this time, I was able to recognize a good song here and there—but I never completely fell in love with this style of music. I was still an old-school rocker at heart. But I started to notice that many of my friends—guys I had tremendous respect for because we all came up through the clubs together—started to fake it. They gave in. They donned flannel shirts and combat boots and cut their hair and stared at their feet while they sang their gloomy songs.

I held firm to my roots. I didn't want to fake it. That seemed disingenuous to me—and it certainly wasn't the image an aspiring MTV-famous guy like myself wanted to portray.

In fairness to the genre, I did own a pair of silver Doc Martin boots. My girlfriend got them for me, and they seemed "Ace Frehley" enough for me to justify wearing them.

I also dyed my hair blue. From about 1994-2000, I went through various stages of different blue hair colors. I don't know why exactly. It was a simpler time.

I got some piercings and grew a goatee…but I couldn't fake the music. My style was sacred to me, and that was that. Maybe my career as a musician might just go down the tubes because the industry had moved away from anything I could (in good conscience) play, but all of a sudden, I had hope—an option that I never knew existed. I could be a record producer and engineer.

I began to focus more and more time & effort on recording other bands. Not that I ever gave up completely on being a musician—it just took a temporary back seat. In fact, at one point I auditioned for Poison. Kind of.

* * *

True story. You don't need to go back and re-read that last sentence. Long before I could have ever imagined *meeting* Bret Michaels—much less playing in his band—I tried out to be in Poison.

And let me be clear: I did not fly anywhere and meet the guys. Nor did I meet with their management, nor did I play in a dueling guitar "shred off" with Richie Kotzen in the finals. But I did submit an audition packet, thanks to a local musician friend of mine,

Michael Fath. Honestly, C.C. DeVille was/is a hero of mine and it was gut wrenching as a Poison fan to hear he wouldn't be with them anymore but...if he wasn't going to be, then in my mind I was the single most deserving guy of that gig on the planet.

Michael was a Northern Virginia guy, which was close enough to Poison's home base in Pennsylvania. He was also a superhero guitar virtuoso who had released two incredible albums by 1991: *Flick of the Wrist* (1989) and *Shake* (1990). To say that Michael was the real deal would have been an understatement…like, he had a *real* shot with Poison. However, he similarly wasn't asked to come meet with the guys in the group. He had to submit an audition packet, just like I did.

For whatever reason, it didn't work out between him and Poison. So, when he got the news he wouldn't be their new member, he called me and said, "Pete…I know you love this band. Here is the number. Call it and give it a shot."

My brain lit up like a flash pot. I had been living under a cloud of grunge for the past few months, and this was a fresh blast of arctic POISON air. First order of business: put together a press packet.

In ONE DAY, I recorded a demo tape, wrote a bio, figured out how to apply basic make-up, convinced my girlfriend (Wendy) to do a photo shoot with me before the make-up smeared off, got my head shots developed at a One Hour Photo, assembled the entire thing into a single coherent package, and flew on the wings of Pegasus to FedEx…

…and on the way to FedEx, Pegasus and I got pulled over for speeding.

There I was, heart thumping a double-bass kick in my chest, sitting on the side of Rte. 234. I could not think of a more colossal waste of my valuable time, but I was still a good kid. All that hubris melted away when the cop approached my window.

I rolled down the window. It took the cop a good three or four Mississippi's before he finally spoke.

"Son…do you have make-up on?"

In a torrent of frenzied word salad, I explained the whole situation to him. To fortify my defense, I showed him the whole press kit and emphasized (maybe seven hundred times?) how Poison was one of my favorite bands and how this was the opportunity of a lifetime and that CC had just left the band and how Michael Fath told me about it and how I couldn't fake it with grunge and…and…and…

And he let me go without giving me a ticket.

The power of the guitar, man. Or in this case, the power of sheer panic…and rock and roll.

I made it to FedEx by closing time and had the press kit in the hands of Poison's management the very next day. I knew I wouldn't hear anything back immediately, which I didn't. A couple weeks later, I got a call.

"Hey Pete…thanks for sending in the audition packet. The demo was great, you looked great…but we're going to go with an L.A. guy named Richie Kotzen."

I was mildly devastated, but I understood. I was young and mostly unknown outside of my little corner of the universe. And besides, now I could tell everyone that I had auditioned for Poison!

Not that it would have mattered. Grunge was in the midst of a full-scale takeover, and the current metal bands were considered the shameful stepchildren. In fact, during that era, I think Poison, Bon Jovi, and Van Halen were the only bands that still played sheds and theaters. So, I put my guitar back in its case (figuratively speaking) and returned to engineering and producing. In fact, I ramped it up a notch.

* * *

Poison audition notwithstanding, I was in the process of making my peace with never being MTV famous. Grunge wasn't my thing, but I was damn good at making records for other people. My basement was a hotbed of music activity, and my parents' patience was probably wearing thin.

Actually, that might not be true. My parents were incredible when it came to supporting my passion for music. But I will say this: I had definitely outgrown the basement studio. So, I approached my dad with another crazy idea. I asked if he would help me—if I rented a warehouse in town and built it out into a *real* recording studio. I wanted to make it on par with the ones you would find in Nashville or Los Angeles or New York.

My parents—God bless them—took out a fucking *second mortgage on their home* to get the cash together for me to build a first-rate recording studio and rehearsal space in Manassas, Virginia. I called it Clear Sound Recording, and it was fabulous.

Someone is going to read that and call me out, so I might as well get this out of the way: the name Clear Sound was derived from the name of my Loudoun County girlfriend, Wendy Clear. Total "puppy love" move, right? Perhaps…but the breakup was ugly (I'll write about it in the next chapter). She and I buried the hatchet in the early 2000s and maintained a distant (but in touch) relationship for about fifteen years. Wendy passed away in 2019.

The studio turned out to be fantastic, but it took a long time to convert the warehouse. My dad helped a lot. Most of the heavy lifting was done by me and my two partners, Chuck (Fanslau) and our friend Paul Lyles (who was nicknamed "Bear"). We also got a shit ton of help from our buddies Bart Harris and Billy Duncan.

Together, we built out the whole thing. Through the sweat of our brow, we built all the walls and wired all the sound systems. Bear was a contractor, so he knew how to build houses. He was the main foreman on our jobsite. He taught us how to do it—and we did it. For months we were in that warehouse, hammering, nailing, wiring, and finishing. Chuck's mom worked for a lighting company, so got us some incredible deals on all that kind of stuff.

But we were all still rock and roll to the core. It took us almost a year to get the thing up and running because before it was finished, we brought in some gear and got distracted. WAY too often we turned "construction time" into "jam time."

Just like the famous line uttered by a disembodied voice in *Field of Dreams*, "If you build it, he will come"—we built it, and they came. They came from miles around, in fact. Clear Sound Studio was open and available 24/7, and artists started to arrive from near and far.

* * *

The first employee I ever hired was a guy named Ed Rodriguez. The background story of our friendship (and the life he has subsequently led) is important to me, so I'm going to devote a page or two to him.

Early on when my studio was still in my basement, I recorded a band called Estranged. They were heavy and modern, but the singer, Steve Selenski, was great and liked Bon Jovi. The band had their roots in my kind of music; they were young and super cool. I remember the bass player was Joe Murray…and the drummer was a guy named Ed Rodriguez.

Ed and I hit it off; I loved him. He eventually came to work at Clear Sound as my first bona fide employee and was a huge part of making it THE SCENE that it became. He would manage the rehearsal section and answer phones and really just be moral support.

Ed met his wife Sara there. They were both so young; we all watched their high school love unfold. And because I was me, I would often get involved when I shouldn't.

I remember that we had one computer in the studio, and we all had AOL accounts. To Ed and Sara, as a display of undying love, they let each other check each other's email. I thought that was crazy and would tell them all the time that wasn't love, that was lack of trust. Hell, they spent more time on each other's account than their own.

But they didn't want my advice…ever. *Even when I was fucking right.*

For example…

At one point, Ed received an offer to join an up-and-coming band (with some promise) in the Chicago area. Everyone—including me—was excited for him at the beginning. But 24 hours before they left, I was secretly told that the Chicago band had gone with a new drummer. Furthermore, they didn't plan on telling Ed—they were literally gonna let him uproot his whole life to get to Chicago and have NO BAND.

I did what any good friend would do. I told Ed and Sara. But instead of gratitude, I was met with total disbelief and negativity. I was accused of trying to ruin Ed's shot at a career.

Well guess what, I was right. They went to Chicago and NO

BAND. To this day, I wish I could find those windy city guys and beat their asses.

Anyway, years went by and a whole other story happens… but Sara and I became really close…like, "best friend" close.

No, this isn't going where you think it is. Get your mind out of the gutter, you maniacs.

Sara became a mainstay in my life…a forgiving soul, although feisty and argumentative like no one else. Years later, when I finally stepped outside the music biz and started Shining Sol Candle Company, she was my only choice for a partner. She and I created something magic; something that led me on a new path. I'll forever be grateful for what she helped me create. I will talk in depth about Sara and Shining Sol in chapter nine.

Ed and Sara are still married today. Their fairy tale came true and is stronger than ever. While not without turmoil, they *made it*. Of all the success stories I've seen in my life, this one is probably the greatest success. Because love is really all that matters in the end, right?

And they found their way.

But let's find our way back to the timeline, and Clear Sound studio.

* * *

Just like my Judd Nelson experience in high school, I had once again created a "Scene." Punkers hung out with Grungers who hung out with Metal Heads. My studio became a musical melting pot, and the epicenter of *cool* in Manassas, Virginia. I was recording and bands were rehearsing and people would show up just to hang out.

This was like my parents' basement all over again—but this was on a much, much larger scale. It was real and it was a thriving business. I was 20 years old and finally feeling like an adult. I had a business license and a lease on a building. I was making money (well…kinda) and doing what I loved: Bringing people together and making music.

Not all of it was caviar wishes and champagne dreams. I built a second-floor loft that acted as a hang-out spot. It was crudely roughed in, but there was a pool table and a stereo. Anyway, the loft was solid and made of wood—but it was surrounded by a soft floor made of foamy ceiling tiles because it acted as the ceiling to the first floor (can you picture what I'm saying?). Picture the attic in your grandmother's house. You step on the joists but not the floor—because often times, the floor is just drywall that acts as the ceiling to the story below.

Anyway, one day a billiard ball jumped the table and rolled out onto the ceiling tiles. A kid who obviously didn't know better ran after the ball—and promptly fell through the floor and crashed into the studio below. He landed on a guitar, and it could have been so, so bad.

I remember freaking out internally. I was 20 years old and figured I was about to get sued and lose everything and probably go to jail. And my parents would get sued too. And lose everything. And then they would go to jail.

Probably not the last thing. But I was in a state of panic.

To my surprise, the kid lifted himself off the floor and said, "This is our place, man. I don't want to lose this place. I'm not going to the hospital and I'm not gonna tell my parents about this."

I couldn't believe it. I don't know if I ever knew the kid's name, but he turned what could have been a tragedy into a moment where I once again recognized the power of music.

This was their place…their *scene*. He didn't want to risk losing it for everyone.

It was magic. I was on top of the world.

* * *

One of the greatest things about Clear Sound was our mascot, my pet iguana, Igor. Igor grew to be over 5 feet long; very rare for a home bred reptile like him. Before we moved into Clear Sound we kept him in my parents' home. My mom kept him by the microwave, so I often joke that he was like Godzilla…a little radiation is what made him so big.

Interesting fact: iguanas have no short-term memory. They

forget everything, just about every 7 seconds. That fact will be relevant in a moment.

We kept Igor in a giant cage habitat my dad built for him. The thing was correspondingly big; 8 feet long by 5 feet high. I put it right at the entrance of Clear Sound; anyone that came in would be greeted by my giant iguana.

The reason I brought up the 7 second thing is because Igor—for as cute and cuddly as he could be—was a bit of a ruffian. He would lunge at the glass in attack formation every time someone walked by. He was not docile or calm in any way, as most iguanas were.

His surly disposition fascinated us; we would often use it as a baseline variable to test the "seven second rule." One of us would walk by and he would lunge in our direction *only once*…but sure enough, wait seven seconds (almost to the dot) and he would lunge again. It was amazing.

Truth be told, I loved that creature more than anyone can imagine. I still think about him every day. As he got older and I knew he had already surpassed his life expectancy (probably due to his radioactive soul), I forced myself to give him away to a friend and frequent client of Clear Sound. His name was Russ and he was a bit of an iguana whisperer. He was the only guy that could get Igor out of the cage and have him rest calmly on his arm. I still remember watching Russ' truck drive away with Igor riding shotgun.

It felt terrible to let him go, but I was touring again. The last thing I wanted was to get a call that my pet was dead in the studio. Russ was able to give him the life he deserved.

And I began to get the life I had always wanted.

* * *

I even recorded some heavy hitters in the music industry. When Kix broke up in the mid-90s, Steve Whiteman (their lead singer) formed his own band called Funny Money. My buddy, Ned Maloney, played bass in Funny Money, so recommended my studio when Steve was looking to record a song.

The song was a Cheap Trick cover that was intended to go on

a tribute album. A pretty simple assignment from my perspective… except I was nervous as Hell when Steve stepped up to the mic. I had never worked with a real "professional" before, so I had no idea what to expect.

I'll never forget—it took him ONE take to nail the vocals. I didn't know what to make of it. The vocalists I typically worked with at Clear Sound were green. Most of the studio time was spent instructing them on what the hell to do, much less trying to fine-tune their performance.

With Steve, all that went out the window. He stepped up to the mic, sang the song, and badda-boom—there you have it.

In fact, I hit the talk-back button and said, "Hey Steve, that was great. Would you like to come in here and have a listen?"

He looked at me through the glass and said, "No…I got it."

He wasn't cocky. He was a professional…and that came with a certain level of confidence. He had done this job so many times before, he knew exactly what to do and prepared himself to do it. It was fantastic.

The next major act that recorded at my studio was the three-piece British metal band, Raven. Ned Maloney made the connection again—because he was friends with their drummer at the time, Joe Hasselvander.

Raven's biggest hit in the U.S. came in 1985 and was called "On and On." I loved that song and was very familiar with the band. In fact, when Metallica was just getting started, they actually opened for Raven during a stretch of tour.

Raven ended up recording and releasing 14 albums during their tenure, and one of them was recorded at Clear Sound Studio in Manassas, Virginia. Check out their 1997 release, *Everything Louder*. It was so damn cool.

I learned a lot about recording from them. The guys in the band produced the album, but I engineered it. They were totally professional, and very nice to me. And that was saying something—I was annoying as shit (I'm sure) because all I wanted to do was ask them stories about Metallica. They tolerated me and were extremely kind and generous.

* * *

Let me throw one more famous band at you…one that came around later in the timeline. This one isn't as radio-friendly, so you may not have heard of them. But they have been nominated for three Grammy Awards—finally winning one in 2022 for "Best Reggae Album" (*Beauty in Silence*). And believe it or not, they got their start at Clear Sound Studio.

The guys in the group came to us in 1997 or 1998. By then, I had started to tour more and became less and less invested in Clear Sound. In order to keep the studio up and running, I had to put my trust in other people. The two I placed at the helm were my childhood guitar teacher, Mike Himmel, and one of my closest friends (at the time), Chris Noel.

Chris eventually came to run the place, as he was just learning to engineer and produce. Mike was a seasoned producer already and took on the jobs that needed actual expertise. But Chris had an ear for talent.

One day while I was on the road, a young bunch of guys who barely knew what they were doing, called Soldiers of Jah Army (SOJA), needed to make a demo. Mike didn't want to do the project, but Chris decided he would take it on. SOJA recorded a demo which eventually became *Creeping In*, their first foray into the music industry.

So… they weren't a famous band back then, but look them up now. Chris Noel and Clear Sound Studio played a small part in launching the career of a Grammy Award winning powerhouse in reggae.

One more band that fascinated me was a band called Enemy Soil. Their genre was called grind core. Their main guy was named Richard Johnson. He would show up with a couple guys and a drum machine, and record an entire record in one night. The first time he came to the studio, I didnt know what to think...then when he came back, he brought me a vinyl pressing of his release. He went on to tell me about how it was on the charts in Germany or Ireland or wherever.

I think maybe at first I didnt believe it—it just didnt make sense to me. But look them up; they are a major part of this brand of music's history. It blows my mind to this day.

* * *

As far as *my* career was concerned, I was transformed into a producer. I still loved to play but could not picture a world where my brand of authentic rock and roll could break through the strangle hold that grunge held over the industry.

And then the world of music changed again. Only this time, it was for the better.

Story Two

In my mind, the Grunge scene was like a dark cloud hanging low over the entire musical landscape. Sure, there were some good songs and incredible musicians and singers that came out of the genre…but in general, the music felt exactly like its dingy flannel shirts.

Speaking of dark clouds, I will add that I survived two near-fatal car crashes during this brief period. I was working at the studio and still held my day job at Melodee Music—so I was burning the candle at both ends.

Incidentally, that's a phrase that's commonly used to describe my lifestyle today—while splitting duty between Bret Michaels and Shining Sol (and now writing a second book). I know…some things never change.

I was basically up all night at the studio, up all day at the music store, and up all in between (trying to find my sanity). My brain eventually gave out because I kept falling asleep while driving.

Both incidents happened around 10am, and both on Rte. 28—my path between the studio and the music store. I was completely sober on both occasions; I was just so exhausted that I couldn't stay awake. So, I drove straight through a red light…twice.

You don't have to tell me how dangerous it is to drive while impaired. I get it. Drowsiness can be just as fatal as alcohol when you slide behind the wheel. When I look back, I grow annoyed at some of the irresponsible decisions I made.

The first wreck scared the crap out of me. Not that it kept me from ultimately falling asleep at the wheel a second time, but it did freak me out. I remember coming to and seeing a baby seat in the back seat of the car I had just rammed into. My first thought was, *Holy fuck...did I just kill a child???*

Not good.

Fortunately, it turned out there was no child in the car. Furthermore, nobody got hurt. I still thank God to this day. Holy fuck is right.

The second time I fell asleep at the wheel happened in February during a snowstorm. Same deal: I fell asleep and flew through a red light. Ended up t-boning a white van and breaking it almost in half. It was an ugly, twisted wreck. Thank God nobody got hurt…and holy fuck all over again.

However, this one was a lot worse for me. When I made impact in *this* wreck, I was knocked from a deep sleep into total unconsciousness. They had to cut me out of the car and lay me on the street to keep me alive.

I came to slowly…and watched snowflakes drift down from the heavens. For a moment, I wasn't sure if I was dead or alive. And then I heard the voice of God.

Except God had changed his name to Paul.

"Pete…? Pete…? Pete—this is Paul Sanders."

I knew Paul Sanders. He was a friend of mine from childhood. He grew up five houses from me. Apparently, he was dead too. It was the only explanation that made sense. After all, he was calling my name from Heaven. What else would Paul be doing way up here in Loudoun County?

Turns out, it *was* Paul—and neither of us were dead. Coincidentally, he was also on Route 28 that morning. Because he was now a paramedic. In Loudoun County. And so happened to get dispatched to my accident. I swear I am not making this up—you can't make this kind of shit up. Anyway, Paul Sanders was trying to revive and keep me calm while (gulp) checking me for a broken neck.

Imagine hearing that in the background. Paramedics discussing the possibility of your neck being broken. All of a sudden,

I was WIDE awake and conscious as can be. I spoke to Paul the paramedic, even though I could barely see him.

"Is…is my neck broke?"

"That's what we're trying to figure out."

Let me say this, dear reader: in that situation, you either want to hear a yes or a no. Either you can rejoice that you are going to escape without a broken neck, or you can start to make your peace with the fact that you will probably live out your days as a quadriplegic. One way or the other—none of this "that's what we're trying to figure out" bullshit.

Magically (and perhaps miraculously), my neck *wasn't* broken. Further, none of my bones were broken. I had torn muscles and ligaments, but nothing permanent.

If you happen to pick up a copy of the EVICK album, *Anachronism*, listen to the second verse to the song "Just the Same." The lyrics go:

I went and drove my car
Right through some guy's van
I woke in a hospital room
With an achin' head.

That whole song is about some of the bad shit I have put myself through—but how I would probably do it all over again if I had the chance. Those particular lyrics referred to that second wreck.

I was working myself almost literally to death. I suppose I can thank my dad for this stupid work ethic. It might be the death of me still…but not back in the days of Clear Sound Studios. And not back in the days when the sunshine returned to music.

* * *

Out of the grunge chaos comes order; out of the darkness came the dawn. Happier music started to poke its head out of the nuclear winter, and bands like Matchbox Twenty, Sugar Ray, and Hootie and the Blowfish found their way onto the radio.

This was music I could relate to again.

Following my second car crash, I coincidentally met a singer named Ryan Gindhart. When Ryan left the Navy, he moved to Washington, DC, from somewhere in Indiana. He was a talented singer, but that wasn't why he was in the area. He had moved to take an unrelated job—but I didn't care about that. Rock music was getting cool again, and I was itching to start playing.

We formally met when Ryan walked into Melodee Music. I was noodling around on the guitar, and he came over to hear me play. We struck up a conversation, during which he mentioned going to a few open mic nights around the area. I'll never forget, he called them "Open Stages." I had never heard that term, but I guess that's what Open Mics are called in Indiana. I let him know that I ran a recording studio, and thus began a beautiful friendship.

To Ryan's credit, he wasn't a jaded old veteran of the music industry. He was fresh-faced and pure… an innocent novice who sang for the love of the notes. In fact, his goal was to record a few songs he had written so he could send them back home to his family in Indiana.

How "Norman Rockwell" is that?

So, he showed up at Clear Sound with an acoustic guitar, and we recorded a song called "If the Shoe Fits." The song was great… but his voice was greater. To me, he sounded exactly like Bryan Adams. And I love Bryan Adams.

When Ryan left the studio, I went immediately to the phone and called everyone I knew from my old days of playing rock and roll. I wanted them to hear his voice. They obliged but weren't nearly as excited as me. They were metal heads and Ryan had a pop voice. Even my friends who had knuckled under and gone grunge were now drifting back to metal via influences like Pantera and Nine Inch Nails.

I didn't care. I just wanted validation that Ryan could sing. And everyone agreed—his voice was wonderful.

And that made me want to start a band with Ryan even more. I needed to woo him into starting a band with me. The timing was right, the chemistry was right, and the talent was right. It felt like we were on the verge of something huge. I was ready to give the music thing another shot. Take aim once again at becoming MTV famous

—even though by then, MTV was starting to fade with regard to its power and influence.

But that didn't matter. I was all-in. Actually, I went a little overboard. I used my newly found talent as an engineer and producer to create something different out of "If the Shoe Fits."

Without his permission, I took Ryan's acoustic song and built a rock song around it. I had a drummer friend of mine (Keith Sarna) lay down a beat underneath the acoustic track; then I played bass and guitar, altering the original arrangement to make a peppier rock/pop song out of a more stripped-down, personal song.

And I've got to tell you, it was pretty good.

I played it for Ryan, and he (luckily) thought it was magical. It was radio-friendly and modern sounding; a tight track that could have been released as a single *that day*.

How could he refuse?

He didn't refuse. We put together a band called Some Odd Reason. Keith Sarna, Spencer, Jaimeson, Ryan Gindhart, and me. I was still active in the music community and had grown my network through the studio. When the band gelled, I swung for the fences.

Keep in mind, Ryan had never been in a real band before. He hadn't played any gigs to speak of; he was a greenhorn in every aspect of the music industry. But he had the look and he had the voice. That was all the clay I needed to mold this kid into a successful front man.

That said, we immediately jumped into the deep end of the pool. The very first gig Some Odd Reason ever played—Ryan's first time singing in a band—was to open for Cheap Trick at Jaxx in Springfield, Virginia, to a sold-out crowd.

We were all so happy and excited by everything that was happening. Imagine if your first car is a Porsche. Or think about if your first date is with Jennifer Aniston. Or if your first job out of high school pays you a million dollars a year. Your expectations would be enormously skewed, right? Like, you would now expect that every step you take from there is upwards—or at least, lateral. You don't want to go backwards. Nobody likes to go backwards.

But for a start-up band like ours, there was no way we could keep opening for national touring acts like Cheap Trick. We had to pay our dues…and that meant going backwards.

Let me say that differently. We weren't going backwards *per se*. Rather, we were returning to where we should have been in the first place. We wrote songs and played clubs all over the place—all the time. It was a Some Odd Reason blitzkrieg.

And look, opening for Cheap Trick was awesome, but it was a bit of a fluke. It was a nice gig I got because I knew some people who were able to hook me up. I understood that. The other guys in the band understood that. But to Ryan, I think we weren't moving forward as fast as he thought we were going to. In the end, he sort of got cold feet and wanted to return to the "real world."

To his credit, he hung in there as long as he could. He got through our first album and the start of the subsequent tour.

Put a pin in the Ryan story for a minute. I have to tell you about how I got our record deal.

* * *

Back at Clear Sound, I produced demos for a band called Scrub. They were signed to a record label called Sol 3 Records, which was owned by a man named Richard Gottehrer. You may not know his name, but Richard was a powerhouse in the industry. He wrote hits like "My Boyfriend's Back" and "Hang on Sloopy" and "I want Candy." He produced and launched the careers of New York bands like Blondie, The Ramones, and the Talking Heads.

Perhaps the crown jewel of his career (other than Some Odd Reason, of course—ha!) was producing the Go-Go's debut album, *Beauty and the Beat*. It went double platinum (over 2,000,000 copies sold in the United States) and launched the career of one of the most powerful all-female groups in history. Incidentally, he also produced their gold follow-up, *Vacation*.

Richard's partner was a man named Scott Cohen. Scott is now in senior management as the Chief Innovations Officer with Warner Music Group worldwide. Not to mention, he and Richard formed The Orchard—a company that was the very first to digitally distribute music. The Orchard was eventually sold to Sony Music.

The muscle to this organization was a guy named Chris

Apostolou. He was partnered with Scott from their old Virginia days managing bands. Chris is a close friend of mine to this day, and he was as much a part of the success of Sol 3 and The Orchard as was Richard and Scott

As one additional tip-of-the-cap to Scott, he is a local guy from Virginia and still one of my favorite people. <Shameless plug alert> If you *sort of* recognize his name, it's probably because he wrote the foreword to my first book.

I don't mean for this to sound like a college lecture. The point is, these guys knew their way around the music industry.

Then it came time to negotiate my record deal. I met Ron Bienstock, who at one time was voted one of the most powerful people in the music business by *BAM* magazine. These three guys (Richard, Scott, and Ron) were my holy trinity of the music business. I had real muscle behind me—real players, real powerhouses. *Everything* was there.

How could this not end perfectly?

*Spoiler alert…it didn't end perfectly.

Anyway, here's how all this came to be.

Scrub was getting ready to record a couple songs in New York. They had recently lost their guitar player, so they asked me to join them and fill in, in the studio. It made sense—they had worked with me at Clear Sound and were comfortable with my playing and my personality.

So, I did. I drove up to New York to work with Scrub. And because I was a recording guy and could geek out on the equipment and the engineering part of making records, I got along really well with Richard.

When all was said and done, the songs were cut and released in Germany—to a rousing success. If memory serves, one song in particular, "Razor Tongue," went to #13 (or so) on the German charts.

I can't end this without saying Scrub was supposed to be THE band that put Northern Virginia on the map. It was special, it was original, it was cool, and it was *great*. We all (everyone in the area, no matter what lifestyle they lived or what other music they loved) believed they were perfect for the time!

* * *

Simultaneous to all of this happening, another member of the Sol 3 family was in my orbit. Jason Miller, singer for the Fairfax, Virginia-based industrial rock band called Godhead (which grew out of Jason's previous band, Blind), worked for me at Clear Sound. In fact, he was the second employee I ever hired at Clear Sound.

Jason, incidentally, went on to a big career in Los Angeles. He runs a studio out there, and also took advantage of some cool opportunities like voicing several characters on the television series, *Avatar: The Last Airbender*. Not to mention he became close friends with Jack Osbourne (Ozzy's son), and Billy Ray Cyrus. I'm proud to have been a small part of his climb in the industry, as he was also a big influence on me with the way he handled his business so professionally. He continues to create original music, travel the world, and do amazing things.

I'm not sure how Jason feels about it all, but I like to believe we helped each other.

It all came together in one neat package. Through the success of Scrub's song, my relationship with Jason, and the fact that everyone in the New York studio got along with me, Richard and Scott became interested in listening to demos from my band.

They liked what they heard but didn't immediately jump in with both feet. First, they sent Scrub's lead singer, Petra, to Manassas to record some tracks with me locally. I don't know for sure if this was all part of the vetting process, but those recording sessions went well and seemed to lead to the next phone call. Scott invited me (and Some Odd Reason) to New York to share our demos with him and Richard Gottehrer.

The band was sent to record in a fantastic studio in Paramus, New Jersey. We arrived and got right to work. Recording in another studio was a trip for me. The place in Paramus was much more high-tech and modern than my place, and I soaked it in. I was in *everyone's* face all the time.

What's this?

How do you do that?

Show me! Show me! Show me!

During our time in New Jersey, we recorded five demos/songs. One was a song I wrote called "Spin" and another was a song Ryan wrote called "All or Nothing." In my mind, both tunes were (of course) smash hits. To this day "Spin" is my baby. It was supposed to be a hit song—and in my mind, it totally is a hit song. Over 20 years later it is still the most requested original I ever wrote. It even sparked its own dance on the night we first played it live.

The lyrics were powerful in their simplicity.

The world keeps spinning around and around,
without you without me without a sound.

I was trying to tell the world, *Don't sweat the little shit*. The world is a fucked-up place but…it goes on tomorrow. Yes, we are important…but we are tiny, and all the things we worry about are insignificant.

I thought I had changed the world; I was coming on strong with the "I'd like to teach the world to sing…in perfect harmony…" kind of message. Have a Coke and a smile, you know?

They loved the demos. We cut more songs. Yadda yadda yadda…we had an album!

Ha! If only. That would have been way too easy. From Richard and Scott's perspective, it certainly was. Scott picked up the phone on a Saturday afternoon, called me, and mentioned they wanted to sign Some Odd reason. All they needed by Monday morning was MORE SONGS.

Easy peasy.

From my perspective, that phone call kicked off a 48-hour hurricane shit show of frenzied, sleepless activity. We already had a handful of songs (five?) that Richard had done with us. But he and Scott wanted more. Long story short, they wanted ten additional songs.

We definitely had the songs written and ready to record—but bear in mind, Some Odd Reason played almost every night of the week. When I got the phone call from Scott, we were booked in Fredericksburg, Virginia, which was roughly 45 minutes from Clear

Sound. It was a "covers" gig, so our contract had us playing until 1:30am.

I remember pulling the guys together and giving them the scoop.

"Look…Richard and Scott need ten more songs by Monday. So, we have to hammer them out between now and then."

To their credit, they were on board. Maybe not enthusiastic… but they agreed to do whatever it took. Our bass player, Spencer Jaimeson (poor guy), agreed too, despite his wife being extremely unhappy about it. He was a schoolteacher in real life, and his wife would constantly put pressure on him when he was away with our band. She was supportive of his dreams but made it very clear this was not what she wanted.

We played the gig and then got back to Clear Sound at about three o'clock in the morning. Our wives and girlfriends joined us, as did about ten people from the Fredericksburg club. It became a Van-Halen-like, all-night party.

Except for me. I was in charge and had to get shit done. I assembled my guys, mapped out the ten songs and the itinerary for getting them done, and began.

The first order of business was to shuffle Ryan away from the party so he could get some sleep and rest his voice. We had played several nights in a row, and he was getting a little raspy because his voice had grown fatigued—which was great for me, because Bryan Adams WAS rasp!

From there, we recorded basic tracks (drums and bass) by noon Sunday. The next three or four hours were spent recording the guitar tracks. I could do this alone, so all the guys took a siesta (that's a lie—they kept the party going) while I strummed and recorded. That took until about 4 or 5pm.

Next order of business was to rustle up Ryan and get him to the microphone. We pushed until the vocal tracks were complete—and he did great. In hindsight, the rasp in his voice was perfect; it gave an edgier tone to the vocals and made for a cool sound.

That took until about 11pm. I took a one-hour break, and we all agreed the guys could go home. Then at midnight—remember, I still hadn't slept since I woke up on Friday morning—I sat down to mix and master the ten songs.

At six in the morning, I was done. I staggered outside and watched the sunrise. I felt like a bus had just hit me, but there was no rest for the weary. I still had to get the songs into Richard and Scott's hands—and it was too late to FedEx the damn things to New York. I had to upload them onto the fledgling internet and deliver them electronically.

I used a new-ish technology called Liquid Audio to compress the music files for upload. Or it might have been mp3—Hell, I don't remember exactly. That whole weekend was a blur.

Making matters worse, these were the early days of stepping onto the information highway. All I remember is the technology was relatively new and I didn't know what I was doing, and the entire process was *insanely* slow—but I got it done. I don't know if anyone remembers telephone modems or dial-up connectivity, but it took almost *ten full hours* to get the songs converted and sent into the etho-sphere. At 4pm, I was half-dead but victorious. I had done the impossible—I had delivered the songs by end-of-business Monday.

In all, we cut ten songs that weekend. And they were good. So good in fact, that we got signed to Sol 3 Records. Some Odd Reason had done it. We had a record deal.

* * *

It felt glorious. We drove to New York City with a bunch of our friends to physically sign the contract. Afterwards, everyone went to dinner with the staff at Sol 3 Records. The universe sent me a strange warning that night, although I was too young and green to take note.

As we were escorted to our table for the celebration dinner, a few of us noticed a metal-looking guy sitting alone at the bar. We filed past and he said to me, "What are you guys celebrating?"

I explained about the record deal.

He turned back to his drink and hissed, "Pfft. Good luck."

I stopped, "Why? What're you doing?"

He took a gulp of his drink but didn't turn back to face me.

"I actually just got dropped from my record label."

Turns out, he was a member of the band, Biohazard.

By this time, the rest of the guys had noticed my conversation and wandered over to join me. We heard the name "Biohazard," and were immediately skeptical.

Just then, the guy turned and showed us a Biohazard tattoo—*on the inside of his bottom lip.*

That was all the proof we needed. Seemed legit.

He was nice to us for the remainder of our interactions with him, but it was such an ironic moment. We were in the midst of our rise, and he was in the midst of his decline. And here was the thing: I should have recognized the fragility of fame. It never occurred to me that this guy was probably scared about his future—he might have a wife or kids or a mortgage (or alimony?). He might be wondering how he is going to earn a living from here on out. He was clearly pissed off and sad…but the world of adulthood is about more than tracking album sales and getting girls to throw panties or flash their boobs at you on stage.

I was too young to connect those dots. In fact, I was too young to think that our lives were ever going to change. I figured my group of guys would be together forever and that we would keep cranking out records and setting the world on fire. In short, I believed wholeheartedly in the Bon Jovi story we were all sold: five kids from Jersey who made it and would be together 4 ever!

I was so naïve.

Actually, let me back up a step. I don't think I *wanted* to think about those types of things. Naivety was more of a choice for me. The reality was, the Biohazard guy's story scared me a little. I didn't want to ever see this thing of ours go away.

But for the moment, we bid Mr. Biohazard adieu and went to bask in the moment. We had a fucking record deal!

* * *

Somewhere in this whirlwind (February, 1998), my mother died. I remember taking the master tape of Some Odd Reason's album (which was released later that year) and placing it in her casket. I wish she could have hung on long enough to see that record come out. She would have been so proud.

Later that year, we released our first album, *To Whom It May Concern*. It was a strong record and got some radio airplay. I am pretty damn proud of that album. In fact, one cut from that record, "Spin," still gets requested today, as I mentioned earlier. I'll be out doing an acoustic set with Chuck, and someone will invariably pull one of us aside and ask if we can do that song.

Humbling, man.

* * *

Once the deal was inked, the guys were over the moon. For me, it was like I had gotten a second lease on life—I had met a lifelong dream. MTV fame couldn't be far behind! We packed up Some Odd Reason, and we hit the road again.

Hard.

We toured *everywhere*, with a record deal in our back pocket—literally. I kept a copy with me so I could show anyone who would listen. We were now able to book better gigs. We would occasionally open for bands like Fuel and The Goo Goo Dolls. But we also played cover clubs on our nights off. It made us more money, but it was a grind.

In fact, the people at the label thought I was crazy to keep pushing my guys out there night after night. They didn't understand why I was having us play cover clubs when they felt the right thing to do was to only play our original music.

That is, until they saw how many CDs we were selling at the cover clubs.

Not to mention, I came up with a brilliant scheme to promote my band nationwide. I started booking us at Spring Break hot spots in Florida.

It sounds terrible nowadays, but I called this technique "Spreading the Disease." We would play to a bunch of kids on Spring Break. They would fall in love with the band, purchase a CD, and then take our name and our music back to wherever they came from. So, in one night, we could play for people from Iowa, North Dakota, Vermont, Ontario, and Idaho. Then they would go home and do the word-of-mouth marketing that is vital to the growth of a band. Then, when we would eventually roll into that town on tour, we would have a fan base that was already established.

It was a ground-breaking idea. I'm quite certain that I am not the only one to ever do this, but in my head at the time, it was all me.

It worked…but it was exhausting. And to be honest, it was a slow go. Building momentum through a grass roots campaign takes time and a tremendous amount of energy. We got signed pretty quickly, but then we hit a bit of a plateau. We kept touring and touring, but nothing new was happening.

For me, stalling was a predictable (albeit frustrating) part of the process. But from what I have learned in life, not everyone has the same single-minded determination that I have.

Eventually, Ryan's patience wore thin.

He hit his wall in Arizona. I have no idea how many nights in a row we were in the middle of, but it was a lot. On this particular night, Ryan approached me before the gig.

"Pete…this is your dream, not mine. When we get back home, I'm out."

It was a humbling moment for me. I had to take a hard look in the mirror and come to a few realizations. For example, I wasn't easy to deal with. I always (secretly—so I assumed) thought that I was the professional and everyone else in the band was an amateur. I wanted everyone to do whatever I said. Heck, I don't think I ever asked for anyone's opinion when I made decisions regarding the band.

This also weighed heavily on my friend and drummer, Keith Sarna. He was well-informed and studied the music business more than anyone else I knew at the time—but I rarely listened to his point of view or took his advice. It's something I really regret now. Maybe he had a better way.

I was young and fiery…and hell bent on becoming a big success.

In the end, my passion probably turned me into an asshole toward Ryan. When he started to wilt under the intensity of our schedule, I was unhappy and let him know it.

Still, when he announced his departure, I was crushed. He was my friend and my brother…and his voice was magic. And now he wanted nothing to do with Some Odd Reason.

Hindsight paints a different picture, of course. At the time, I was just angry that he wasn't willing to give all I was giving. But the truth is, Ryan had changed his entire life and lifestyle. Had sang till he basically ruined his voice due to me pushing him. Furthermore, he knew he would be killing himself if he kept following my dream. He spent all his money on having the best gear, and… had multiple surgeries on his throat and nose due to the damage our constant touring had done to his voice. Yes, dear reader, in hindsight he seems to have sacrificed way more than me.

A couple years later, I wrote a song about this moment with Ryan. It is called "Frankenstein," and the lyrics read:

Now I feel like Doctor Frankenstein.
I've lost my monster; I've lost my mind.

It wasn't a hate thing toward Ryan. I was more disappointed in myself. In fact, I was fucking devastated. Some Odd Reason was on the decline.

Despite my funk and pissy disposition, I was able to grab onto a life raft floating by—my wife and I married on September 6, 1998, which breathed life back into my soul. I desperately wanted to grab her and run off into the sunset as a successful rock star.

When none of that happened, it was brutal.

But as they say in the biz, the show must go on. I knew Ryan was gone…so I had to find a replacement singer. I made some calls and talked to some friends. By the time we returned to Virginia, I had lined up a new guy. He was a buddy of mine named Bart Harris.

And we began a new era in the life of Some Odd Reason.

Story Three

We didn't stay home for long. Returning from Arizona, we dropped Ryan off, shoved Bart into the van, and got right back on the road.

It wasn't exactly that quick, but it sure felt that way. If memory serves, we had two days home before we were slated to start a tour as the opening band for the group, Fuel. It was a huge deal for us—Bart didn't have long to learn the songs. The reality was, most of what we did was covers. He knew 80% of our set list by heart just by virtue of listening to the radio.

With Bart, the dynamics changed within Some Odd Reason. He had a more "metal" voice than Ryan. To this end, he was an amazing singer. He wasn't faking it—and our band could feel it. When we sat down to write new original material, it felt like we headed in a new, very exciting direction.

From my point of view, it seemed like every time we took a hit, we came back stronger. In fact, our drummer left the band somewhere along the way during this crazy period. When he quit, we replaced him (literally overnight) with a band mate of Bart's, Eric Spencer, and kept on slugging—without leaving the road. We were paying our bills (well…kinda) and kicking some ass.

Back in New York however, Richard and Scott were not exactly 100% behind the change. They were tracking our sales and felt things could be better. Don't get me wrong—CD sales were fine, and our live shows were packed, but they just didn't like the sound as much. They felt it had changed too much. They knew that Bart had a killer voice—but to them, Ryan had a more marketable pop voice. Bart didn't have a grunge voice per se…but it was definitely edgier and harder than Ryan's. Again, this was the direction in which the whole band seemed to be going.

Grunge swept through the rock scene like a scourge in late 1991, but pop music never went away. Artists like Bryan Adams were still alive and kicking. In fact, Bryan's album, *Waking Up the Neighbors*, was released on exactly the same day as Nirvana's *Nevermind*—September 24, 1991. While Nirvana's world-changing album went on to sell over ten million copies in the U.S. alone (10x platinum), Bryan's album sold over four million (4x platinum).

Not too shabby.

Add this to the fact that grunge had pretty much worn out its welcome by 1995. Nirvana released their final album, *In Utero*, in 1993. It went on to sell over five million copies (5x platinum). But in early April 1994, their front man, Kurt Cobain, committed suicide… and the music world started to change back.

Soundgarden's last huge album, *Superunknown*, (six times platinum) was released a month before Cobain died. Alice in Chains, who had sold over a combined seven million albums in 1990 (*Facelift* – five million copies) and 1992 (*Dirt* – two million copies), gave it one last shot—1995's self-titled release, which went double platinum—before calling it quits for the time being.

And that's the point. By the time we picked up Bart Harris in 1998, pop music had made a roaring comeback. Hootie and the Blowfish had released their world-changing album, *Cracked Rear View*, during the summer of 1994, three months after Cobain's death. It went on to sell a mind-boggling TWENTY-ONE million copies in the U.S. (21x platinum, or double diamond). Matchbox Twenty followed suit a couple years later, releasing their album, *Yourself or Someone Like You*, in October of 1996. It sold over twelve million copies (12x platinum, or diamond) in the U.S. alone.

Grunge was a faze. Pop was eternal.

Richard and Scott knew this, and wanted to steer Some Odd Reason back into a lane that could make some money. Harder-edged metal was still around, of course. Metallica's *Load* (1996; 5x platinum) and *Reload* (1997; 3x platinum) proved there would always be a market for their style of music. But they were the exception rather than the rule. Sales have always been driven mostly by pop/rock music, and that was what we were tapped to be.

Ultimately, the label didn't like our new direction. They weren't enthusiastic about the newer, edgier songs…which put me in a horrible position that almost ended Bart's and my friendship. Dude, it was *rough*. Bart and I are brothers to this day, but it was a long, long road to recover from this blow.

Anyway, Ryan Gindhart wasn't about to return to the fold. We needed a different option. Frankly, the proposal Richard and Scott made to me was preposterous at best.

They told *me* to sing.

Story Four

When it comes to writing songs, I'm pretty good. Or at the

very least, *I* like what I write. I'm no John Lennon, but I could always hold my own. And I will add this: I loved Bart and loved the way our band had been. The most interesting and ironic thing about this story is that Bart formed a band called Junkfood. For over 20 years they have continuously put out world class pop/rock that was more commercially viable than anything I could ever write.

When it came to singing however, I was a ten-car pile-up. When Richard and Scott looked over the options and decided that I was going to sing, it was the single worst thing I could have ever imagined coming out of their mouths. I had never sung a song in my life.

Okay, to say I had never sung in my life is an exaggeration… but you get my point. I couldn't carry a tune with a shovel, and now I was supposed to step up to the mic and deliver like Ryan or Bart?!? That was fucking Looney Tunes to me.

I remember the aftermath of that meeting with Richard and Scott. I was with my lawyer, Ron Bienstock—who was also present at the meeting in New York. I turned to them and said, "How could you do that to me? You know I can't sing."

Ron, God bless him, didn't fire back. He remained steady and talked me through my emotions. He reminded me that I *wrote* the songs…and then used Nirvana to make his point.

"You know, Pete…Kurt Cobain wasn't a good singer either. But his voice was perfect for the songs he wrote because his *passion* came through, loud and clear."

That thought set me on my heels for a moment. He was right. Nirvana had a legion of fans around the world. In fact, they *still do today*—almost thirty years after Kurt killed himself. Those fans think Kurt is the greatest thing in the world because of his passion. His voice will never be compared to Freddie Mercury or Steven Tyler… but he changed the music world.

So, there I was. I was almost 26 years old, and I was at a major crossroad. I could either lose my record deal or I could learn to sing.

I think you know what happened from there.

For the next nine months, I took singing lessons from a teacher named Don Lawrence. We met at his office/studio on

Broadway in New York. He was a big fish in the world of singing—having worked with the likes of Mick Jagger, Jon Bon Jovi, Dee Snider, and Sebastian Bach (to name a few).

In fact, try this one on for size:

My lesson time happened to fall between a somewhat unknown young girl named Christina Aguilera—and Ally Sheedy (from *The Breakfast Club*). Christina had been on the revamped version of *The Mickey Mouse Club*, but was still largely unknown outside of a small, very specific demographic.

On some days, Ally would show up early for her lesson. She and I would sit in the waiting room together, marveling at how Christina Aguilera could flat-out *sing*. I remember Don would often say to me, "That little girl is going to be a star someday."

He wasn't wrong.

Anyway, Don worked with me and started to mold me into a decent singer. Not a good singer—not yet. Hell, not even a passable singer for several months. It took a while before I sounded anywhere near how I was supposed to sound. That would have been okay—Rome was not built in a day. But the problem was, I couldn't stop touring while going through this rough process of growth and change.

This change kicked off the absolute worst period of my musical life. I lost my band. The guys in the group were pro-level players. They didn't believe in me…and the proof was in the pudding. Audiences let me have it. I couldn't blame them. My vocals were all over the road.

When Some Odd Reason lost every member except me, I had to find replacement players on the fly. As I have said before, it wasn't easy to find high caliber musicians in Northern Virginia that were willing to go on the road. Yes, there were a lot of great musicians, but most had day jobs. The task is even tougher when you don't have a heck of a lot of time to do the looking. The band ended up being populated with guys who were pretty good at what they did…but they were nowhere near the level of the guys they replaced.

*The only exception was my best friend, Chuck, who is easily THE GREATEST DRUMMER OF ALL TIME. And like a true friend, he came back to me in my time of need.

All in all, it was devastating. I'd spent years on the road creating a family bond with those guys

All the years I had put in to growing the brand and toiling away on the road...all of it was dissolving like water through my fingers. It felt like a horrible mistake to have left Clear Sound Studio and try my hand at rock and roll again. MTV fame was all bullshit anyway. MTV was bullshit. The whole music industry was total bullshit. Rock and roll was a steaming pile of bulls--

Hang on…I would never go *that* far.

But I had entered a pretty deep depression.

In just one year's time, I had gone from touring the country with a record deal and some burgeoning radio airplay—to being the front man of a C-level local cover band. A band that had a terrible lead singer (me) and was drawing a smattering of boos by the time we left the stage each night.

This was a dark, dark time for me. Frankly, this was a difficult part of the book for me to write because the details and timeline get a little fuzzy throughout this period. Days and weeks and months bled together while I just tried to keep my head above water.

Man, I had to have been a truly miserable fuck to be around back then. Still, I had to keep strapping on my guitar and stepping onto the stage. I clung desperately to the dream of somehow making it. More importantly, I had bills to pay. I had to keep trotting out there and doing my best to entertain the people who were kind enough to pay a cover charge and watch us play.

The entire world watched me learn to sing. I didn't have the luxury of time to practice in my basement before unleashing myself onto the scene. I had to work out the kinks and the bugs in real time. I had to just push myself up there and do it.

I will tell you this: without a doubt, these were the most awful years of my life. I knew full well what it was like to be great—and this wasn't it. In fact, it was quite the opposite. I was literally embarrassing myself every night. I remember feeling such anguish before going on stage some nights, that it turned into actual physical pain. On most nights, the band would take a break and I would struggle to try to find a reason to return to the stage. I just wanted the nightmare to end.

To their credit, the band itself got real good, real fast. My amateur guys stepped up to the plate and took their roles very seriously. I took my role seriously too…but I was certainly not good.

As the old saying goes, it's always darkest before dawn. Something good started to happen. I noticed a small but loyal fan base beginning to grow. Because we were playing locally, the same people started to show up night after night to see us play. And these people…they watched me get better and better over time. They were completely behind me and completely supportive. They cheered my victories and cringed at my sour notes. But all in all, they became "Team Pete." They rooted for me; they believed in me.

I don't like to come across as overly dramatic, but they probably saved my life. And even if that's overstated, I certainly wouldn't be where I am professionally without them. I have to add that my ex-wife, her sister, brother, mother, father, and their giant extended family were so incredibly supportive. It was amazing. This was not the life they wanted for Kristen (more on her in the next chapter), but they knew how it was. They knew how *I* was. They all showed up whenever they could.

Unfortunately, the universe wasn't quite ready to stop pummeling me. By the time I got good at singing and was ready to start our second album (with me at the mic), the record label folded. It turned into The Orchard and was no longer operating as a label, but rather a distribution avenue. Not that you should cry a tear for Richard Gottehrer or Scott Cohen—those cats landed on their feet. But for me, the demise of Sol 3 Records kicked off another anxiety spiral. I didn't know what or how we were going to survive this loss.

But here was the thing: Some Odd Reason (now called EVICK) didn't exist because a royal record executive tapped it on both shoulders with a sword. The band wasn't the brainchild of a record label. And more importantly, the band's primary function was not to serve the whims or fancy of a corporate entity.

No…the band existed because *I* put it together and loved it and nurtured it and did everything I could to keep it going. It stayed alive because of the fans; the people who paid money every night to come and see us play. And lastly, the band was not a static monolith. It was a living organism, capable of change and adaptation.

So that's exactly what I decided to do. With me at the helm, I assembled a crew. Chuck Fanslau was back on board, as were a new wave of true professionals. I grabbed the wheel and steered the mothership toward a brighter future. No longer the SS Some Odd Reason, I rebranded the vessel to reflect this new voyage. We were now sailing through the stars aboard the SS EVICK. We jumped back on the road and wrote fresh songs and honed our craft over the next several years. And as with every new vessel, we held a christening. For us, that meant a new album.

* * *

Anachronism was finally released on Potomac Records in 2002. The title reflects the singer; I was a child of the 80s, but writing and performing in this new frontier of music. Digital was king, and as a result, album sales across the board plummeted precipitously. Napster had created a new underground of free music sharing (read: theft). Fans were now able to snatch songs from their favorite artists off the internet. No $14.99 for a CD, no sales tax…no royalty for the artist. Artists and record labels scrambled to shame and guilt fans into stopping this practice. Federal law enforcement intervened briefly, making a few high-profile arrests of kids who were caught with too much pirated music on their hard drives. But it was all to no avail; the genie was out of the bottle.

The business model of the music business had to adjust accordingly. Not that the adjustment came easily—it took a full decade of kicking and screaming. At the time, there was no means of generating income through digital streams or downloads—neither of those concepts had been invented yet. MySpace didn't exist until 2003. YouTube wasn't online until 2005. For now, there was a sucking black hole and almost no money changing hands.

And I totally understood. Millions (billions?) of dollars were lost when fans no longer had to pony up at the cash register. So now, The Big Change in music economic philosophy started. Rather than touring to entice fans to purchase albums, artists began putting out albums to entice fans to their concerts. The money was in live events, not album sales.

This ideological shift was perfect for me and my guys. Our work ethic matched the requirements of the new climate. We were relentless when it came to touring; it was our primary source of income from Day 1. We understood the value of generating new music, but shifted seamlessly into a world of tour, tour, tour. Not that I didn't hope *Anachronism* would sell a million copies—I was just well-suited for this new era in music.

Incidentally, Potomac Records was not a household name in 2002. In fact, the label didn't even exist before 2002. I know this because I founded the label, along with my buddy, Dave Shaffer.

And from here, the story gets even more…*interesting*. We definitely hit highs and lows—but I kept fighting. Let me give you a few examples of things that kept me going…even during the darkest times.

CHAPTER 5:
MOTIVATION

I hit you with an agonizingly long chapter four, so I'll give you a breather with a shorter chapter five. I'm going to frame this chapter in terms of some of the clubs we played back in the day. Looking at history, you can figure out that EVICK never made it as big as Van Halen or Kiss (not YET, anyway) …so there had to be something that kept us and kept me going. We worked so hard and didn't reach the mountain top we were climbing toward. As young men, this was extremely trying at times.

So here are a few stories of things and moments that buoyed our spirits and gave us a reason to keep pushing.

Sully's

I was a white trash kid from the wrong side of Manassas, but the rest of my band mates were not. Ryan was a wholesome kid out of Indiana. The rest of the guys were not nearly the angels Ryan was, but they were still a far cry from the serial killer I could have been. They were more upscale; more hip and more cool than me.

That said, Sully's was in Fairfax County, one of the richest counties in the country, and the owner originally saw it as a fine dining place. But the bands that played there were more southern rock based and that alone drew a more blue-collar crowd. The owners and the staff were far from white trash or redneck. These were strange times, but Sully's became home for us.

Despite all the cultural mismatch, we always did really well at Sully's. In fact, the crowd loved us right from our very first show —which was on a slow Wednesday night. I remember arriving and thinking, *This is going to suck. They're going to hate us—we're out of place.*

Nothing could have been further from the truth. After the

show, I was flying high—another job well done—when one of the bartenders, Roy Crawford approached me.

"Hey Pete—we're looking to add more bands like you guys. We'd like to make this place feel more modern and new."

Roy was a fan. That was awesome. I appreciated anyone who was willing to hire us. Plus, it always puts a little more wind beneath my wings when somebody tells me we're great. We immediately became the Wednesday night house band and a mainstay at Sully's.

I didn't drink alcohol yet (seriously) but needed to wet my whistle. So, I stopped packing up and went to order a Sprite. Fortunately, this also gave me a chance to engage with one of the bartenders. It was a girl I had known from around the local music scene. We hadn't ever really talked, but she was cute and I was thirsty.

Her name was Kristen, and we hit it off like peas in a pod that night. She was friends with a lot of the same people I was friends with and would often be out seeing bands that we played with. She and her friend Katie (who ended up being the maid of honor at our wedding) were both working that night, and we ended up chatting for the first time. Both of us had just come out of long-term relationships and both were gun shy about jumping into something new. We would often joke that we were just "spending time alone together."

And thus began an amazing love story…and eventually a sad divorce.

No, I'm not going to lie to you and say that everything turned out like roses. If you know anything about me, you know that Kristen and I divorced twelve years ago (as of the writing of this book). But I will also not lie and throw shade on our courtship—she was *really* cool. She was really cool, really pretty, and I was smitten. I honestly thought I loved her more than I had ever loved anyone in my life.

Funny enough, we were sort of like Tommy and Gina that Bon Jovi sang about. We were young, in love, and didn't have a pot to piss in. I never had to put my six-string in hoc (thank God), but we struggled to stay afloat while I lived out my rock and roll dreams.

The crowd at Sully's helped. They knew of our growing relationship and cheered us on every step of the way. When I tell you that I felt a sense of family at certain places, Sully's was one of them. These were our people; this was our home…these were our kin.

Some Odd Reason became the biggest draw Sully's had on their roster. We would pack them in every time we took the stage. It was gritty, nasty…and absolutely fabulous. It didn't matter how much frustration or anxiety I was feeling about the future of my career; walking into Sully's gave me a boost and the shot of confidence I needed to keep pushing.

I loved that place right up until the second they closed. And that was a shame.

The Golden Phoenix

We played everywhere. Some Odd Reason had a residency to play every Wednesday night at Sully's, which we did for a few years.

When we formed EVICK, I started doing Thursdays at Sully's, and then switched Wednesdays to a place called The Golden Phoenix. The place was owned by a wonderful woman named Susie, and I still remember the bartenders' names: Joanie and BJ. In fact, I'm still friends with the bartenders to this day.

By all accounts, you would think it was an Asian place by the name…and you'd be wrong. Dead balls wrong. The Golden Phoenix was a full-on biker bar. It's also the place where I met my lifelong friend and most trustworthy favor granter, Tracy Melvin. I probably literally couldn't exist without the help he has given me over the past twenty years.

Most of my Some Odd Reason and EVICK history is tied to Sully's the way the Ramones' history is tied to CBGBs; or how Van Halen's history is tied to the Whiskey a Go Go. Our tie to Sully's is so strong that people sometimes mis-attribute a line from one of EVICK's songs. In a song called "Used to Be," I have a line that reads:

And now on Wednesdays
I play this local club
Right down the street
from where I grew up

Again, almost everyone directly relates that to Sully's—but in fact the line refers to The Golden Phoenix.

I have one killer story from our time at The Golden Phoenix. It is a story that both tells of how we used to pack the place, but also tells of how I should probably be dead right now (as many of the best stories tend to do).

To give you some perspective on how life was back then, the band consisted of me, Kyle Stokes on bass and Dan Duff on guitar. Keeping a good drummer around was a nightmare. Our drummer would either be Chuck Fanslau, Ed Rodriquez, or this guy named Josh Teade. The drummer spot literally became "whoever could show up on any given night." I needed the work so badly; I had 2nd and 3rd string players…just in case.

Anyway, Susie would sometimes assess the crowd, and then lock the door to shut out anybody who wasn't already in. She was probably concerned that the Fire Marshall would show up and shut the place down for good. We packed them in like sardines on many of the nights we played. And to fully complete the scene, picture that the band was set up against the front window.

One night there was a drunk guy who got *super* pissed that the door was locked. He could clearly see through the front window and wanted to be a part of the off-the-chain, full-on rock and roll debauchery melting down right in front of his whiskey-lit, bloodshot eyes.

So, he did what any rational alcoholic would do. He decided he was gonna drive through the window—and (I guess) kill us all.

Anyway, I turned and happened to catch a glimpse of his car —which was coming right at us. I was a little tipsy at the time but sobered up immediately. It was the craziest shit I'd ever seen at that point in my life. Luckily, The Golden Phoenix was in a shopping center that had a sidewalk and big brick pillars protecting the façade. The drunk guy's car got the pillar before it got us.

Following the loud BANG, the bar fell silent. Everyone looked out the window in shock…and then cheered and resumed their total face-melting party mode.

Ah, the good ol' days…

Sunset Grill

When Don Henley released the song, "Sunset Grill" in 1984

(from his *Building the Perfect Beast* album), I was surprised to think that he had been to Annandale, Virginia.

What did I know? I was twelve.

Once I grew older, it occurred to me there might be more than one Sunset Grill in the world, and that he was probably singing about the other one.

Ironically, the second CD put out by my band, EVICK, was called *Sunset to Sunset*. The album art featured a street sign that read: "2667 miles"—the exact measurement from the door of the Sunset Grill in Annandale to the Sunset Strip in Los Angeles.

That had nothing to do with Don Henley or any other establishments with identical names. But it does show how big of an impact this particular bar and grill had on me.

Whatever the case, the Sunset Grill *I* knew was a tiny, rickety biker bar. And when I say "tiny," I mean that place was a shoebox. We had to set up in a corner (there was a *tiny* stage) and we couldn't even wedge in a full PA system.

That said, the Sunset Grill was also a coveted venue to play. Bands *loved* to get booked into that place. It was a feather in your cap if you got to play there. I used to beg our agent, Rob Casey, to put us there.

I'll never forget the phone call when I got the news. Rob sounded concerned—and actually laid out the ground rules. He had never given us any rules or guidelines to playing a venue. He knew we were professionals and would show up—on time—and play our full set. Something about this place had him concerned. He explained the proper protocol to me like Jerry explained The Soup Nazi's protocol to George and Elaine.

"Don't go in there thinking that you're a rock star. Get in there early, sit at the bar, order a burger, eat that burger, and tell Kay, the manager, thanks for having you. Then you set your gear up and do your job."

I was like, *Fuck, dude...what the hell?*

Fast forward to our arrival. I was a little concerned as we walked in. Not so much because of "the rules," but more because I didn't know if we would fit in. This place was more of a "classic rock" establishment. 80s rock had completely disappeared from the face of the Earth by then, so cover bands doing classic rock would pull songs by Lynyrd Skynyrd, Foghat, and CCR. We were doing a few originals, and also covering bands like Hootie and the Blowfish and the Goo Goo Dolls.

But here was the deal: *the crowd loved us*. We were invited back time and time again. And when I write about moments that gave me a boost and a shot of confidence to keep going, the Sunset Grill provided one powerful moment that will forever be burned into my memory.

The stage was set up near the front of the building, with a small window framed in the wall behind us. During our sound check one night, I looked out the window and saw a line out the door and into the parking lot—people waiting in the cold to try and get in to see us.

At some point, the line stopped moving—nobody else could fit in the place.

What an achievement! This wasn't Madison Square Garden, but we had fucking sold the place out. It was wall-to-wall, asses to elbows. To my brain, that felt like an affirmation of success. We had grown so big; fans were lining up to see us—and—people were being turned away at the door.

* * *

Here's another random memory that just popped into my head. When I think back on the Sunset Grill, I cannot leave out the fond memory of the first time I was ever punched full-on in the face. I know it sounds like this shouldn't be one of the moments that feels uplifting, but it was one of those nights I will label as "redneck-level fun."

I will get out ahead of you critics who will point out that I had been in many fights by this point in my life. So yes, it would stand to reason that I had been punched in the face numerous times before the night I am getting ready to tell you about. But my father always taught me that (basically) a good strategy in fights is to have an aggressive offense. Ergo, I would strike first and end the ruckus before it had a chance to get out of hand.

So there's that.

Anyway, our drummer's (Keith Sarna) father showed up at one of our Sunset Grill shows. I remember he was recovering from surgery to help quell a pretty bad bout with cancer, but he wanted to see his son play. We were all happy to host him…despite the club's surly reputation.

True to form, Keith's dad ended up getting into a fight with one of the bikers. To this day, I have no idea how it started or who said what to whom. But fists started flying and Mr. Sarna was smack dab in the middle of it.

Knowing about the cancer and the fact that Keith's dad (an older gentleman, let's be honest) was compromised, I felt an immediate surge of protective valor. Without missing a beat, I put down my guitar and dove into the crowd.

Dear reader, when I tell you that what ensued was a good ol' fashioned "western saloon" bar brawl, I mean that in every sense of the word. All that was missing was a piano player in the corner and guys getting thrown into the street through a pair of swinging doors.

It was an all-out WWE Smackdown MELEE. Like, a "chairs getting smashed across people's backs and bottles getting smashed over people's heads" level melee. This scene would have rivaled anything ever filmed for an episode of *Gunsmoke*.

And then it happened.

At one point during my involvement, I got shoved from behind and lurched forward. At precisely the same moment, I saw stars. Someone cold-cocked me right in my fucking jaw with a roundhouse right that would have taken down any lesser of a man, Fortunately, I had the stature and the presence of a great white rhino —I stood tall when other men would have fallen.

Kidding, of course. Hell, I'm the guitar player in a rock band. Plus…look at me.

My knees buckled and I wasn't completely certain if I was afoot or horseback, but that detail will never make it into the box score. I had taken my first real punch to the face and lived on to tell the tale.

However, history will not be kind because of one minor detail. The person who slugged me was Keith's sister, Jennifer

Sarna. It was friendly fire (we were on the same side, after all), but it was an unabated shot to my face. And it definitely got my attention.

I don't know if Jennifer ever kicked Keith's ass when they were growing up, but she sure as shit hammered me onto Wobbly-Leg Street. I would have hit her back—except I was a little bit scared about what might happen if I REALLY pissed her off.

And we were on the same team. And she was Keith's sister.

And good lord, she was WAY meaner than me.

Kidding aside, I loved Jennifer. She felt horrible when she saw who she just hit. In the end, Keith's dad was okay. And that was all that really mattered. Some Odd Reason was no stranger to rough and tumble biker bars, so we were fine.

And I had a great story to tell. Although in my version, the guy who hit me was *enormous*—he was heavily tatted, wearing an eye patch, and out on parole after killing an entire motorcycle gang using only his bare hands and a Slinky.

You got something different to say?

Fight me.

* * *

Lastly, the Sunset Grill is where I took my very first sip of alcohol. I'll keep this story short because it turned into such a massive shit show. It was on my 25th birthday. Not a huge deal, but that quiet moment turned into a roaring wildfire.

We had just signed our deal with Sol 3 Records, and I felt this would be a good time to open up and properly celebrate. Roy (from Sully's) was there, as was Kristen and a bunch of other people who were important fixtures in my life. I felt it was only proper for Roy to serve me my very first drink, to which he obliged.

Because I was a novice, I think he started me out with some fruity wimpy drink. Think the trashy biker bar version of a Zima mixed with Hawaiian Punch.

I drank it down and felt wholly underwhelmed. I remember staring at the empty glass and thinking, *Huh. Alcohol must not work on me.*

So, I made the executive decision that, despite having built up no tolerance whatsoever, I was an alcohol heavyweight. I instructed the staff at the Sunset Grill to "KEEP 'EM COMING!"

There is a big chunk of that night that is missing from my brain. I *think* I had a good time—but thank my lucky stars that cell phones didn't have video cameras back then and YouTube wasn't yet a thing.

All I know is that I woke up at 2am, lying on the bar like it was a hospital gurney. I was happy, I wasn't mean to anyone, and most importantly—I HAD A RECORD DEAL!

So far, all good…right?

Welp, let me remind you about Kay—and "the rules."

Right up until this very moment, Kay had always been cool with me and with the band. In fact, I think I remember earlier that night, she was laughing and serving me drinks. As far as I was concerned, everything was great.

Anyway, I saw her face. And she was *pissed.*

I was confused. Wasn't she part of the fiesta the night before?

Apparently, I read the room wrong. Because Kay leaned over my prostrate body and said, "You won't be playing here anymore if this is how it's going to be."

What a sobering moment.

I had a headache, I couldn't think clearly, and I felt slow. I guess you could call it a hangover, but I (honestly) feel like I damaged something that night that I have never been able to get back. I know that's physically impossible, but it freaked me out enough that I made a vow to never drink that much again.

But as I alluded to earlier, the floodgates had opened. Drinking was a very difficult activity to stop. Hell, it became difficult for me to even slow it down.

Remember the album cover I wrote about at the beginning of this segment? For the album, *Sunset to Sunset*? The first single off that album was a song called "This Ain't the Life." The opening lyrics discuss the ensuing battle I had with alcohol. They read:

All the years have passed me by way too fast

And every drink I take I swear it'll be my last
But my will is not as strong as my want
And right now, I want to get fucked up

The next chapter will be devoted to the debauchery of being a wanna-be rock star. Just because we never got to be MTV famous doesn't mean we didn't fall into some of the same patterns as those who did. The fact is, we might have partied harder and gotten into just as much trouble as some of the most hedonistic bands of the 80s.

I'll save the rest for Chapter Six. For now, let me get back to the good times. The times that kept me excited to keep climbing.

Bad Habits

And then there was the time a HUGE rock star shoved a note into my locker after study hall!

That's not true.

Sort of.

But I was as giddy as a middle school kid after it happened. Here's the story.

Back in the day (1990-2006), there was an annual Washington DC music festival called the HFStival. It was a giant event thrown by local rock station, WHFS. The festival ended when the station basically went out of business in 2005—when they abruptly changed to a Tropical Latin format. Interestingly, the scheduled 2006 festival was already selling a ton of tickets—so organizers decided to go ahead with it (despite WHFS basically disappearing).

As an asterisk, the HFStival was reinvigorated in 2010 and 2011 in dedication to the old station and the good times had by all. In the festival's heyday, upwards of 90,000 people would grace the turnstiles of RFK Stadium (its most frequent venue) and rock themselves into oblivion.

The Foo Fighters played the festival three times during this stretch. Their front man, Dave Grohl, was from the area (Springfield, VA), so probably considered it a homecoming of sorts.

Now, before you think that Some Odd Reason was invited to

perform in front of 90,000 people at our area's premier music extravaganza, think again. But we *were* booked to play on the same weekend. At a local club called Bad Habits.

In the spirit of full disclosure, we had no idea that any of what I am about to tell you was going to happen. In fact, it was just another night as far as we were concerned. Obviously, we knew the festival was going on, but that was neither here nor there. We set up and did our thing.

At one point during our gig, Dave Grohl showed up. The place wasn't fully packed—we weren't exactly in competition for the WHFS fans at the stadium. But a nice crowd had gathered, nonetheless.

For me personally, I was aware of Dave's presence. I could kind of see him in the back of the bar, surrounded by a bunch of people who immediately recognized him, even out of context. Rock stars of his status have a hard time blending in, particularly in a bar filled with rock music fans.

He never approached the stage, never announced himself… never made any overtures toward the band in general. It seemed he wanted to be as incognito as he could be, given the circumstances. That was cool with me. I had been around enough higher-profile musicians by then that I understood their balance of public vs. private selves.

Back in that iteration of our band, we always ended gigs with the Kiss song, "Rock and Roll All Nite." That seemed appropriate, given how important Kiss was to me as a kid. In fact, even they closed nearly every show with that song—and have since it was released.

And that is what happened. We played the gig and ended with the Kiss song. No big deal. But on this night, the bartender came up to the stage while we were packing up our gear and handed me a napkin. On it was a brief notation:

Great Kiss cover.
-Dave Grohl

I was over the moon. I passed around the napkin and

everyone shared the same sentiment: "Oh look! We've made it! Dave Grohl thinks we're great!"

Sure, he had just played in front of a sold-out stadium of diehard fans and we just played in front of 39 drunken patrons at Bad Habits. But what the hell—it was all the same when it came to rock and roll. And it probably gave me enough of a fuel injection to keep me going for another year.

Long Wong's

Ah, the pride of Tempe, Arizona. Located on the outskirts of the Arizona State University campus, I always thought of Long Wong's as "The CBGBs of Arizona." And I meant that in a complimentary way. My friend Peter, who was the singer in a band called The Robbies, got me our first gig there.

Our *To Whom It May Concern* album had just come out, and we were feeling pretty good on tour. When we got to town, we were reminded that Tempe was the home of The Gin Blossoms, who had already sold over 5,000,000 albums and were huge at the time.

We sounded enough like the Gin Blossoms (and their other successful contemporaries) that we were a big hit in Tempe. We used to get booked there a LOT.

Things really took off for us from there. In fact, we were invited to return to Tempe to open for Robin Wilson's (Gin Blossom's lead singer) side band, Gas Giants.

In my mind, Long Wong's sort of became our west-coast anchor. Long Wong's always provided a nice boost to our spirits when we were in the middle of a long road trip.

Coconut Teaser

When we finally got to play Los Angeles and the fabled Sunset Strip, we weren't quite big enough to make it into the marquis venues like The Whiskey a Go Go, The Rainbow, the Roxy or The Viper Room. Still, we managed to get booked into a cool venue close to those landmarks—a little club called the Coconut Teaser, across the street from the Virgin Records mega store.

When we pulled into the Teaser, it felt like we had truly arrived. We had made it onto The Strip—and that was an enormous milestone achieved, as far as I was concerned.

We played the club, and we did great. But even more important than that, on the afternoon of the show we walked across the street to the Virgin Records store. And listen, I'm not going to say that I expected to find the Some Odd Reason record there…but it would have been nice.

The four of us flipped through the stacks—and there it was. *To Whom it May Concern* was available and for sale in the fucking Virgin Records mega store.

We were ecstatic. We took a bunch of pictures; each of us posing with the album in the store. Yeah, we probably looked like stupid tourists from another planet, but we didn't care. This was another indicator that we had finally arrived and that we were on our way to something even *more* huge.

My ego was out of control. But give me a little grace. There were *so many* moments when all I could do was focus on how things *weren't* happening and how everything was harder than it should be —I needed a win. And the few stories I have just told provided those brief windows of victory.

I will end this chapter with an example of how bad things could get. There are a lot of these stories, but I will only tell one. It was early on in the life of Some Odd Reason, and it was probably the worst I've ever felt.

Triple BBB's

When Some Odd Reason first hit the road as a group, getting booked into an out-of-state venue was a huge deal. It meant that we were no longer merely a bunch of local yokels—we were now a nationally touring rock band. So, when our agent got us a gig in High Pointe, North Carolina, we were chomping at the bit.

Being young and completely inexperienced at this sort of thing, none of us knew exactly what to expect. It never occurred to us that different places had different ways of doing things—or that we were about to go from "big fish in a little pond" to "fish nobody gives a shit about in an even littler pond." Such was the case at Triple BBB's.

It was about a five-hour drive from Manassas to High Pointe, and a handful of our friends (and our girlfriends) made the drive to celebrate the opening of our *almost* MTV fame. The five hours flew by—this was going to be the greatest show on Earth, and we were going to kill it from coast to coast.

What could *possibly* go wrong?

When we pulled up to the place, I was confused. Maybe the directions given to me were wrong. Maybe we took a wrong turn somewhere on a back highway of this freakishly remote little town. Maybe this was an episode of *Candid Camera*, and Allen Funt was about to jump out and inform us that they had replaced the extravagant rock and roll venue with this shitty little cinder-block gardening shed.

Before you run to Google, Allen Funt didn't pass away until 1999—so the last scenario was still entirely possible.

There we were, cars idling on a pitted gravel parking lot in the middle of the woods in God-knows-where, North Carolina. I couldn't wrap my brain around what I was looking at. Like, I couldn't comprehend what the fuck was happening. The difference between what I expected and what I was looking at was about as far apart as a finely-tuned Italian sports car—and a shitty little cinder block gardening shed.

The ONLY door to the place opened, and a guy (straight from central casting—if you requested a scary psycho dude who looked like he should be in the next version of *Texas Chainsaw Massacre*) yelled, "Are you the band tonight?"

"Yeah."

Inside, it was totally on brand. There was no stage. It was a big (ha!) empty room with a few troughs near the walls. And when I say troughs, I literally mean the things that cows drink out of. The troughs were getting filled with bags of ice—they would eventually be stocked with beer and liquor bottles and act as the bar.

That's right, kids. There was no "bar" per se. Just a trough, filled with ice and semi-cold bottles of beer. In a nutshell, all of us were in a pretty bad mood. This wasn't what the touring lifestyle was supposed to be like. Definitely not for a band that was on course to be MTV famous.

And don't forget, we had a nice little posse with us. It was embarrassing.

But we dutifully set up our gear in the corner. We were professionals if nothing else. And when this place threw open its doors (well, its "door"), and the crowd came streaming in, we would rock like it was Armageddon.

And that is exactly what we did. To our girlfriends, four friends from Manassas…and about six locals. Not even kidding. Literally six people showed up to get drunk and listen to our music.

It was *soul* crushing. I remember packing up after the show and thinking, *I don't know if I can go on like this. Why did my agent even put us here?*

The band felt it too. Our eyes were opened wide to the fact that not everything was like home—and some things were positively shitty. The energy we carried out of that place was as dark and as negative as anything we had ever experienced. Being a bunch of young men, we didn't know how to handle it.

Wendy (my girlfriend at the time) and I got into a huge fight in the parking lot. We broke up for good that night. The girl with whom I had spent a few years with; the girl for whom Clear Sound Studio was named…we were no more.

Fortunately, we got the worst out of our system early. I don't think we *ever* played in a shithole that bad again. Fucking Triple BBB's.

There's a song on the *To Whom It May Concern* record called "Disappear." It was about our breakup. The opening line reads:

And her world came crashing down
In the middle of a summer's night
200 miles from nowhere
Across the Carolina state line

* * *

Okay, that night sucked. But it was up and up from there. When Bart joined Some Odd Reason and we really hit our stride, things heated up—and full-blown alcoholism replaced common sense. We entered an era of pure decadence…and it got bad.

I will tell a few of the stories to give you an idea of how things can get out of control very quickly. We were young, reasonably successful…and had no idea how to conduct ourselves when alcohol flowed like the Ohio River.

CHAPTER 6:
HEDONISM

When I set out to write this book, I didn't want it to resemble the book of lies and exaggerations written by Neil Strauss and Mötley Crüe, called *The Dirt*.

Their book's full title is *The Dirt: Confessions of the World's Most Notorious Rock Band*. It chronicles many over-the-top moments of pure debauchery and excess in which the band engaged throughout their drug-and-stripper-addled history—a history which Vince Neil has said many times is probably bullshit and that he doesn't remember half of it.

However…

It occurred to me one day that I should at least include a few of these kinds of stories in my book. Even bands that reached the level of my band have opportunities (and related stories) that might surprise casual fans. Particularly when you mix a shit ton of alcohol with late nights, pretty women, and no reason to get up early… you've got a recipe for excess. Believe it or not, the world of rock and roll at *any* level is a wicked world unto itself.

I'm not a generally vulgar guy. So, I'll keep it as classy as I can.

Story One

The first story takes place during Spring Break, at Club La Vela in Panama City, Florida. Their property was billed as the "Largest nightclub in the USA" at the time, and MTV would famously film segments for their *Spring Break* shows on the beach near the club. We played more than once at this club, so got used to some of the idiosyncrasies of the place…but that familiarity grew over time. It was definitely a stressful learning curve. In fact, our first gig at Club La Vela got booked while we were still too young and inexperienced to know what the fuck we were doing.

In my experience, cover bands would have all day to figure out when they wanted to arrive at a bar or club, and then have an open window of time to set up and sound check their equipment. If we were scheduled to begin at 9pm, we could show up at noon or 3 or 5 or 7pm—it didn't matter as long as we were ready to fire up the engines and play at 9.

Club La Vela was so professional, bands were assigned exact times to load in.

I didn't know that. Because *nobody fucking told me*.

On our way down to Florida, the guys decided they wanted to stop at a big strip club in Atlanta. Nothing more "rock and roll" than strippers, I suppose…except not for me. I was never into the whole strip club scene. In fact, to this day I do not go to strip clubs. Watching a stripper makes me feel uncomfortable and super sleazy. I've been in a strip club exactly ONCE in my life. No offense to anyone who makes a living doing it, I actually have several stripper friends and friends that own strip clubs. It's just not my thing.

But if my guys want to dip into a strip club for a while, more power to them. I sat in the van and worked on some promotional materials for the band while they were inside.

We didn't have cell phones back in those days, but I carried a pager. And while I waited for the other three guys to get tired of the strip club, my pager went off. It was our booking agent, Joe Guida.

I frowned and checked my watch. Twelve noon. I called back from the pay phone in the strip club parking lot.

"What's up, Joe?"

He copped an attitude with me, "You're late. Load-in is at noon at Club La Vela."

"What do you mean, load-in? We're playing covers." I had no idea what he was talking about.

And that is when he decided to tell me about how the club worked. It would have been nice to be made aware of this PRIOR to leaving Virginia, but there was no time to sit around and point fingers. We had five or six more hours of driving ahead of us before we even set foot on the club property. It was time for action. Truth be told, I'll bet the contract said something about the load in…but I never looked. Joe was a pretty thorough agent so I'm sure it was my fault.

Anyway, I ran into the strip club and scraped the other three guys out of there—and we promptly hauled ass down to Panama City.

* * *

When we arrived at Club La Vela, it was like the first time a person walks down the street in Times Square. The enormity is hard to process—like, total sensory overload. The indoor capacity of the club hovers around 10,000 people, plus they had a parking lot the size of an amusement park.

The Entertainment Director, Rob Yaegar, met me at the entrance…and he was pissed.

"You were supposed to be here at noon to load in!"

He continued rattling off their protocol—everything that *should* have happened but didn't. I was only half listening. In the background, I was trying to wrap my brain around what I was seeing—this place was *huge*. Inside the club/rock room was a pretty big stage. The pool deck, on the other hand, had a big stage for bands like Aerosmith and (eventually) The Bret Michaels Band. During the height of *Rock of Love* we played the BIG MTV stage. Chuck, Ray, and I would officially become the only cover band from the rock room to actually make it onto the MTV Famous Stage.

The place was like Madison Square Garden, without the Knicks' locker room underneath.

Hell, that might be an understatement. For all I knew, there could have been three or four professional sports teams that called this place home. It was certainly big enough.

Anyway, we got everything settled and set up. As our call time drew near, thousands and of kids were lined up to get in and begin the Spring Break bash. They weren't there to see our band per se, but our lives certainly changed in that moment. It was time to PAR-TAY.

Jäger shots flowed from the moment we hit the stage until the moment we walked off at 4am. We loved it; we made this place our home. Despite getting off on the wrong foot, Rob ended up hiring us to play for seven straight nights, over and over again. And the money was good. Damn good (*well...good for a starving rock band!).

That's when the proverbial bus started to slide off the road. We made a big mistake—which led to an avalanche of other big mistakes.

On paper, this was a golden opportunity to completely immerse ourselves into our music. We had no responsibilities all day. As long as we showed up and played all night, we could basically rehearse, write new songs, and dive into the music all day, every day, for a whole week at a time!

Instead, we chose to dive into a bottle all day, every day.

On day one, we woke up raring to go. It was time to put on our best Jon Bon Jovi thinking caps and pen some hit songs. But first, a couple guys decided they wanted to have a few drinks before we started working. The next thing I knew (and it is a big blur), we were chest-deep in the Gulf of Mexico, with a cooler full of alcohol floating beside us. We proceeded to drink until show time.

Day one was a total bust.

But then came day two.

Another total bust.

Day three…four…five… At some point, we decided that we *deserved* this break from real life. And therefore we unanimously decided to lean in and go with the flow.

And buddy, did the alcohol ever flow.

There was a night when I got so drunk, I decided it was a good idea to swim in the Gulf after one of our shows. It was 4am, still dark, and I stripped down to my underpants and paddled out into the inky sea…

I didn't know anything about bull sharks back then. Not that I would have been able to remember anyway. Long story short, I lived to tell the tale. But I should probably be dead.

I wish I had a nickel for every time I've uttered those words.

For the remainder of our shows at Club la Vela, we were literally drunk off our asses every night when we walked onto the stage. We still played and did our job—that part never changed. But from that week forward, this band could never quite get its shit together. We were having fun, we played all over the country—and we wanted to show the world that it was more important to party than it was to grow up.

I was never completely comfortable with this new development. But we were still getting hired and still just as popular as ever, anywhere we went. So we just kept pushing the limits.

Story Two

We drank our way across the country, eventually finding ourselves back at Long Wong's, in Tempe, Arizona. Remember, this club felt like our western home. In fact, we talked about it so much that our wives and girlfriends tagged along to soak in the majesty that was our live show. Kristen was there with me.

On the day of the show, we were delighted to find that one of our local good friends was throwing a party to celebrate our arrival. It was an off-the-chain, *Project X* kind of party that would have made any of the guys in Van Halen say, "Dude…you need to settle the fuck down."

Somewhere along the way, I decided to try a pot brownie. It was a big step for me. Up until this moment in my life, I had never done a drug other than alcohol—but a pot brownie seemed innocuous enough. Other people were eating them and having a good time. How bad could it be?

Down the hatch it went…and I waited.

Fifteen minutes went by.

Nothing.

What a major letdown. I knew how alcohol felt, and this was definitely not that. In fact, this was the total opposite. It was a big fat ZERO burger.

So, I ate another half of one.

One of the party goers floated by and told me these brownies had peyote in them. Not that I cared—I really wasn't affected anyway. They could have been laced with some weird alien drug that Luke Skywalker brought back from Dagobah, but that wouldn't have mattered. Whatever drug it was that I just ate, I was evidently immune to it—just like when I took my first drink.

But then it kicked in. And ho-lee SHIT; I lost my fucking mind.

Have you ever had a really bad fever—and sometime in the middle of the night, you start hallucinating? Like, it's impossible to tell if you're asleep or awake? You're sort of in an in-between reality, where the rules of reason and reality go right out the window.

That's where I was.

I remember bits and pieces. I remember riding to the show in our van, crying my eyes out. I was convinced that my legs had fallen off. It didn't hurt, which was weird in and of itself. But I was mostly upset because I somehow thought it was the next day already, and that (because my legs had fallen off) we missed the gig.

And this was a super important gig. The show was completely sold out. We were on the bill with the Gas Giants (featuring Robin Wilson from the Gin Blossoms) and Roger Clyne, another local Tempe guy who was from a band called The Refreshments—the band that did the theme song for the show, *King of the Hill.*

The crowd was packed in and buzzing with pure pent-up energy; a giant coiled rattlesnake ready to strike. It was the kind of concert scenario straight out of a budding rock star's dream. But for peyote-laced me, it was drawn straight from my nightmares.

I couldn't go in. I was slobbering and whimpering and apologizing to the guys for fucking up the gig. I was inconsolable—and to their credit, they tried.

Over time, they convinced me that my legs were still attached to my body. Then my brother-in-law, Bobby (our merch guy), took me up the street to a Jack in the Box so I could get cleaned up and grab some food.

As we walked in, I kicked off my shoes and started to take off my shirt. I had decided that I was going to get naked in this public restaurant. Fortunately, Bobby was able to wrestle me into the bathroom—just in time for me to start throwing up.

Here is the most insane part of the story: I was further exacerbating the situation because I was intermittently spinning in circles too. Hence, I would throw up, spin in circles, and then throw up some more.

Lather, rinse, repeat.

I am being dead serious when I tell you that I spun in circles because I was trying to turn into Wonder Woman.

Mm-hmm.

Say no to drugs, kids.

I'm not talking about the new Gal Gadot version of Wonder Woman. I'm talking about the campy 1970s television version of *Wonder Woman*, starring Lynda Carter. If you remember, Diana Prince would start turning in circles—and then there was a flash of light, and Diana would miraculously transform into Wonder Woman.

That's what I wanted to be. My god…I so badly wanted to be Wonder Woman. But instead, I was a naked, spinning, vomiting, high-as-fuck Pete Evick.

Poor Bobby. By the grace of God, he was somehow able to get me cleaned up and pull my shit together well enough to stumble back down the street to Long Wong's.

And here was a strange quirk about the club itself: Long Wong's had a backstage door that led directly to the stage from a sidewalk behind the club. Except there was no space between the door and the stage. In other words, you opened the door and literally stepped from the sidewalk onto the stage.

Bobby led me to the door, where Bart Harris and our guitar tech (a guy we called "Elbow") stood waiting. Bart splashed a bottle of water in my face, Elbow hung my guitar around my neck, and then the three of them shoved me through the door and into the show.

Dear reader, you can ask any member of that band—I played *flawlessly*. I didn't miss a note. Not even kidding. I've heard people wonder aloud how bands like Van Halen or Guns n' Roses could do so many drugs and drink so much booze—and yet still get up and play every night.

Now I know.

There is something deep in our brain—call it muscle memory—that combines with our desire to entertain. When it kicks in, there is almost nothing that can stop us from putting on the show. I felt it that night.

When we hit the last note of the gig, Elbow took my guitar from me—and I crashed, face first, onto the dance floor. I smashed my head on the concrete, but I have no memory of anything after. The next thing I remember was waking up in my hotel room at about 4 pm the next afternoon.

You'd think that might be enough to scare all of us into slowing down.

You'd think that...but you'd be wrong.

Story Three

A couple nights later, we played a gig in Houston. Bart had smuggled the rest of the pot brownies out of the *Project X* house in Tempe and slammed one before the Houston show. On this night (thankfully) he was the only one who did the chocolate peyote specials.

When the gig ended, Bart decided that the gig wasn't going to end. He kept playing and playing. We asked him to stop, but he grabbed an acoustic guitar and played a few more songs. So the rest of us joined the crowd and kept partying.

This story doesn't have any funny anecdotes of drug-induced insanity, but we did get thrown out of the bar and were never invited back. And lest we forget, there were still some pot brownies left over.

Until a few nights later in Hattiesburg, MS.

We were slated to play at a converted movie theater with a band called Opal Dial. They sounded a lot like Three Doors Down, another band from the Hattiesburg area. In fact, for years and years we all assumed that it was some kind of pre-incarnation of Three Doors Down. However, in 2023 The Bret Michaels Band played with Three Doors Down, and I sat and talked with Brad Arnold for a while. He remembered the name Opal Dial but assured me it was not his band.

Anyway, there were barely any people in the crowd that night —so all four of us decided to wolf down a pot brownie.

And I will repeat, the crowd was *sparse*. Like, there were probably only 35 people milling about the club. It was the total opposite of what we had recently experienced in Tempe. While Opal Dial was on stage, we walked out into the theater to watch them play.

What happened next cannot be explained...it can only be

described.

At one point during Opal Dial's set, Spencer (our bass player) decided it would be a good idea to take a piss. Except he wasn't too keen about walking all the way back to the bathrooms. So, he did what any of us would do. He pulled it out and started to take a piss. Right there in front of God and everyone.

I sincerely hope his decision was guided by the pot brownies.

The other three of us stared, aghast.

And then decided we would take a piss too.

Call it camaraderie; call it brotherhood…call it "stupid shit people do when they're high on peyote." But there was a moment when all four of us sat in movie-theater-style seats, shoulder to shoulder, and pissed down the floor of this poor club.

Needless to say, were not invited back to *that* club, either.

Our tour of decadence was in full swing—and this was totally NOT the cultural norm. The days of rock stars acting like whacked out three-year-olds was long behind us by this time. These were the days that Matchbox Twenty was considered "edgy," if you catch my drift.

There are SO many more stories during the Bart era of the band, but I think you've got the idea. Let's fast-forward to when I revamped the band into EVICK.

Story Four

With EVICK up and running, I somehow managed to swing a deal with Jägermeister, the German alcoholic beverage company. We loved Jäger, so this felt like a huge win for me.

Is Jäger a beer? A spirit? A wine?

Who the fuck knows. It's Jägermeister.

Basically, I signed a marketing agreement that would have us promote their brand wherever we went. In return, they gave us a lot of professional-grade promotional material. Cross-branded banners, posters, and swag that we would wear, carry, and/or hang around the clubs while we played.

They figured they would move a lot of product if we pushed Jäger at the clubs. And buddy, they were not wrong. My band alone probably caused the company to requisition an extra cargo ship to bring back-up Jäger to the U.S. while we toured.

All 100% true. We took our end of the bargain seriously. To this day, I don't know how we're not dead. (YES, I SAID IT AGAIN)

For example, my 30th birthday party at Sully's.

We drank so much that night, we outdid ourselves. I remember (barely) that during our third set, a friend of mine (Tracy Melvin) brought a shot up to the stage.

I don't know if any of you have ever seen the pewter shot glasses that Jäger used to sell. They were shaped like a deer head—and they were extremely cool. But in the right state of mind, they could also resemble a medieval goblet. Like a chalice straight out of *Game of Thrones*.

Anyway, Tracy brought one of these pewter Jäger shots to me.

Here's how extraordinarily drunk I was: I began to hallucinate. In my brain, Tracy was the devil. Like the real devil… Satan himself. And he was making me drink blood from his goblet.

Therefore, I did what any normal person would do. I hid behind my amp.

I (literally) crouched down behind my amp. But the show must go on, so I took my microphone with me.

Keep in mind, this is all perfectly normal.

I sang the rest of the night from that exact location. I finished the last five songs of the night while playing and singing on the floor behind my amp.

HA! IN YER FACE, SATAN!

I was nothing if not a survivor. The devil was NOT about to get me that night.

(**remember, all perfectly normal)

As a footnote to this story, I will defend my honor by saying this was the last time I saw Satan. Unfortunately, that's about as far as my dignity is allowed to stray.

From that night forward, I would often get so drunk, I would freak the fuck out and grow deathly afraid of *something*. The "something" could vary from night to night, but I would routinely do songs—or entire sets—while camped out under a table or behind the bar, hiding from whatever nefarious entity was trying to get me.

I would still sing and play my guitar. I never missed a lick or a lyric. The show must go on, man…the show must go on.

Story Five

Nestled on the southern tip of Maryland, where the Patuxent River meets the glorious Chesapeake Bay, there is a cool little plot of land known as Solomons Island. There, roughly 1,500 souls live a quiet existence, enjoying the fruits of the ocean water and the moderate climate.

Solomons Island is home to several businesses that cater to the summer tourists. Gift shops, seafood restaurants, and marinas dot the landscape—and what was an amazing club called "Harbor Sounds." EVICK headlined their biggest event one summer…and things have never been the same.

The event was called the "Tiki Bar Opening." The Tiki Bar was a club next to Harbor Sounds, but the shared parking lot overflowed with patrons from both establishments—as well as most of the island residents. It was an unbelievably big party (given the small-town feel of the area itself), where the owners would kick off the new season by throwing an all-day music festival to signal the outdoor venue's readiness for another rockin' summer.

By the time they booked me, our reputation had grown legendary in two distinct areas: First, we were known to be a big draw. We were popular in the Virginia/Eastern Maryland area and would pack the house wherever we went. But second, we were also known as a major party band. I don't know if anyone else was comparing us to major party bands coming off the Sunset Strip in the 80s, but I certainly was. Pound for pound, we would have given a go to any of those dudes.

Let me tell you dear reader, we pulled into Harbor Sounds at 1 or 2 in the afternoon, and the crowd looked like Woodstock. DC had to have been a ghost town that night. Baltimore was surely vacant. The only people left in Maryland and Virginia must have either been too infirm to travel, or too stiff to enjoy a good ol' fashioned hootenanny.

A sales rep from Jägermeister must have called ahead and arranged something with Harbor Sounds. Because their owner, Jimmy Z, had pulled his Jäger machine out into the parking lot (where the stage was set up), and started feeding me shots.

We were booked to start at 9pm.

My sobriety ended around 3:30. My sanity left about 7.

At some point during the 8 o'clock hour, a town official pulled me aside. It could have been the mayor or a town councilman or the President of the United States. I just didn't know. I had no idea who *I* was by that time, much less who this suit happened to be.

Anyway, he pulled me aside and said, "Mr. Evick, we are so glad to have you here in our town. We're also delighted to have your band here to help kick off this big night for the island."

His smile remained firmly in place, but then his tone grew less friendly.

"But I need to lay out some ground rules."

I nodded along while he laid it out.

"I need you to *not* bring girls up onto the stage. I also need you to not use profanity, and really not say the word *fuck*."

He enunciated the last word like a nun at catholic school. Still smiling, his tone returned to friendly.

"I need all this from you because this is a family event, and we are outdoors. We'd like to keep it clean and enjoyable for everyone."

He met my eyes, "Okay?"

I nodded again and eyed the Jäger machine.

I knew what he was saying. This was a tourist town and there were a lot of parents walking around with their kids. But at this point in my life, the asshole part of my brain was running loose and carrying a bota bag full of Jägermeister.

The city official walked away satisfied with our conversation. I walked away pissed and plotting rebellion.

At 9 o'clock sharp, EVICK took the stage. I strutted up to the microphone, and before playing a note, said, "The fuckin' mayor told me I couldn't say FUCK."

The crowd went ape-shit crazy. It was going to be one of those nights.

"He also said I can't bring any fuckin' girls on stage."

I proceeded to hit the first note of our opening number and started picking out girls to bring on stage. Usually, I would bring up about twenty girls. My goal tonight was to have fifty.

I never got that far because security people started pulling the girls back *off* the stage. We went back and forth with a few, but I eventually relented. I was defiant as fuck, but I wasn't about to compromise the show.

The town administrators let us keep playing, but had their people maintain a tight perimeter around the stage.

Not that it stopped our antics.

About six or songs into our set, the drums stopped.

Weird.

I looked behind me, and Chuck had fallen off the drum riser. Keep in mind, this was a big event with a big stage—the riser held the drum kit about six feet off the actual ground. Chuck, drunk as a pirate at Tortuga, must have leaned back and fallen six feet onto his head.

I was concerned—not so much about Chuck (he would be fine), but about playing the rest of our set. Fortunately, an old friend was in the audience. Bart Harris was there because his new band, Junk Food, was scheduled to play the after party inside Harbor Sounds once we were done.

Long story short, his drummer jumped onto the riser and started to play. Chuck was crumpled in a heap somewhere behind the drums, I was hammered out of my mind, and the show must go on.

But it got worse.

Back then, I used to love stage diving into the crowd. It was a thing. But under normal circumstances, I would dive out, the crowd would catch me, and then everyone would work to wriggle me back onto the stage.

Tonight, there was a bit of a miscommunication.

I dove into the crowd, and felt gravity reverse when dozens of outstretched hands reached up and held me afloat. Then they started working me from one set of hands to the next—but in the wrong direction. Instead of getting eased back toward the stage, I was surfed toward the rear of the crowd. By the time I was placed onto my feet, I was all the way in the back, standing in the parking lot.

I looked toward the stage—and saw that it was (what seemed to be) about a mile away Probably realistically it was about 50 yards away, but Jäger has a way with bending the map. I also saw that Bart had apparently jumped on stage in my place, and picked up where I left off. He was now singing, and the crowd was going crazy.

What a fucking night.

Anyway, my brain was still being held captive by several gallons of Jägermeister. My first thought when assessing my options was, "Welp…I'll never get back to that stage."

Then I did what any rational human being would do. I found my car and fell asleep in the driver's seat.

After this gig, one of my good friends (Zane)—who was incredibly supportive of EVICK and was instrumental and having us headline this festival—expressed his disappointment in my behavior. Zane loved my band and knew what we were all about…but I had pushed the limits. This affected me in a very negative way. Zane, Jimmy and the people of Solomons Island had become FAMILY to me. As much as I liked my Van Halen-esque reputation, that kid in me that doesn't like to disappoint people was crushed.

It's not like this was the first time I fucked up. The previous year, we also played at Harbor Sounds. This time wasn't for the Tiki Bar Opening, but it was still outdoors and near the water. Anyway, I was so drunk and so focused on myself, I grabbed the mic, ran down the dock, and started jumping from boat to boat while singing. I didn't know whose boats these were, and definitely didn't have permission to trespass. It never occurred to me that the owners might have been on board, sleeping or relaxing or whatever. It didn't cross my mind that I was doing something incredibly invasive.

I got in trouble for that stunt, of course. I was always afraid to not get invited back to Harbor Sounds. But we always got invited back. The power of the guitar, remember? Jimmy, the owner, seemed to love our antics. We made them money, so they put up with our bullshit.

Well after the fact, I knew that through all these antics I let the band down, I let the crowd down. I let the whole town down. But at the time, I wanted to take EVICK to the level of Guns N'Roses or Poison or Van Halen. And not just in terms of record sales—I wanted to party as hard (or *harder*) than any of those guys. Ergo, everything we were doing was perfectly in line with that goal.

I've been fortunate enough to have the opportunity to tell some of these stories to members of those aforementioned bands. One member (not Bret) remarked, "Well…you guys actually took it a little farther than we did."

In a strange way, I suppose that meant "mission accomplished." But on the other hand, it spoke to my level of disregard for anyone other than myself. There was nothing rock and roll about my behavior. I acted like a selfish, petulant child. I had to start considering what I was gonna lose versus win with this way of life.

Story Six

We would do summer on the coast and winter at a ski lodge.

As pretentious as that sounds, it is exactly what happened. EVICK would play at the Harbor Sounds when the weather was nice, and then we became one of the house bands at The Black Bear Tavern near Deep Creek Lake—a bar adjacent to the Wisp Ski Resort in McHenry, Maryland—during the winter months.

The Black Bear had kind of a unique feature insofar as they had an apartment to house the band between gigs. Think about the bunk house in *Dirty Dancing*, where the staff would reside. Then remove all semblance of the place being gross or uninhabitable. The apartment at Black Bear was actually really nice.

That is, it was nice until we got there. Hell, we didn't give a shit. Not having to drive anywhere after a gig meant extra party time for us.

Buddy, the owners and the staff were so nice to us…but we would flagrantly disregard their rules and their serenity. We always held giant knock-down-drag-out rock and roll parties in the guest apartment. We would *trash* the place. I remember one time we smashed their toilet to bits. I have no idea why. We were drunk and living the rock and roll lifestyle.

EVICK held the record for alcohol sales at almost every bar or club we ever played. Our crowd liked to party as hard as we did, and booze flowed like a sluice off the Mississippi River. In my brain, that meant we were successful. We hadn't grown to the level of playing theaters or sheds (amphitheaters), so I had to measure success the only way I knew how. That meant partying *as if* we were Poison.

We had a free pass for decadence.

Story Seven

Here's a quick story to further illustrate our legendary status when it came to pounding down alcohol.

EVICK started touring the country hard core, zigzagging from coast to coast. Long Wong's had closed for good by this point, so our Phoenix-area stop became a club in the Ahwatukee Foothills, called Cactus Jack's.

Cactus Jack's was new to us; likewise, we were new to them. All they knew was that we were popular in the greater Phoenix metro area—if for no other reason, for being from the east coast. So they welcomed the band with open arms. In our honor, they hung as much Jäger promotional material as they could find.

As was our custom, the drinking started the moment we arrived.

And the truth of the matter was, I really wanted to love Cactus Jack's. I missed Long Wong's and knew a lot of the same people would be at this new venue to cheer us on and provide support. More importantly, I wanted everyone here to love us—and to love me in particular.

When we walked on stage that night, I ordered 50 (yes, FIFTY) shots of Jägermeister to the stage. It was enough to kill an entire platoon of gladiators, but I wanted to give a suitable gift to our fans. I paid for the drinks and proceeded to hand them out to the crowd.

In return, the crowd started buying shots for us. It became the most fucked up love story ever told. Before long, we were completely out of our minds and out of control.

We were jumping on tables and knocking over chairs—we

basically started wrecking the place. But the cash register never stopped ringing. It sounded like a pinball machine throughout the entire night. We ended up making Cactus Jack's more money than they had ever seen for one single show.

By the end of the night, I was at least coherent enough to talk with the manager while she paid me. I will never forget her words as she passed the envelope across the bar.

"I will tell you, we've never seen anything like this in our lives."

In my brain, I figured it was a compliment. She was clearly impressed with our "rock star" level of partying. Every band that came before us was a bunch of lightweights. We were the real deal.

But looking back, I think her comment was far from complimentary. I think her underlying message was, "I'm never doing this again."

And to her credit, she didn't. We were never invited back.

Story Eight

Before leaving that night at Cactus Jack's, I must add one footnote to the story. I also have to add that during this era of the band, we toured with a background singer named Rachel.

And here is the rest of the story:

Still brimming with pride over the manager's comment about how we were the hardest partying band in the world (or something to that effect), we decided to purchase a full bottle of Jäger on our way out the door. No sense ending the party just yet.

The manager—despite her words of admiration a few moments before—sold us the bottle…but by the shot. In other words, she calculated how many shots were in a full bottle, and then multiplied that by the retail price per shot. I think we ended up paying $175 for the bottle of Jäger.

When we arrived at the hotel, I decided we were going to have a little pool party. Long story short, I ended up rescuing Chuck's drunk ass—three times—from the bottom of the pool. After the third rescue, I put Chuck far enough away that he could not accidentally roll back in.

However, this seemed to give new life to Chuck. Before I knew it, he had stripped naked and come over to hover above me (I was in the pool). When I saw him, and I swear I am not making this up, I freaked out. I screamed—which caused Chuck to run (still naked) into the pitch-black Arizona night. The hotel was on the edge of the arid wilderness, so Chuck was wandering like Moses in the Desert of Paran.

And here is how drunk I was: I was horrified. In my wet brain, I thought Chuck was no longer a human being. I thought he had turned into a Bigfoot and would return to terrorize us. Probably kill us, as naked Bigfoots are prone to do.

Therefore, I did what any rational person would do. I climbed a tree, hugged the trunk, and fell fast asleep. I was nothing if not safety conscious.

I was awakened the next morning by the manager of the hotel. He was throwing random garbage at me (literally), trying to get me out of the tree without having to climb up and retrieve me himself.

Now let's get back to Rachel.

I finally woke up, Chuck finally returned (and put on some pants), and we finally packed up and got ready to leave. As we walked to the van, we noticed the entire walkway from our room to the parking lot was punctuated by little piles of vomit…and it was a dark, dark black. Piles of black yak, if you will.

It was all compliments of Rachel. She was so drunk the night before that she had thrown up eleven or twelve times while trying to walk from the parking lot to the room. And she was sick as fuck—so much so, that she thought she was dying and about to meet Jesus.

From that day forward, we started calling Jägermeister, "Black Liquid Jesus."

Remember my song, "This Ain't the Life"? Another lyric reads:

Black liquid Jesus
Gonna come numb my brain.

And that's how we rolled.

Story Nine

Alas, all the partying was taking its toll on me. Yes, I was living the life, but no—I wasn't functioning like a real adult. Things began to come to a head for me at a club called Oasis, in Occoquan, Virginia.

(**author's note: don't try to pronounce "Occoquan" while drunk)

A few days prior to this gig, Ray (our bass player) had just gotten a brand-new Chevy Suburban. Beautiful vehicle—big enough to haul a bunch of gear in our trailer, but luxurious enough to be comfortable while doing so.

Anyway, we played the gig that night and got annihilated beyond belief. The Jägermeister Company probably added an EVICK wing to their corporate headquarters after that show. We were drunk enough that we decided (mercifully so) that it would be a bad idea to drive home. However, we did have to move Ray's Suburban to the front of the club in order to load out our gear.

We got it loaded, and Ray hopped in so he could return the vehicle to the side of the club. All told, it was a drive of *maybe* two hundred feet.

Somehow—and I wish there would have been video security cameras back then—Ray managed to run the Suburban square into a concrete pylon that held up a light post. To this day I cannot figure out how he got up enough speed to accomplish this, but he hit the concrete so hard, he lurched forward and split his head open on the steering wheel. Like, split open down to his skull.

In my mind, he was driving slower than we could have walked around the building. In reality, he must have been going like Jeff Gordon down a straightaway at Talladega.

But here is a testimony to just how soul-less Chuck Fanslau can be (I love you, Chuck!). Imagine the scene: Ray is bleeding all down his face and onto his chest. Someone from the bar is yelling to call an ambulance. There is chaos in the parking lot. I'm freaking out, trying to figure out what to do next.

And up walks Chuck.

He surveyed the situation and said, "We've got to get the gear off this fucking trailer."

Everyone turned, confused.

"We've got a gig tomorrow night," Chuck continued, "And the cops are probably going to impound the trailer."

We all looked at each other, confused. Ray was probably going to die a twisted, bloody death—and all Chuck could think about was salvaging the gear.

Fortunately, the ambulance arrived pronto. And the cops were incredibly cool about the whole thing. They basically looked the other way and let me and Ray go to the emergency room. Holy shit…that was a relief. Once again, the power of rock and roll!

And to sum up how amazingly soul-less and callous I can be, I did something about an hour later that got me kicked out of the hospital.

Ray got wheeled into a room, and I sidled up to the bed. He was split from the top of his forehead to the bridge of his nose—and the split was clean. You could literally see his skull between the flaps of skin that had folded back.

I couldn't control myself. In my brain, I thought, *This is a once in a lifetime opportunity to touch a human skull…while the person is still alive!*

And while my friend lay dying of a skull split in a hospital room outside of Occoquan, I placed my finger onto his skull.

Just then, because this could not have happened any other way, the nurse walked in—and I was immediately removed from the hospital. I was forced to wait in the parking lot while Ray got patched up.

When he walked out of the ER, Ray had his head bandaged like Dengar, a bounty hunter in the *Star Wars* story. I found that to be hilarious.

We gigged in Pittsburgh the next night, as planned. Ray was up there, playing bass and sporting his new Dengar look with pride.

The show must go on, man. Ray is, if nothing else, a true rock and roll trooper and to this day one of the greatest guys you could ever meet.

But the wheels were coming off the cart.

Story Ten

I think we bottomed out a few years later. I was already playing in Bret's band, as was the rest of EVICK. My first year with Bret, I was fortunate enough to bring the whole band with me. But I also know that Bret had used a different band every year. That was a dark thought for me. I was getting older, EVICK hadn't made it out of the bars and clubs, and now I was about to lose an opportunity to play with one of the biggest rock stars in history.

It was bad. And it was time to grow up and get more serious.

Except we couldn't.

Between Bret's gigs, EVICK would play clubs. It was just what we did. We didn't know any other way to live.

One such opportunity happened on St. Patrick's Day, 2005. Bret was off for the holiday, so EVICK accepted a gig at The Black Bear. As per usual, the place was packed, and the Jäger was coming in hot.

Chuck managed to get so drunk he was unable to finish the show. I was drunk too (duh)—but I was able to function well enough to keep playing. When Chuck faded, I was angry. However, I was not nearly as coherent as I thought.

Out of the well of drunken good ideas, I drew a suitable plan. It seemed that an appropriate punishment for a drunk-as-fuck drummer would be to piss in his bass drum. Not that it was going to be pretty, but who was I to argue with a perfectly reasonable plan?

So right there—in front of the band, the sold-out crowd, and the almighty God above—I whipped it out and started pissing in Chuck's bass drum.

As anyone executing a good plan would have to do.

By this point in the evening, I had consumed my body weight in Jäger bombs, so the piss stream could have put out the California wildfires. In fact, the golden arch continued to awe the crowd for six or eight minutes.

In retrospect, it probably wasn't six or eight minutes—but I was hammered, and I didn't check my watch before I started.

Anyway, at some point during the feat, the other guitar (Brad

Puckett) and bass (Ray Sherring) players took it upon themselves to aid and abet. Perhaps they too understood that Chuck had to be punished, and that mine was the most reasonable approach to achieve that goal. They wandered over, joined me in my act, and created the *golden arches*.

No way McDonalds could say no to *this* endorsement opportunity!

Incidentally, I had recently hired a new keyboard player prior to this show. Robbie Jozwiak bore witness to the whole thing. It was his first ever gig with us. I can't imagine what he must have been thinking. To his credit (and perhaps due to his level of dismay and disgust), he kept himself firmly secured in his pants.

The spectacle couldn't have scarred him too much. To this day, Robbie is the only original EVICK member to remain (with me) in the Bret Michaels Band.

At some point, Chuck regained consciousness and realized what was going on. He must have agreed with our overall premise: that it was necessary to punish him. Ergo, he did what he had to do. He stood up and pissed onto the wall.

(**this move, now including *four* of us arching it gracefully, can be referred to as "the double McDonalds")

After we were all empty, we managed to get our shit together well enough for one last song. We closed the night with Bob Seger's "Old Time Rock and Roll." The crowd was fantastic…but this night had to end.

As we finished, I had come to my senses enough to remember that it was getting to be time to grow up and become more serious about the band and our career. More specifically, it was time for *me* to get more serious about the band and *my* career.

After the show, I put my arm around Chuck, my best friend in the world, and said, "Buddy…we have to stop this. I have to support my kids. We have to pull ourselves out of this."

Unfortunately, Chuck was not in a state of mind that would allow him to process my words like an adult would do. Instead, he got into an insane argument with me over what I had just said. I was in no way sober myself—so when I reached my limit, I started swinging. It was on the dance floor in front of the stage, and in full view of the audience. I didn't care. I was tired of living like a sixteen-year-old that just found the keys to his old man's liquor cabinet. I was a husband and a father and could no longer live solely for myself.

I viciously attacked my best friend. And that's when shit really got out of control.

As Chuck was falling, his head hit the stage. It made a loud THUNK; like a scene in a movie where the character dies from the fall. But I was incensed. When Chuck landed on the floor, I pounced on him like a gorilla and continued to pommel his lifeless body with punches.

A few guys pulled me off of him. Luckily, Chuck wasn't dead. And I do mean I was lucky. It could have gone way, *way* worse than it did. We were so fucking out of control.

Some of the kind folks (who came out to have a good time and watch us play) now took the initiative to carry Chuck to the on-site apartment. The rest of us stayed behind to clean up the mess we made.

Not that we were done with Chuck. I guess the rest of the band decided that he hadn't quite made up for his transgression.

I honestly don't remember how we got our hands on a green Sharpie, but there it was. All I know is that for some reason Chuck's pants were down…and Ray took the Sharpie and drew a dot on Chuck's balls. I had to top that (of course), so I colored his entire scrotum green. Before you rush to judgment, remember that it was St. Patrick's Day. Sporting a set of green balls was as "leprechaun" as you can get!

Anyway, Chuck stumbled into the bathroom when he came to the next morning. I was already wide awake—because I was still fuming about what happened the night before. All I could think about was that our band was called EVICK—which is my name. I alone would bear the brunt of consequences whenever we messed up. Nobody was ever going to remember that Chuck Fanslau got drunk and ruined a gig at The Black Bear. Rather, they would all think to themselves, "We're never hiring Pete's band again."

All that rage disappeared in a heartbeat.

When Chuck walked out of the bathroom, he was visibly

upset. He had a giant bruise on his chest (the result of our fight), and he had just found out that his balls had been colored green with a permanent marker.

Through bloodshot eyes, he looked at me and said, "I need help."

Those three words really struck a chord in me because Chuck was no longer the drunken asshole. Now he was my best friend—and he was in trouble.

Honestly, we all needed help. Chuck didn't have a drinking problem—the entire band had a drinking problem.

But Chuck was the one backed into a corner. He went on to say, "There is no lie I can tell, there is no truth I can tell. There is no acceptable explanation I can give my wife as to why my balls are green."

As I stated but never explained in my first book, Chuck is one of my best friends and one of the most important people in the world to me…because he STAYED. When I read these stories back, I can't understand why he has and still does. When I'm angry, I would say he deserved such treatment. But when I'm sober, I'm utterly embarrassed that he and I have fought like we have. There will never be enough ways to apologize and never enough words to thank him for still being here.

And frankly, Chuck was right when he alerted me to how we really needed to do things differently—to become better versions of ourselves. It was time to make a change. I was about to sober up and grow up.

PART 2:

MY LIFE...IN THE BRET MICHAELS BAND

CHAPTER 7:
AND THEN I WAS IN BRET MICHAELS'S BAND

C'mon…would this even be a book if I didn't talk about my relationship with Bret? For my life and my career, I can't talk about kindness without talking about Bret (and not just because he's going to read this book). He doesn't just hold a bust in my personal "Rock and Roll Hero Hall of Fame," he holds an entire *wing*.

I will add one caveat to our quasi-timeline. One or two of the stories in Chapter Six reflect a time during our first year playing in Bret's band. The real grow up and sober up moment happened in almost a flash—but it happened as we were preparing to tour with him for year number two.

I'll get to that story in good time; for now, I will tell the story I have told a million times on podcasts and in radio interviews: *How I Met the Bret*. The story's cold open is compliments of a mutual connection, HK Management.

* * *

To set the context for this fortuitous meeting, I will remind you of two important facts. First, I was a huge Poison fan. No two ways about it. And second, I auditioned for Poison several years earlier. Back when I, along with hundreds of other applicants, lost the job to Richie Kotzen.

Having said that, Poison was being managed by a company called HK Management. It was to them that I sent my audition tape. And because I'm me, I held on to HK Management's contact information…just in case.

And then "just in case" happened.

In 2003, Bret was bursting with creative ideas that reached outside the boundaries of Poison. He wanted to do country, he wanted to do metal, he wanted to do pop, he wanted to do whatever he wanted to do.

Bret is not a man who sits still. I will speak more about this in a few pages when I spell out the recipe for success in the music industry…but Bret is THAT guy. Rather than sit home and count his money and yell at the gardener to keep the damned gate closed, Bret wrote and recorded a solo album. *Songs of Life*, which was released on April 22, 2003—and featured a similar bluesy-hard-rock style that Poison played, but without boundaries. There were keyboards and percussion and funk parts; there was *anything* Bret wanted, without compromise.

Personally, I thought the album was awesome. The fans loved it, and the song "Raine" (written about his first daughter) gained critical acclaim by the press. But Bret was diving deeper and deeper into his country music influences and was enjoying the freedom to do exactly what he wanted musically

So Bret moved toward a more country-rock style. He re-arranged some Poison classics, and wrote some new material to reflect this ideological shift. Off this record came a song called "All I Ever Needed," which instantly made the Counrty charts and gained airplay all over the country. To many, this WAS the sequel to "Every Rose…" that millions of fans had been waiting for.

And that's where I come in.

The country-tinged album, *Freedom of Sound*, was released on New Year's Day, 2005. Leading up to the launch, Bret toured as a solo artist. In fact, he never actually *stopped* touring. He would assemble a band, hit the road, take a short break, and then get right back out on the road.

As Bret was preparing to hit the road in 2003, I called Jay Nedry, the owner of Jaxx.

Using my gift of gab (and more than a little begging), I was able to finagle EVICK onto the bill when The Bret Michaels Band played at Jaxx. I've written about Jaxx already, but suffice it to say that this club was our people. Opening for Bret was a natural, and we helped pack the house that night.

(I'm sure Bret is forever grateful that we helped him out—

HA!)

With the old Pete Evick, that night would have been enough. But there was a new sheriff in town. I was tired of being a glorified bar band. I wanted to take EVICK to the next level, and that would require more work and more exposure.

When I looked over Bret's touring schedule, an opportunity presented itself.

I called my contact at HK Management. Squeaky wheel gets the most grease, right?

Either that or it gets replaced and pitched into the garbage. But let's not find a grey lining in this silver cloud.

I called HK Management and worked my charm.

Honestly, I say that because I don't remember exactly what was said or what the terms of the agreement ended up being. But they gave me the info I needed and I got EVICK established on several of the east coast dates remaining on Bret's tour.

We played a lot of dates with The Bret Michaels Band. We were out promoting the *Anachronism* CD, and got a ton of exposure —compliments of hard work and hustle. It was a dream come true.

* * *

Smash cut to 2004. Bret hits the road again, and this time with a completely different band than the one he toured with in 2003.

As for me, I let my fingers do the walking and kept close touch with as many of my connections as I could. Just like 2003, the Evick charm was impossible to resist. Except this time, EVICK got booked as the opening act for even MORE dates on The Bret Michaels Band tour.

By this point in our career, EVICK is getting ready to release its second CD, *Sunset to Sunset*. When I confirmed the dates, I kicked it into high gear. It was time to market the shit out of this album and try to ride the wave of new fans and old friends. A part of that marketing bonanza was to shoot a video for the lead single, "This Ain't the Life."

The details of this next part are a little fuzzy because they are bent through the prism of time and storytelling. Frankly, I wasn't aware the next event even *happened*. Bret told me about it years later. But behind the scenes, it became a seminal moment for me personally.

* * *

By that point in Bret's career, he'd probably encountered over a thousand musicians in bands that had opened for his solo band or for Poison. I was just another local yokel.

From the story Bret tells, he was sitting on his bus one day before a show. He was playing back-to-back nights, first in Springfield, VA, and then in Baltimore, MD. At the time, I'm sure he had no idea that EVICK had a record deal or that we were a nationally touring act. He would have no reason to know that.

My band arrived early that day so we could do the video shoot. Matt Weglean directed the video, but I (admittedly) constantly had my nose in it. I took this opportunity very seriously. From what I'm told, Bret watched the shoot from the window of his tour bus. I don't think he was necessarily looking for a guitar player. Rather, he was probably entertained by the beehive of activity.

As Bret watched me conduct myself in a professional setting like that, he was impressed with my drive and my composure. There was something about me that stood out from what he considered the "normal" way for local guys to act.

Bret no longer saw me as a local bar guy who would inevitably blow his chance opening for the band. He now saw me as a go-getter, and a guy who could get shit done.

Frankly, I was in tight with the entire Bret Michaels Band crew. I was buddies with his guitar tech, Fast Tommy. I hung out with his security guy, Big John. I had made friends with his tour manager, Janna, and with the members of his bands from both years.

I was living my best life.

I dropped hint after hint that I was interested in joining the band if there came an opening. As luck would have it, the guitar player (Steve) was unable to return when Bret hit the road again in 2005.

Steve really went to bat for me. So did Bret's guitar tech (Fast Tommy) and his head of security (Big John). I was thoroughly vetted by the "non star" personnel on the tour. That was important, but there eventually came the time that Bret wanted to know what kind of guy I was. Obviously, he knew I could play the guitar. No problem there. But being a part of a band requires more than just my playing. Bret wanted to see if I treated other people with respect when he wasn't around.

If I made the band, I represented the band.

And if I represented the band, I represented Bret Michaels.

* * *

The call finally came. Bret called me personally because, as he put it, he needed a guitar player for a little radio gig he was doing in Detroit. It was called The Downtown Hoedown, and I (of course) said yes.

In my mind, a "little radio gig" means playing under a pop-up tent in a mostly-deserted parking lot next to an intern roasting weenies. For Bret, the "little radio gig" was a huge event, hosted by 99.5, WYCD, Detroit's home for Young Country. To this day, the Hoedown represents one of the largest country music festivals in the country.

It was the very definition of "Trial by Fire," in front of *at least* 50,000 people.

Oh—and we didn't have time to rehearse with Bret. So that was fun.

It all came out okay…but it wasn't great. We played the songs, but we just didn't gel. And if you recall, Bret is not a man who is satisfied with "okay."

A day that should have been thrilling for me became (instead) a pity party. I was convinced that I had blown the chance of a lifetime.

* * *

When I got back home, I was surrounded by my friends and family and other local musicians…and they made me feel a little better. Actually, they made me feel like a returning hero. The people I loved gathered 'round and begged me to tell some tales of my adventure to the far-away lands of enchantment. I spoke of magical wizards and dragons and unicorns…

Not really. But I might as well have. They hung on my every word. Although frankly, the story I told was not one they necessarily wanted to hear.

I told them that I now understood what was required to "make it" in the music business. It wasn't about how well you could play or the clothes you wore on stage. It was about the sheer energy you would spend on the stage. It's exactly how Bob Seger sang it in "Turn the Page":

Out there in the spotlight
You're a million miles away.
Every ounce of energy
You try to give away…

And buddy, that was Bret Michaels in a nutshell. He had the "IT" factor. Yes, he was good looking and talented—but he also gets on stage and gives 100% of what he has to the audience *every single night.*

My guys definitely *think* we give it all away…but we don't. At least, we hadn't up to that point. I told them that I could do three sets with EVICK and leave the venue feeling like I was king of the world. However, I just played ONE set with Bret Michaels, and felt like a fucking freight train just hit me.

That sounds dramatic, but it is absolutely true.

Obviously, my anxiety had a bit to do with how drained I felt, but I wasn't wrong. Bret taught me something that day in Detroit that I could have never gotten by reading a book or watching a concert from the audience. This was something you would never understand until you actually experience it—until you literally *feel* it.

I remember thinking the exact words, *Oh…so that's why we never made it. I know how to make it now.*

I figured the gig with Bret was probably a one-off. After all, I was just "okay." But it clicked in my head that I now knew exactly what it took to make it. So even if it wasn't going to be with Bret's band, I could take that knowledge home and apply it to EVICK.

That really didn't happen. Not only because I ended up staying with Bret (which was the best possible outcome, to be honest), but also because there was yet *another* aspect of "professionalism" that everyone in EVICK was not aware of. Not yet, anyway. It probably represented a second important reason that we never ascended past the level we were at. I'll write about it in just a minute.

For now, let me get back to the timeline.

* * *

A couple days after the Detroit Hoedown, my phone rang. It was Bret.

"How do think that went, Pete?"

I underplayed my hand. "It went terrible I am so, so sorry…"

Bret picked up what I was putting down.

"Well, if you had thought it went good, then you and I would have had a problem. Fortunately, I think we're on the same page."

Bret knew we hadn't rehearsed with him, and that might have been part of the issue.

But instead of getting together to rehearse, he figured we should just get back on stage and try again. No rehearsal…no problem solving…no troubleshooting. He had a show coming up at the Starwood Amphitheater, in Nashville, TN. The epicenter of country music. We were the opening act for Lynyrd Skynyrd, in front of a sold-out crowd of roughly 38,000 screaming fans.

Backstage, I was pretty excited. Anxious too—I had no desire to blow another chance. And Bret, being the leader and mentor that he is, pulled me aside.

"Listen, Pete—I've seen your band a bunch of times. I know how good you are, and I know what you can do. Just go out there and be yourself. Don't try to be what you think I want. Have fun and be you."

As I write that line, it sounds so cliché. Like some trope out of a Disney movie, just before the hero pulls through and saves the day.

But I'll tell you why it was so important to me. It took all the pressure off. And once I got out of my head and out of my own damn way, I played…and it was great.

We ended the night with "Nothin' but a Good Time." While we held the last note, Bret high-fived me…and the rest is history. We're still together, nineteen years later (and counting).

* * *

The Starwood show was the front end of a four-day run of shows. Bret trusted us to perform all four days, and it went well. From there, we played gigs in Myrtle Beach, Cincinnati, and Pottsville, Pennsylvania (outside of Philly). I might add that the guitar player I was going to be replacing, my good friend Steve Frangadakis, was with us on this run to kinda help break us in.

We got better each night—although I could tell that we had a ways to go.

After the Pottsville gig, we went home for a few days to decompress. There was a *lot* going on, and my head was spinning. But as Ozzy reminded us in 1988, there is no rest for the wicked. My phone rang. And I was informed that Bret wanted me—and the rest of the guys in EVICK—to be his band for the next tour.

Originally, Bret was just going to take me. Now, he rounded out his roster with the rest of my guys.

This was still our first year with Bret—and with that came a steep learning curve. Once again Bret, being the true leader he is, made it all snap into focus for us in a single moment.

* * *

To put it into perspective, consider this. EVICK was coming out of the world of bar and club bands. Throughout our history, there has been an allowable amount of improvisation and creativity on the stage. We reacted and adjusted to the crowd, rather than the other way around. If the audience was grooving with a particular song, we stretched it out and let them go nuts. If something happened that needed addressing, we could stop on a dime (sometimes in the middle of a song) and address it right there and then.

We were drunk as shit, and basically made almost no distinction between us and the rest of the patrons.

We brought some of that mindset to The Bret Michaels Band. I thought I knew what "the next level" meant—it meant giving 100% of your energy to the show and to the audience every night. But as I mentioned earlier, it also meant something else. It meant changing our *self-perception* when we were on stage,

It happened during a show in Waynesboro, Virginia. We were having a great time—we definitely had the home field advantage. Waynesboro is only a two-hour drive from Manassas, so much of the crowd was made up of our family, friends, and fans. We played the shit out of every song and brought all of our antics on stage with us. It was party time, and we were the life of it.

After the last song, we walked off stage to grab some water and prepare for the encore. However, Bret stopped short of the dressing room area. He gathered us behind the drum riser and delivered a message.

Before I tell you what he said (and its subsequent impact on us), I will say that Bret delivered this message with a certain amount of force. He wasn't angry per se—he was frustrated and red-lining at "10" because he was just coming off stage.

We huddled around and he said, "If we're going to keep doing this, I need 100% consistency, every night."

In other words, he needed a little more than we had been giving. It wasn't just that night in Virginia. We were all comfortable with a little bit of "slop" every night. We added little musical signatures to songs and played around with some different, ad-libbed components.

We did what a bar band would do. Except we weren't in a bar anymore. We were playing behind the incomparable Bret Michaels.

Bret walked off and I said to my guys, "Okay. This is what

we have to do…"

It was time to grow up. We had been talking the talk for a good long while. I made the conscious decision to completely revamp my self-image. My band did the same—we were at a crossroad. Either walk the walk or get the hell out of the game.

Dear reader, from that night forward, we became a *machine.* We hit every note and gave every ounce of energy every fucking night. It only took Bret telling us that ONE time, and just like magic, we were a professional, A-list type of band.

Now, whenever we took the stage behind Bret, we had our shit together on a whole different level. We no longer carried ourselves as the same drunken idiots as everyone else in a bar. We carried ourselves as the musicians—disciplined and dedicated to our job.

It should have been a straight line to success from here. But my existence as a musician became confusing.

I've said it a number of times already, but I figured we were only going to be in Bret's band for one year. So, we kept playing bar and club gigs as EVICK during the times we weren't on the road with Bret. Hell, we were going to *need* those fans to keep our income flowing once we got let go.

Except we became a Jekyll and Hyde sort of band. When we played with Bret, we were polished, professional, and disciplined. When we would play as EVICK, all hell would break loose. We partied and acted like a bunch of slobbering idiots. It's like we never thought of EVICK as anything *but* a party band—and that was the final answer I needed.

The reason we never made it, when I looked at all the lessons I learned from Bret, was because I didn't walk the walk with EVICK. Our internal identity was that of a bar band. We never actually thought of ourselves as "real" rock stars, so we never thought to carry ourselves as such.

That knowledge made me crazy. I would scream at my guys, "Why do we give Bret what we give him—but we don't give the same thing to *our own* fucking band?!?"

There was never a good answer. Thus, there was never an elevation of EVICK to the next level. At some point, I gave up on it.

I was having fun; so I accepted the fact that "fun" was all I would ever have with EVICK. BMB became the job and EVICK became the vacation.

It was a hard lesson, man…but now that I knew "the secret," I was not about to personally remain in place.

* * *

That rounded out our first year with The Bret Michaels Band. In a gesture that I can only attribute to dumb luck (because I'm me), we were invited back for a second year. This was unprecedented, and exciting for me.

To start that year of touring, we assembled in Nashville—and the talk between Bret and me that I opened this book with (the prologue) took place at the Nashville area hotel.

The rest of the year was torn straight from my rock and roll dreams. We toured a ton—I would wake up in a different city every morning and marvel at how I had finally achieved the life I had always wanted. Every day was filled with music and touring and meet-and-greets and fans…good lord, there were *so many fans.*

We had always thought EVICK toured everywhere—but that just wasn't true. We thought it was true, but we were wrong. Bret Michaels toured *everywhere*. He didn't stick to the east coast and the I-40 or I-10 corridor. Bret toured from Miami to San Diego to Seattle to Boston—and every city and town in between.

I remember sitting with Chuck and saying, "Holy shit dude… we're in SOUTH DAKOTA!"

We also played alongside our heroes. We played with the guys in Foreigner and Warrant and Vince Neil (to name a few). And to top it all off, we weren't just opening for these guys. *They were opening for us!*

Obviously, they were opening for Bret Michaels and not Pete, Ray & Chuck…but still.

To me, it wasn't an ego trip. It was more about being the greatest honor in my life. Guys whose records I had listened to until they were worn out…guys I had purchased concert tickets to watch when they came to town…these guys were now casually chatting with me about gear or songs or whatever.

They became my friends.

And here was the most interesting thing: having them as my friends made me feel like I was finally at ease with who I was. These were my "people." Even the lifelong friends I thought I'd had, I never felt like I was completely in place. In other words, I still felt out of place. Even in my group of beloved outcasts, I always felt like an outcast. I was the one malfunctioning Gameboy that was never fully accepted on the Island of Misfit Toys.

Until now.

Hanging out with guys who had made their living as rock stars gave me that sense. I got where they were coming from, and I was convinced that they understood where I was coming from. They believed things that I believed; they felt things that I felt.

I finally found my island. I *do* belong here.

I don't want to come across as arrogant, or that my friends back home didn't matter. Nothing could be further from the truth. How I felt was more like how E.T. must have felt when the ship came to take him home. He dearly loved Elliott and Gertie…but he felt a sadness; a longing to be among *his* people.

**I realize that E.T. wasn't a person. Just go with it.

**I also realize that I didn't use a *Star Wars* reference. But it was still "outer space themed."

Anyway, it was all great. Truly, seriously great. But my friendship with Bret was about to take an even sharper turn toward the sky. Somewhere in the middle of that second year, Bret's tour manager quit. In a pinch, Bret turned to me—and I came through.

* * *

When I first joined Bret, a man named Big John was his acting tour manager. As I mentioned earlier, he was also the head of security. The two of them had a long history and I was the new guy—so I didn't think much of it.

Nor did I completely understand the main function of a tour manager and head of security…but more on that in a moment.

This story opens with a scheduled gig in Milwaukee, Wisconsin. We were playing an enormous music festival called Summerfest, on the shores of Lake Michigan. The grounds were spectacular—but even more impressive were the attendance figures. Summerfest was named in the 1999 *Guinness Book of World Records* as the "World's Largest Outdoor Music Festival."

Because of the scale of the show, we all felt a little pressure. Well, probably not Bret. I don't think his heart rate ever gets above 65. But among the rest of us, there was an ambient stress in the air. No sense making any mistakes in front of a giant crowd.

At some point before the show, Bret and Big John got into an argument about something. I don't have any idea what it was all about because I was not there when it went down. No big deal. John and Bret had been friends for a number of years. They would squabble here and there as friends often do.

Something about this argument was different. Big John couldn't let it go.

I will mention here that among John's duties with the band (in addition to being the tour manager and security guy) is to film parts of the show. He would basically move around the stage with a hand-held camera and capture different songs or different moments.

We hit the stage and started tearing it up. It was the dead of summer and (to misquote Bob Seger), the sweat poured out our bodies like the music that we played. The crowd was lit, the music was tight…it was one of those shows that transcended our earth-bound souls…

Bret could feel it too. We were about to transition into a song we knew would make the crowd lose their minds, when Bret turned and yelled to John, "HEY! GET THE FUCK OUT HERE AND FILM THIS!"

I know I wrote that in all caps, but I will say this: when Bret yelled, it wasn't out of anger. He was totally pumped up and excited with the energy of the show. However, it didn't seem as though John took it in the spirit from which it was intended.

We hit the opening notes (I can't remember which song it was—sorry) and the crowd *did* lose their minds. I momentarily forgot about Bret yelling toward John. Honestly, it didn't involve me anyway, so I had just sort of moved on.

That is, until a video camera crashed across the stage and slid past my feet.

I saw it go by and thought, *Oh boy…*

I immediately knew what was happening. But I was just the guitar player. I had no intention of getting in the middle of those two—despite their airing of grievances in such a public forum.

Anyway, we finished the show as per usual. The crowd loved it. I loved it. I wasn't involved in the fracas between Bret and John, so I was free to have a good time and play with all the reckless abandon that Bret had taught me to harness.

Back on the bus, things were not so happy. John was so pissed off at whatever was going on, he quit on the spot. He had a car come pick him up and that was the last we saw of him. He left the tour in a huff.

Before I go on, I will add that John came back into the fold a bit later. In Bret's reality television series, *Rock of Love with Bret Michaels*, on VH-1, John was a recurring character.

In the moment however, Bret had to be thinking through a real "how do I fix this fast" kind of moment. He was basically left with his bus driver (named Rat) and me. He wasn't particularly close to anyone else on the tour. My band was with me, but Bret hadn't bonded with them the same way he bonded with me. I was the next closest thing to a trusted friend that he had out on the road at that moment.

In a nutshell, he was left with two choices. Either turn over the responsibilities of tour management and security to his bus driver…or take a chance on his semi-new guitar player.

His was not an enviable position to be in.

In short, he made an executive decision on the spot. Right there in front of God and every lost drunk looking for a bathroom near the backstage area of Summerfest, Bret anointed me his new tour manager.

There wasn't much of a choice. At the very least, somebody had to collect the money and make sure everything was right.

He sat me down and went over everything he needed me to do. Obviously, I had been the tour manager for Some Odd Reason and for EVICK, but managing a bar band is WAY different than managing a rolling *Fortune* 500 company like Bret Michaels.

Quick example: when you are a bar band, you play your gig and then pick up your payment from the manager or the bartender at the end of the night—usually in cash. You then divvy up the meager pittance among the band members, cry softly in your Jäger bomb, and head out to the next town.

With a major production like Bret, the process is altogether different. The promoter pays a deposit months ahead of the gig. Then you collect the balance from said promoter before you even hit the stage for the show. It was a whole new way of doing business from what I was used to.

Most of the rest of the job is detail-oriented but self-explanatory if you've ever traveled. Making sure reservations are confirmed; getting everyone settled in a new city; arranging for bus call, etc. But the business end of tour managing was a whole new world to me.

For example, venues and promoters almost always pay big acts with a check, but merchandise money is *always* in the form of cash. Many people pay with debit and with credit cards, but nobody pays with a check these days. If it isn't a card transaction, it will be green cash.

Incidentally, green cash creates a lot of temptation for skimming. I have heard many horror stories over the years of artists losing money because of employees pocketing thousands of dollars in merch money. Bret has his cousin Bobby overseeing the merch table—it's hard to find people you trust when that much green cash is involved.

And therein lies the rub. This was an opportunity to really make a contribution and fast-track up the list of people Bret trusted. But there was also a chance that things could go sideways real fast. Honesty is everything to me, but everyone in the industry knows that a lot of unscrupulous people have wound up as tour managers. As I said, money corrupts.

A lot was at stake, and I had never done anything like this—particularly at this level. I didn't think I would be able to do it all without some help. So I turned to the only guy I knew who was also doing double duty—playing in the band AND acting as tour manager: Dana Strum.

Remember I mentioned briefly that we would sometimes play on a bill with Vince Neil? When Vince plays shows as a solo artist, he uses half of Slaughter as his backing band; Jeff Blando on guitar, and Dana on bass. As a consequence, Dana also fills the role of tour manager for Vince.

I had bumped into Dana backstage a time or two, but we had never formally been introduced. I mention that because I don't know how it was that I got his number.

Anyway, in a fit of panic, I dialed.

I was super nervous while the phone rang on his end. I didn't know what to expect…but I was in dire straits.

Dana picked up, and he was the absolute nicest guy in the world. I am dead serious when I tell you that he had no earthly idea who I was at the time. Yes, I had Bret's clout behind me, but I was Pete Evick, not Bret Michaels.

Dana mentored me. He walked me through every step of what to do and how to do it. Everything from the money (the original reason I called), to his tricks of the trade. In all, he spent *hours* on the phone with me. Then year after year, if I had a question, I would call Dana. And he would always put aside whatever he was doing to help me out.

I don't know how I would have done it without him.

To this day, he takes my call. He'll ask about me and my family; he likes to hear about my candle company; we'll talk about things related to music and things not related to music. He is a prime example of how I wish everyone would be—not just industry people.

I will also add that Dana has become more of a friend than a mentor over the years. I talk to a lot of guys in the business for one reason or the other. Mostly, these reasons involve something specific and pragmatic. It's the nature of the beast—we're all busy so respect each other's time when it comes to communications.

With Dana however, he is a guy I can call and just say, "Hey man, how's it going?" We'll talk for a while and then move on. He's relaxed and open to being a friend.

* * *

With Dana's guidance, I became more comfortable with my dual roles as guitar player and tour manager. Over time, I grew deeper and deeper into the inner workings of Michaels Entertainment, LLC. I also climbed the ranks of his organizational structure. For years I was a full-time employee, intimately involved with advancing his shows, promoting his shows, and marketing his shows. It was a tremendous amount of responsibility, but I handled it to the best of my ability. These days, our sound man, Bob Poole, does a lot of the tour managing duties and my focus is on being the Music Director and doing marketing.

I was a bit overwhelmed after that fateful night at Summerfest but loved every minute of it. The second year with Bret sailed by—I was so damn busy; I didn't have a lot of time to slow down and smell any roses. Before I knew it, the tour was over and we had to make plans for the future.

One of those plans culminated with me being on television. And then I got to my darkest place ever…just before I found the light.

CHAPTER 8:
ROCK OF LOVE

2007 started with an unexpected twist. I was on tour with Bret (as usual), and the bus was chugging along through the hills and dales of Montana, one of the most beautiful places on Earth. I was up early, watching the sun rise through the mountains. Bret was up too —he and I were the same that way. Most mornings, we were the only ones up to watch the rest of the world awaken.

A bottle of Mountain Dew in my hand, I sat at a window in the front of the bus. My grin extended from ear to ear as I reflected on how perfect the moment was. I had reached my lifelong goals.

Plus, I'm in Montana. How many people get to do *that*???

I took a sip and sunk deeper into the leather couch. But just then, my brow furrowed…I could hear muttering. Bret was in the back of the bus, talking quietly on the phone.

I was the full-fledged tour manager, but I was still getting my legs under me when it came to the rhythm of everyone and everything. Bret was no exception to this rule—I was still getting used to his quirks and routines.

One thing I had learned was that Bret did a lot of business over the phone from his perch in the back of the bus. No problem. But today, he was being…weird. Not "weird" like I thought he was plotting my murder, but weird insofar as he was making an effort to keep his voice low in the back of the bus. And he wasn't saying much about the calls when he would return to the front.

In a word, he was being more secretive than normal. Not that any of his business was anyone else's business, just on this particular morning things felt different.

I've never been much for middle school drama, but I have to say—I was getting a little paranoid about the whole deal. *Was* he plotting my murder? Or even worse, fire me and leave me in

Montana?

I eyed him suspiciously as he emerged from the rear lounge. He took a seat across from me and paused, collecting his thoughts. Despite the gorgeous scenery passing outside the window, he looked directly at me.

“Have you ever heard of a show called *Flavor of Love*?

I had. Despite being a super cool rock star and MTV famous, I was still aware enough to be plugged into all the trappings of pop culture. I told him what I knew.

“Yeah…It’s not particularly my thing, but it’s a huge hit.”

He asked me to describe the show, in my own words.

Okay. This doesn’t sound like the opening salvo to a “murder for hire” scheme. I’ll play along. I said it was a dating show and that it was well done. I added that it made Flavor Flav (of the rap group, Public Enemy) look a little silly, but it was all good fun. The show was a smash hit and most everyone seemed to know about it.

Bret took it all in and remained reserved. He didn’t mention why he wanted to know. Instead, he thanked me and returned to the back of the bus.

Totally weird. But I was still alive and that was good.

Of course, later I found out that he had been pitched the idea for *Rock of Love with Bret Michaels*. Furthermore, I also found out that Bret already knew everything I told him in the front of the bus that morning. In typical Bret fashion, he was being methodical and cautious as he researched this new idea, and had already made his decision before even talking to me.

In a later chapter, I’ll mention more lessons that Bret has taught me along the way. But his over-arching philosophy—about being well-informed and deliberate when making important decisions—was taught to my impulsive ass over and over again.

Regarding this decision specifically, Bret had been negotiating the concept over the course of several months. He wanted his version of the show (if there was going to be “his version of the show”) to be laid out a little differently than Flavor Flav’s show.

For example, Bret wanted the girls to be the stars of the show, rather than himself. He wanted to be the host…and the grand prize, so to speak. Similar to Flav's version, the girls would all compete to win his affection. Each week would feature a different competition, with a couple girls being eliminated at the end of the episode. Bret was insistent that the challenge be more exciting and interesting than any other dating show. When there was only one girl left, Bret would be the spoils awarded to the victor.

And I will say this about the man: Bret has never been a guy who says, "Yeah yeah yeah…let's just grab the money and run!" Rather, he does things the right way. Bret is one of the most sincere and genuine people you'll ever meet—both on and off the stage. And that comes through in everything he does.

Believe me when I say, Bret Michaels is not famous by accident. Nor is he one of the most beloved superhero rock stars of all time by accident.

Anyway, Bret was okay doing a little bit of self-effacing humor, but the tone had to be carefully constructed so as to not make him look like an idiot. As trite as that sounds, it is an extremely important detail. Reality show producers have tremendous power when they cut a show together. They search for storylines and plot arcs—sometimes making them up out of whole cloth in order to ensure that the characters and each episode are compelling.

To me, the entire process is amazing. The editors take hundreds or *thousands* of hours of video and then condense them into a single 42-minute episode. In order to do this, they are very selective about which moments they use. And if the moments they choose frame you as a hero or as a villain, then that shall be your "framing" for the rest of the season and the rest of your celebrity career.

Bret wanted to be very clear about his expectations on the front end and made sure (contractually) to have a say in the editing process. The more you get in writing, the better off you are.

Interestingly, one point he negotiated affected me directly. He got the producers to agree to let him write the music for the show. So, when everyone signed on the dotted line, Bret and I set off to write some songs.

* * *

Concurrent to all of this happening, Bret had purchased and moved into a sprawling ranch in Arizona. I grew up in a shitty part of Manassas, Virginia—so I have always been appreciative of the splendor that is the nice homes and nice cars and nice yards of wealthy people. And I must say, I have been in a few insanely fabulous places in my life.

In a word, Bret's place was awesome.

Not only did he have a beautiful house and nice cars and a nice yard, but he built a recording studio to use when he was home. For now, it was about to serve as the first place I wrote and recorded music with Bret.

It didn't take long for us to come up with a theme song for *Rock of Love*. The two of us have a chemistry when it comes to writing. We're each stubbornly creative—but so eye-to-eye in our collective vision that beautiful music merges from the synergy. The first song we ever wrote together became "Go That Far," which was the theme song for the entire three seasons of the show.

I was giddy, man. Yes, I had engineered songs with Steve Whiteman and with the guys from Raven—but now, I was legitimately writing and recording with one of my childhood heroes. And the tunes we came up with were (in my humble opinion) undeniably hit songs. The proof was in the pudding. "Go That Far" was on the front end of a weekly show watched by millions of people.

While the entire process was cool beyond belief, one moment in particular stands out to me. A few days into the process, Bret said, "Man…you're really good at producing and engineering."

I knew I was pretty good at it. And honestly, I really enjoyed doing it. But to hear somebody with the stature of Bret Michaels reinforce my talents in this area was awe-inspiring to me. Not to mention, Bret isn't the kind of guy who blows sunshine up anyone's ass. When he speaks, he means what he says and says what he means.

In any case, his words solidified my identity as a true "professional" when it came to working in the studio.

I mixed and mastered the song and presented it to Bret—who

loved it. He sent it along to VH-1, and they approved it to be the theme to the show.

Let me tell you people, there is nothing more thrilling to a songwriter than to hear your tune coming out of the television. And there it was. My guitar licks (well…mine AND Bret's) flowed from the small speakers like *Musica Universalis* (or, "Music of the Universe") first proposed by the Greek philosopher, Pythagoras.

It was beautiful. My confidence soared.

I had waited a lifetime to be MTV famous—and to hear my music flow from speakers. And at long last, here it was. It was VH-1 and not MTV, but what the Hell. I had co-written and produced the theme song for a hit TV show. Later (in 2009), I received an ASCAP Award for my contribution to reality television. Once again, I remember thinking, *Well, here we are. If it all ends tomorrow, I've had a super successful run.*

Bret, God bless him, took a very level-headed approach to the whole process. He helped me keep my ego in check.

He pulled me aside and said, "I know you produce records and do a lot for a lot of different people. I also know you're probably thinking this song will open doors for you to produce more and more records for other artists going forward."

I nodded. He continued.

"Don't think that doing this song with me will make you the next Mutt Lang."

Bret wasn't being mean—he was being honest. And he was sending me a strong message I needed to hear. The music industry is devastatingly competitive. Of course, I knew this at some level already, but nobody knew that better than Bret Michaels. He had been to the top of the mountain. He knew what it took to play the game and to keep winning.

In short, he didn't want my high expectations to end up breaking my own heart.

* * *

I accompanied Bret (in early 2007) when he "checked in" to

the *Rock of Love* mansion. This was the actual house that was about to be on television. Up until this point in my life, I had never been on the set for a television program before. In my brain, it was sort of like walking up to the *Brady Bunch* house…which was very cool.

Obviously, I had watched reality television programs before. However, the grand scale of the production caught me by surprise. The cameras were installed in virtually every nook and cranny of the house—and they ran 24/7. This means that each week, EVERY camera produced *168 hours of footage*. If there were, say, thirty cameras in and around the house (which would have been a conservative estimate), the producers and editors would have to wade through over 5,000 hours of video in order to find 42 minutes of coherent and cohesive content.

Holy fuck.

Plus, I felt a little bit of fear. Not from the magnitude of the production, but more because I didn't know what to expect for Bret. I'm pretty sure he felt it too. The show was planned as well as it could have been before filming—but you could not predict what would happen once 25 women with 25 separate personalities were thrown into the mix.

This could end really well…or really poorly. The last thing in the world we wanted was for this whole concept to backfire—and for Bret to end up looking foolish.

Dude…it was so surreal when I left the house that night. I had to say goodbye to my friend.

I remember thinking, *I'm not going to see this guy for two and a half months. What's going to happen to him?*

In a strange way, it felt as if my friend was being walked into prison. Like I was saying goodbye to him at the front gate of Riker's Island or San Quentin. He was going to have to deal with whatever dangers awaited behind the barbed wire and stone walls…

Metaphorically speaking, of course.

Godspeed, my friend…Godspeed.

He disappeared into the bowels of the mansion. And I went home to wait.

* * *

When my phone rang in Manassas, I answered it like any other day. Probably our booking agent. He would be excited about getting us into some dive bar or small club…maybe play in some rich guy's backyard for their kid's bar mitzvah. It wasn't easy to go back and forth between Bret Michaels and EVICK. I wasn't an egotistical asshole by any means—but it was sure easy to get used to the rock star lifestyle, afforded by a bona fide rock star.

But it wasn't our agent. It was one of the producers of *Rock of Love*. When I heard her voice, I grew nervous. What was she about to tell me? Did something happen? Was Bret dead? Did he get crushed under an avalanche of hot girls, perishing in a manner torn from every teenage boy's fantasies?

Turned out, Bret wasn't dead. Quite the opposite. They were extremely happy with how the show was progressing and pitched me an idea for one of the episodes.

Bret's solo band would play a show in Las Vegas. Afterwards, Bret would do his normal meet and greet then return to his hotel room…while the guys from EVICK (who were still his band at the time) stayed back and partied with the contestants until he was ready to see them.

At first, I was over the moon. My band and I were going to be featured in a reality television episode. But then I realized why they were arranging the episode in this odd manner: they had gotten wind of our ability to drink and party like no other band in history. So, they hoped that if hot women were mixed with a band that can consume its body weight in alcohol, entertaining hijinks will result.

They were correct.

The episode ("Vegas, Baby!") is infamous to this day. And I will add this: everything you see in the episode is absolutely real. The girls tried their best to keep up with us…but dude, we were the thing legends were made of. Nicolas Cage, in *Leaving Las Vegas*, would have been like, "Holy shit, guys…slow down. What the fuck is *wrong* with you???"

I will also say that the cultural zeitgeist in 2023 would never allow for an episode like this to be pitched, much less filmed and aired. But in 2007, it got green-lit. We partied with a bunch of hot television show women like the End of Days was coming tomorrow.

The girls were so drunk, they were a literal mess. They couldn't walk; they couldn't *speak*. By the time they made it back to Bret's room, it was amazing they were even conscious. One had to crawl because she couldn't stand without falling. Another one collapsed in his bathroom, puking her guts out for the next several hours. One stumbled over the food table and knocked buffet items all over the floor.

One of the girls made a statement that still gets quoted among my friends to this day. When asked about us, she said, "Bret's band…those guys can *drink*."

I don't know if that makes me proud or embarrassed…but I was on television!

I feel the need to add that nobody got hurt. Nowadays, the villagers would probably grab torches and pitchforks and come to burn down our castle for participating in something so exploitative. But back then, it was all good fun. And that was the thing…*everyone* had fun. That episode was one of the most popular in the show's entire three-season run.

Being on television was something I had never dreamed of nor desired. I had never once awakened thinking, *I want to be on TV!*

Obviously, I wanted to be MTV famous. But to me, MTV was *not* TV—it somehow transcended television.

And yet, once I called everyone I knew and had them all watch me on VH-1…it was fantastic. I was the luckiest guy in the world.

Let me say that differently: I *am* the luckiest guy in the world. Whenever anyone asks me about what it was like to do this or that, I always say, "I now have the answer to every question I ever asked."

And it just kept getting better.

* * *

In June 2007, Poison kicked off a 50-date tour behind their *Poison'd* album. Ratt was on the bill with them, as was Dokken. Bret had finished filming the first season of *Rock of Love*, and the mountain of video footage was in the capable hands of the editors and producers. The show was scheduled to run on VH-1 beginning in July. A hushed anticipation hung over the entire Poison crew as they waited to see how it would affect the image of their lead singer —and possibly the fate of the band.

I was with Bret throughout the entirety of the tour that summer. Bret wanted me along so we could write songs together. He and I were close friends by that point, and I think he actually enjoyed my company.

On July 15, we were parked at the Verizon Wireless Amphitheater in Bonner Springs, Kansas—just outside of Kansas City. *Rock of Love* was set to premier that night. The setting in the back lot was surreal—at 7pm, *nothing* was moving. Poison had over forty band and crew members along for that tour, end every single man was plopped down in one bus or another, eyes glued to their television sets.

The Moment of Truth. We watched, with bated breath.

When the show ended, Bret and I looked at each other. I told him what I thought.

"Bret…that was great."

Considering that he's a major rock star in every sense of the word, Bret is a seriously humble guy. He tends to remain uncertain until he receives feedback from the people around him. Bret understands that the fans will ultimately decide whether something (like a song or a television program) works or doesn't work. In other words, his opinion is not nearly as important as the opinion of the people he's trying to entertain. But… at the same time he doesn't ever FAKE IT. He is always 100% Bret Michaels.

I kept going, and tried to provide more specific feedback.

"The show is going to be a hit. It was amazing. It was funny and charming…it was great."

Not two seconds later, there was a knock at the bus door. I got up to see who it was. The door opened, and there stood C.C. DeVille.

I backed up to give him enough space to come up the steps and onto the bus. As he passed me, I held my breath. This was either going to go really well or really poorly. He and Bret have gone through a series of ups and downs during the long run of their relationship in Poison. It was no secret the two of them maintained a love-hate sort of brotherhood.

I could tell Bret was metaphorically holding his breath too. But I'll be darned, CC came through like a champ. He stood over Bret and gushed.

"Hey—that show is going to be the most amazing thing in the world!"

CC's opinion had more weight than anyone else's at this point because he had recent experience with reality television. He was fresh off Season 6 of *The Surreal Life*, which aired in 2006—and then the one-season spin-off, *The Surreal Life: Fame Games*, which had just finished its on-air run in March 2007.

Not only did CC have an informed point of view, but his words came across as 100% genuine. And that was extremely cool to see. For as tumultuous as their relationship had been, I could tell that CC had just hit a home run.

I've got to say, I felt honored to be there for that moment. The camaraderie between the two rock warriors was touching to experience.

And then Bret's phone started ringing. One by one, he fielded calls from friends and family. They were equally as positive. Poison gave a killer performance that night—but I don't remember much about it. Getting the series premier under his belt was monumental.

* * *

CC was correct. The show was an incredible hit. And for all the worry that doing a reality television show might tarnish the image of Bret or the band, the *exact opposite* happened. Within two weeks, there was a noticeable shift in the fans attending the concerts.

Historically, Poison has never had much of a problem selling tickets. They put on an amazing, high-octane show. Even today (this book is being written in 2022), as the four guys in the band hover around 60 years old, they are insanely energetic and entertaining on stage.

The shows in 2007 were generally packed. But following the premier of *Rock of Love*, the shows were *extremely* packed. Not only that, but the fan base was significantly younger than when the tour launched in June. This was a full twenty years after Poison's rise to fame, and their typical fan base reflected that era. Now because of Bret's constant ability to reinvent himself, Poison and the solo band experienced a multi-generational audience. There is no age expectancy. It's a party for everyone, all the time.

I probably shouldn't tell this story, but it's funny to me. And frankly, it's been 15 years—so everyone just relax.

Dokken opened for Poison during that tour. On August 4th and 6th, they shared a bill in Des Moines at the Iowa Speedway. As per usual, the grandstands were filled with screaming kids who loved Poison's music—but had probably never heard of Dokken.

That did not go unnoticed…and was certainly not appreciated.

I remember Don Dokken getting mad about it. He was playing to a full house—but not a full house of Dokken fans.

"I didn't come here to play in front of all these kids," he groused.

Earlier, Don had approached Bret and expressed how proud he was of the show and Bret's success. But once it became clear that the fans were there to see Poison (or more specifically, to see BRET) and not Dokken, his mood darkened a bit. Don's audience might have gotten shut out of ticket sales because there was a run on the box office by young kids seeking an audience with the new pop culture icon, Bret Michaels.

And behind the scenes, it was just as crazy. Bret's tour bus couldn't go anywhere without crowds of people surrounding it. Any car that Bret got in was followed by fans wanting a photo or an autograph. I imagined this was similar to the mass hysteria the Beatles felt.

Once the Poison tour wrapped over Labor Day weekend in Atlanta, Georgia, Bret resumed his solo tour. And it was just as hyperbolic as the Poison crowds. Suddenly, we sold out large venues and sheds (amphitheaters) ourselves—Bret didn't need Poison anymore. He could sustain a headlining tour in 15,000-seat (and larger!) venues all by himself.

He had fully come into his own. He became a household

name.

For me, this was utterly fantastic. I felt MTV famous whenever I stepped out onto Bret's stage. I started having fans follow me and know who I was. In fact, even today there are several people out there with tattoos of my likeness somewhere on their body.

Is it weird that I take a certain amount of pride in that?

Not to mention, the video for "Go That Far" remained in the #1 spot on the *VH-1 Top 20 Video Countdown* for TWELVE weeks in 2007.

I grew up watching these video countdown shows on MTV. I was a huge fan of *Headbangers Ball.* I wanted to be MTV famous—and now I was. The video for "Go That Far" opens with a "frozen" shot of the band—and I am the focal point. I am in an "action" pose holding my guitar upright; my mouth gaping wide open and my tongue wagging out. Then Bret walks into frame, and the scene comes to life.

But that's the point—this was Bret's video of course…but I was there. I was in a video that hit number one for twelve weeks on VH-1. MTV had long since given up on playing music videos by 2007. This was as "MTV famous" as anyone would ever get again.

And I had made it.

It's hard to put into words how awesome that was for me. It didn't punch my ego into high gear. It was tough to keep it all in check at times, but I did it. I always know that it's Bret's fame I'm riding. But dude…there I was! And I had a hand in writing the song that was number one for twelve Sundays in 2007. It was like Christmas morning every week for three months.

PS – the video for "Go That Far" was shot on the same soundstage as many of the scenes filmed for *The Goonies* in 1985. For uber nerd Pete Evick, that was incredibly cool.

One last thing about that song: it was picked up by Activision, and included on the soundtrack to the video game, *Guitar Hero III: Legends of Rock*. If you recall, the Guitar Hero series was enormously popular, generating (literally) billions of dollars in revenue. Anyway, the third installment of the game became the best-selling video game of 2007 and was the first video game to ever earn over a billion dollars *single-handedly*. My good friend Aaron

Habibipour was a huge part of making this happen. He worked on the game and to this day is a huge part of the gaming industry.

73 songs were available for the game. "Go That Far" was one of the 25 bonus songs you could unlock to augment the initial 39 single-player songs that came with the game. Then, there were three "boss battle" songs, and six "co-op career exclusive" songs. Presumably, once the player mastered the initial 39 songs, they would seek out more difficult songs to keep challenging them.

Bret was especially tickled by the game because the developers brought him in to do some motion-capture filming. From that footage, they computer-generated an animated "Bret" that moved along and sang with the track while the user played along.

Once again, this wasn't a burned-out rocker from twenty years ago. Bret Michaels was on the cutting edge of pop culture in 2007. And I was along for the ride. It was an amazing run.

Being on a top television program…writing a hit song…having a video that went to number one…flying on a private plane…playing in front of sold-out arenas…having a song picked up for a multi-billion-dollar video game series…it was all happening.

I hadn't just achieved my goals and lived my dreams.

I had *exceeded* them.

* * *

Season Two of *Rock of Love* began with the same format as Season One. This year, there would be 14 episodes instead of 10, and there would be 20 girls instead of 25. But they all lived in a big house together and competed each week with eliminations along the way. "Go That Far" returned as the theme song. "Dating Bret" would be the grand prize.

Season One had been such a runaway hit, everyone was totally pumped and eager to begin Season Two. I was particularly pumped because I was invited back to be featured in another episode.

In short, the episode's competition centered around each woman writing a song for Bret. More specifically, they had to write lyrics for a musical track that Bret and I had written and produced (for the show) earlier. My job was to record each girl singing her song, and then basically produce them into demos. Bret and I would listen to each song later and judge them on the quality of their lyrics.

I had a blast. It was a hell of a lot of work in a very short time frame. Also, I am happy to report that nobody threw up into a napkin during the filming of this episode.

And yes, that really did happen during the infamous Las Vegas episode of Season One.

Anyway, the remainder of Season Two went off without a hitch. Bret continued to take the world by storm, and I toured with him in big venues around the country.

When filming began for Season Three of *Rock of Love*, things started to happen that I did not expect, nor could I stop or control. My mental health began slipping into a dark chasm. Life was about to change...until my darkest hour led to a shining sunrise.

* * *

Bret decided to change things up a bit regarding the format for Season Three. They also changed the title slightly, calling this season *Rock of Love Bus*.

Rather than have everyone live together in a giant house, they opted instead for the girls to join Bret on the road. They would then film all the video footage from tour buses, backstage areas, and various other road stops.

To do this, they had to have cameras on everyone, all the time. Cameras were fucking *everywhere*. They were almost literally in our faces 24/7. There were still cameras installed on the bus, cameras shoved in our faces, and cameras floating around each venue.

The tour itself was booked for a nine-month run. If I remember correctly, we were filmed for a solid three of those nine months. Doesn't sound like much, I know. But believe me—it became a *chore*.

Bret was used to all the attention. The girls lapped it up. But for the band and the crew, it got to be very difficult to manage. We weren't the focus of the show—we weren't even characters, really. We were just background noise; ancillary bodies floating in and out of frame. So the fact that we *still* had to be aware of what we said and did every second of every day was a burden.

I will speak for myself here. For me, I started to grow paranoid. Think about it this way: if you were on film 24 hours per day, what kind of dirt would the owner of that tape have on you? How many times have you made an off-color joke? Or picked your nose?

You get the point. I knew the producers wanted to create drama so they could make each episode interesting to watch. I am already anxious enough as a human being—but then I started to worry constantly about doing or saying something that would get twisted on the air and then rub Bret the wrong way.

Then I would get fired over something that was probably a big misunderstanding in the first place. The producers would love that, wouldn't they? More good footage for their show. They would love for me to slip up and give them good content.

In fact, the words of C.C. DeVille echoed in the back of my mind. He told me, "Those cameras…you gotta watch yourself, man. They'll catch ya—and turn you into the bad guy in a *second.*"

I found myself looking over my shoulder constantly. I grew to hate the cameras…resented the guys carrying the cameras. I stopped talking; hell, I stopped *breathing*. I would be damned before I gave anyone a reason to get pissed at me.

All of this was WAY overblown in my head, of course. Yes, the producers would probably sell me out in order to generate more viewers…but that was certainly not their intent. And frankly, I was well down their list of "people they give a shit about." They were primarily there to film the girls and Bret. The guitar player was an afterthought.

Still, I descended the staircase and into the cellar of my brain. And it was fucking dark down there. It was exhausting. Rationally, I understood all the positive aspects of being on a TV show. But that wasn't enough to outweigh the deepening agitation and depression I was experiencing.

I retreated fully into myself. I (seriously) became a recluse. In fact, I was the closest thing to a hermit that you will ever find on a rock and roll tour. The residue of that tour still affects me today. I used to be extremely gregarious and outgoing. Today, I remain a bit more reserved than I used to be. Something in my brain got permanently broken by that tour and those cameras.

But again, it's a huge reason why any of you are even reading this book…so I'm still strangely grateful.

There was safety in solitude. So that is what I chose; I isolated myself from the rest of the world. Internally, I sank into the darkness. Externally, I was a lot less likeable than ever.

In the end, that season of *Rock of Love Bus* had a profound impact on my marriage. For whatever reason, I became impossible to be around. I was surly, I was withdrawn…I was a terrible friend and partner. I had basically become someone else.

My wife persevered for as long as she could, but in the end, she had to go.

I can't say I blame her. I would have left me too if I could have. But the aftermath of her departure with the kids pushed my head even further under the water. I'll devote an entire chapter (later in this book) to the loneliest moments I have ever experienced while on the road. But nothing prepared me for how soul-crushingly lonely life became in my own house.

CHAPTER 9:
SHINING SOL

I remember coming home from a gig on the first night after my family moved out of my house. I sat in my living room, but this wasn't my living room anymore. The lights were on—except they couldn't fend off the darkness. It was so fucking *quiet*. It was the kind of quiet that makes you want to tear off your own skin to try to shed the loneliness.

The light was gone.

My children were gone.

That night was easily the worst night of my entire life. I mean, by FAR.

I wasn't suicidal per se; I just didn't want to exist. Even when the sun was shining, it felt utterly and completely dark.

For the time being, I wanted to sleep. Go to sleep and wake up in a different life.

But it was not meant to be. My mind crawled through the wreckage of my current situation. I tried to drink myself to sleep, but to no avail. Fucking tolerance. I thought about grabbing my guitar—except I had no desire to ever play my guitar again.

That was interesting. Playing the guitar was all I had ever wanted to do since I was five years old. Guitar, guitar, guitar. And sometimes *Star Wars*. This marked the first time in my life that I *didn't* want to play the guitar.

Probably not a good sign.

I thought about how I had achieved everything I ever wanted to achieve. But for what? I made a deal with the Devil, and now here I was…all the fuck alone.

As a last resort, I grabbed a candle from one of the cupboards. It was a gift that we shoved into a box a while ago, but I didn't care. I just wanted to do something active to take my mind off whatever fucked up script it was running.

The candle was supposed to smell like a wood-burning fireplace.

Cool. I like that smell.

Except it didn't smell like anything. I wouldn't have cared if it smelled like ass—at least my brain would have had something to do. I lit the candle, and it smelled like absolutely nothing.

I didn't get pissed off about it. I watched the flame dance on the tiny wick and had a strange thought: *I wonder if I could make a candle?* Seemed reasonable. If this giant candle company couldn't make a decent candle, maybe I could.

The next day—I swear to God this is true—I went to Michaels craft store. I hadn't showered for three or four days; I hadn't brushed my teeth or come near my hair with a comb. I surely looked (and reeked) like a hobo that had been riding the rails for the past several years.

As I wandered up and down the aisles, mothers would pull their children close. The clerks probably pushed the silent alarm button under the counter. When the cops showed up, they would likely be disgusted by the sight of me too.

If the apocalypse was a person, it would have looked like me.

I found an employee and asked if they sold candle making kits. Her frightened eyes never left my face. I can imagine what it felt like to be confronted with death incarnate. Without moving her torso, she held out a trembling arm and pointed to a corner of the store.

Anyway, I bought all the ingredients and took them home. The planets lined up that day. I had some space available in my brain, now that guitar playing and music were no longer there. In their absence, my internal hard drive was filled with candle making. I became obsessed.

Maybe my anxiety requires that I am constantly obsessed with *something*. Be it music or playing guitar or *Star Wars*, I am always hyper-focused on one of those and nothing else. And that's the point. I cannot stress enough how (without music) there was *nothing* else in my life.

I had no hobbies. I had no interests. Hell, I don't even follow (nor know anything about) sports—I had no outlets. On that day however, I became obsessed with candles—which may have saved my life.

Over the next three months, I didn't touch my guitar. I was on the longest musical hiatus of my career because Bret was involved with a different television show. He turned down a fourth season of *Rock of Love* and focused instead on a new show called *Bret Michaels: Life as I Know It*. That show wasn't a competition/elimination program. It was more of a true "behind the scenes" reality show that focused on his family life and personal life. Think *The Osbournes* (featuring Ozzy Osbourne) or *Gene Simmons Family Jewels*.

As for me, I poured all my money and energy into learning how to make candles. It was just like how I felt about music when I was a kid. Back when I would run home from school every day and shut my door and play guitar for hours and hours. It was like that—except with making candles.

I would still keep up with daily errands and chores. I would still take my kids to and from school and help them with their homework. But when all was said and done, the rest of the world faded into the background. I would obsess like a mad scientist over the art and science of candle making.

Helping me along this journey was the internet. I bought dozens of e-books and devoured countless videos about the candle production process and the industry itself. I learned that there was a hole in the industry—and an important one needing to be filled.

This was the dawn of the soy revolution regarding candles. Up until the 2000s, paraffin wax was the main ingredient that made up almost every candle on the market. However, Paraffin wax is made from petroleum, coal, or oil shale. In other words, breathing the smoke coming from a paraffin wax candle is somewhat akin to breathing the discharge from your car's exhaust system.

Don't hammer me for the analogy—I know they are not 1:1. But in my defense, the National Institute for Occupational Safety and Health has set a Recommended Exposure Limit for paraffin wax fumes over an 8-hour workday because of the potential harmful effects.

In any case, making candles out of soy is far less problematic regarding health. Soy wax is all natural and won't harm you or your pets. I'm not an "eco-warrior," but being eco-friendly has always been important to me.

Plus, soy wax is made from soybean plants, which are grown in the great Midwestern states of the U.S. I've traveled through (and played music in) those states many, many times. I have formed deep friendships with tons of people who are truly the salt of the earth.

Using soy wax became important to me. It helps the environment and also helps farmers and economies in a part of the world that I care about. I am a lot like John Mellencamp in that sense. Not even kidding. I have admired and emulated him in a lot of ways.

In short, making candles out of soy felt like I was doing something meaningful, something positive. Music felt negative…felt dark. I was starting to question whether the music industry had *ever* been good for me—or wondering if making music was even meaningful at all—the candle idea felt like the right thing to do.

I climbed into the life raft and was able to breathe. I started to think about my two boys. I knew they might very well follow my path (of not going to college) for their chosen careers. They didn't seem destined for a "normal" route—college, career, two and a half kids plus a white picket fence. They were free spirits, man.

I will add this: the one thing I am most proud of in my life is how I stepped up as a father in the aftermath of my divorce. I don't know if I could have done this if I had stayed married to their mother. Once she was gone, I *had* to get my shit together and step up.

I was never a bad dad…don't get that idea in your mind. But my wife had always taken care of the day-to-day stuff. There was always a parent in the house with them. There was no need for me to be there as much. Once she left, there was no other adult in the house *except* me. I had to step up and take care of all their day-to-day needs when they were in my custody.

Custody was never contested between the two of us. We shared as 50/50 as we could (given my schedule), and neither of us protested if the other wanted or needed the kids for whatever was going on at the time. So, when I was home from the road, the boys were with me—and I took care of their daily needs like a mother and father put together. I learned to cook. I learned to do laundry. I learned to do seventh grade math (that's a lie—I still suck). The normalcy of everyday life was strangely as rewarding to me as anything I had ever done with music.

I think it's also important that I say this: just before the divorce, I had been seriously considering leaving Bret's band. Being on the road and feeling disconnected from my children was eating me alive. I loved to play and travel and hang with the guys—but I could never shake the gnawing awareness that I was leaving something behind.

I was prepared to leave the music industry behind. What I wasn't willing to lose was the friendship I had made with Bret.

My plan (at the time) was to find a replacement for myself in Bret's band. Then I would come home and teach guitar or work at a music store or drive for Uber so I could cobble together a decent living and be there for my kids.

I don't know if Uber was even around back then.

But my kids, man…they are the life of me.

And that brings us back to candles. I decided that I could start a small, online business. Through it, I could teach my kids about entrepreneurialism and how to run a business. Marketing, accounting, inventory production and management, fulfillment, distribution, scaling…everything they'd need to know to start, run, and grow a small business of their own.

Real world education, right?

But I needed a name. To wit, I needed the *right* name. So, I agonized over that decision for five or six weeks; turning words and concepts in my mind like an endless Tetris game.

The answer came from some kind of divine intervention.

I'll never forget. I was out with Bret. We were in a hotel, getting ready to play a gig in North Dakota. I was pacing around my hotel room, and it suddenly came into frame. And I mean it just like I wrote it—it was like a voice came out of thin air and said, "Shining Sol."

It was perfect. I was extremely excited—not only does "sol" mean "sun" in Spanish, but it also connects me to my history—my early days in the music industry (Sol 3 Records).

Not that I told anyone in the music industry about my new passion.

I do remember the first music person I ever told. It was my buddy (and Bret's former bass player), Bart Harris. When I mentioned my new candle company, he whirled around and looked at me like I had just said I was going to start an underwater welding company…or that I was thinking about working on a bomb squad or becoming a cattle rancher.

In any case, it confirmed all the reasons I had kept this new idea under my hat.

By the way, the international candle industry is a multi-*billion*-dollar industry. It is dominated by two giants: Yankee Candles, and candles produced by Bath and Body Works. Not that they have the market cornered—there are hundreds (thousands?) of smaller, boutique-style candle companies that do just fine with regard to finding a customer base and making money.

But here was the deal: there is no real marketing or branding in the candle industry. When was the last time you saw a commercial for Yankee Candles? Who is the spokesperson for Bath and Body Works candles?

For that matter, when have you EVER seen an ad for candles *anywhere*?

Right?

Regarding branding, you all know the bowtie logo for Chevy…you know the font on Coca-Cola cans and bottles…you all recognize Flo as the main character on the Progressive Insurance commercials and Tony the Tiger on boxes of Frosted Flakes.

Do Yankee Candles even *have* a logo? Do they have a face?

*Well, they do…but nothing that gives them brand recognition. It's just their unique font.

I went to an artist friend of mine, Keith Sarna. You may remember Keith from an earlier chapter because he was the drummer in Some Odd Reason. Since that group broke up, Keith had gone to work as an AWESOME graphic artist and designer.

Anyway, I asked him to design the logo. It needed to say something about candles but could also be unique. The logo started with clip art because I wanted something everyone would feel like they had already seen—and then had him alter it enough that it was original and all ours.

He nailed it. It's simple…and it's fabulous. I will say with a certain level of pride that my logo is the only candle company logo in the known universe to be tattooed on people's bodies.

It felt like success.

Next order of business: find a face for the company. It didn't seem likely that anyone would want to buy a wholesome candle from a dirty rock and roller such as myself. The right person had to be more welcoming…and more in line with the target demographic: women.

I called Brad Pitt. I called George Clooney. I showed up at their houses. I posed as their gardeners. The restraining orders are still a matter of public record.

That's a joke, people.

Those records got expunged.

(*another joke…calm down)

I called an old friend, Sara Rodriguez. She was a mom, which was ideal. She was also attractive and looked friendly…like a neighbor you'd like to live next door to, but also full of spirit. Not to mention, she had her finger on the pulse of pop culture like no one I have ever known. She was the perfect candidate to be the face of the company.

She agreed, and the last piece fell into place. I told everyone it was Sara's company and left myself out of it. She was the focal point of my marketing campaign. People saw her as the face and the energy behind the entire operation.

Again, I felt it was more palatable for people to buy from a woman like her than from a guy who looked like me. And honestly, I wanted this candle company to succeed on its own. I didn't want it to be tied to music or anything I had done up to that point.

I launched the website and was officially in business on January 1, 2012. It had been a long, long journey. But at the end of this journey came my candle company, Shining Sol.

Shining Sol's slogan is "Share the light"—because these candles created a happiness in me that I had not felt for at least a year prior to them. I wanted to share that happiness with everyone…and in turn, have them share it with each other.

Be positive and be bright, man.

I still get emotional when I tell this story. To be honest, I am glad it turned out like it did. Not that running a candle company is without its stresses.

* * *

Following the launch, we plodded along for a while. We did okay…but not really. Everyone who purchased the candles loved them—but we were struggling to find a foothold in the market.

One day, Sara came to me and said, “Pete…you’ve got to tell everyone this is yours. It’s the only way to get us to the next level.”

I reluctantly agreed. One night in August or September 2012, we announced on Facebook that the company was actually mine. Furthermore, we were going to have a special through the website: For anyone who buys a candle within the next 24 hours, I would autograph the lid.

That night, we sold hundreds of candles. We literally did more business that night than we had done during all the previous months *combined.* Sara was right. It was a bit of a kick to my gut—I wanted to succeed differently. I didn’t want to tie it in with my music career.

But what the hell. Here we were.

The company changed overnight. Customers purchased through the website. Different stores around Manassas (and beyond) started to carry my candles in their brick-and-mortar locations. We started to sell more and more candles…we grew at a rate that was eternally gratifying.

And by the way—all this while my kids thought I was stupid.

In fact, they probably thought I was stupid in a more universal way. But in this case, they couldn’t wrap their brains around the fact that their rock star dad was lowering himself to sell something dumb like candles. Their dad had played with the guy from Poison. Their dad had toured all over North America. Their dad was on several episodes of reality television. Their dad had been on fucking *Larry King Live* (with Rikki Rockett, to talk about Bret's brain hemorrhage).

And now he's selling *candles*? WTF?

It didn't make any sense to them. And God bless them, they didn't pull any punches. My hope to inspire them by showing them how to run a successful business? Well, that part didn't seem to be working out.

Kids notwithstanding, many people thought this was a *great* idea. I was approached by several people over the next few years that wanted to invest in Shining Sol. I turned them all down—my intention (once again) was to demonstrate for my kids how to start and run a small business.

But then in 2015, my buddy, Deron, called.

Deron had been my friend since we were eight years old and trying to earn our Wolf badge in Cub Scouts. The music industry had made it difficult for me to trust anyone…but I trusted Deron.

He was the proverbial Cub Scout. He was married, had a beautiful family, attended church on Sundays, and always had his head screwed on straight. He was also ambitious and had an entrepreneurial spirit—but made good choices. He never got ahead of himself in business…he was thoughtful, methodical, and rational. And he was very good with people—a rare trait of those who can remove emotion from financial decisions.

Honest…trustworthy…nice.

It was the weirdest trifecta I had seen since 1980.

Deron was also a creative type. He owned a marketing company and had done business with me during the Some Odd Reason days. I hired him to make all our merch designs and help to market the band and the album.

I could go on and on. In any case, he came to me with interest in Shining Sol.

His initial interest was to revamp the company's website. Yes, he was also a web designer.

He did a great job with the website and eventually sat down with Sara and I to discuss making him a partner in the business. I was eager to bring him on board because I felt as though I needed a wholesome influence in my life. Again, the music industry made me jaded and calloused when it came to dealing with other people. Deron was the exact opposite of all that darkness.

We brought him on board…and then leveled our candle game up a notch.

* * *

Old Town Manassas is a super cool, historic part of town. I've always liked it and was interested when an opportunity became available.

We received word that one of the shops on Main Street, Love Charlie, was about to contract their footprint. Love Charlie was a boutique home store, selling high end knick-knacks and accent furnishings. They also happened to carry Shining Sol candles as a part of their inventory.

They had occupied two adjacent retail spaces along Center Street and were now planning to reduce their presence to one retail space. The owner was nice enough to approach me ahead of time and give us first right of refusal on the space she was about to vacate.

Leasing a brick-and-mortar space had never been my idea. I wanted a slick and modern internet company…so I didn't have to keep up with personnel and inventory and customer relations and building maintenance…dude, that was a challenge I just didn't want to take on.

Had this space been anywhere else in the world, we would have nixed the idea outright. But this was Old Town. This was the coolest place on Earth.

We took the plunge…and the buzz was incredible.

That store's grand opening in 2016 marked the first—and ONLY—time I have ever missed a Bret Michaels gig. I had to be there because it wasn't just a store opening its doors…it became a *Project X* level event.

I am not exaggerating when I say that the crowd we drew for the grand opening was so massive, the cops had to shut down Main Street to all vehicular traffic. It was like the U2 video for "Where the Streets Have No Name," when they played live on the rooftop of the

Republic Liquor Store on 7th and Main in Los Angeles.

**If you haven't seen that video in a while, go back and check it out on YouTube. It's worth watching.

The city was quite impressed. The mayor of Manassas showed up (no sense wasting a photo-op) as did Old Town's Head of Economic Development. They all told me they had never ever seen anything like this before.

In fairness to them, practically nobody in Old Town Manassas had any idea of what I did for a living. They didn't know that a local ruffian had made good with his life. That was all well and good with me—but it created some intense cognitive dissonance for them when people flew in from all over the US and Canada to attend the grand opening of a candle store.

It was powerful, man.

We opened the store for three hours that day, 5-8pm. My goal was to sell a thousand dollars' worth of candles.

We ended up selling over *four* thousand dollars' worth. Once again, it felt like a success.

But it didn't stop there.

* * *

The very next day, the three of us (Sara, Deron, and Me) were still riding the wave of excitement from the night before. We reconvened at the Center Street shop and shared a collective idea: What if we opened a second store?

Preposterous, right?

Hell no.

I threw out the idea for a Myrtle Beach location. There was an area in North Myrtle Beach (near the Intracoastal Waterway) called Barefoot Landing, which was a shopping district that catered to the tourist crowd. Sporting over 100 shops and restaurants, the foot traffic alone would be insane. Deron mentioned he had vacationed there and liked the idea a lot.

That very day, we called down to Barefoot Landing and put our name on a list to secure a retail space. That's how crazy popular

Barefoot Landing was—there was a waiting list to lease space within their confines; and the list was *several years* long.

The wait time seemed ridiculous to me, but it worked out perfectly. The "cooling off period" allowed for us to make clear, strategic decisions going forward. We had time to let the heightened emotions of our Manassas grand opening fade before committing to jump into a second store.

The call came in October of 2019. A space had opened, and it was ours if we wanted it. We did.

The three of us jumped into a car and made the six-and-a-half-hour drive down to Barefoot Landing. The space was ideal, but we wanted to be strategic rather than impulsive. In short, we made several trips and held several meetings before making the final decision.

When the time was right, we signed the lease and felt a warm rush of anticipation. The space was cool—but needed to be built out according to our specifications. That would require contractors and permits and building materials.

No problem. We were flush with cash from the first store, and ready to accept the challenge.

And then COVID hit. And the world stopped.

To compound our distress, Sara had to leave our company. I don't want to say a lot about her private affairs, but long story short, her young child was born with a rare genetic disorder called SCID (Severe Combined Immunodeficiency Disorder). Sara had to decide between running a company with Deron and I, or protecting her child from the pandemic.

The decision was not a decision at all. Sara was a great mom and did whatever she had to do to care for her child. Her sole focus became the health of her family, and she moved on from Shining Sol.

So, Deron and I were down one partner and trying to keep our heads above water at both locations. To the credit of Barefoot Landing, they were cool with us. They didn't charge us rent during the early stage of the pandemic. It was all well and good…but we were ultimately on the hook for that space and felt dead in the water regarding moving forward with our business.

A few months into the pandemic, in June 2020, we went

down and decided to build the damn thing out ourselves. Construction had begun before COVID, so it was not a complete build out—but it was enough that we had to put some serious sweat-equity into the place. We were fucking monsters, along with our friends Rick, Tracey, Dan and Bruce. In actuality Deron spent most of the time down there until the very end, and I stayed up in Manassas with Tina running the warehouse.

Over the next three weeks, my friends put their noses to the grindstone and hammered out a fully decked-out Shining Sol candle store. Tina and I cranked out enough product to fill the shelves of the new store. Our Myrtle Beach grand opening was held in July 2020.

It was a gamble, I'm not gonna lie. We got extremely lucky in one respect: Myrtle Beach remained functional during COVID. I don't know all that went into their decision, but they did not fully shut down their tourist season in 2020. That decision, mixed in with our hustle to build out the store, gave us a modest grand opening.

Despite not holding a candle to Old Town (pardon the pun), even the modest grand opening felt like success to me. We were able to remain afloat while the rest of the world was totally under water.

It was exciting. We were in two states and profitable. Eventually, a third opportunity presented itself. It was met with resistance on our part...but you can probably guess what happened from there.

* * *

Rehoboth Beach, Delaware; a sleepy town during the winter months...but a booming resort destination during the summer months. It's also a fairly wealthy part of the country, as affluent people own summer homes in the area (including current president, Joe Biden).

More importantly, the retail area is right on the ocean. Like, you walk out the front door of your shop and turn to your right—and the Atlantic Ocean is *maybe* 150 yards away. You can smell the salty sea and hear the waves...

I love the sand and the shore—and I love Rehoboth Beach.

Anyway, a friend of mine owned a store in Rehoboth Beach

and was nice enough to carry my candles in her place. One day, I approached her with a somewhat morbid—yet business savvy—request.

I said, "Hey…I know this sounds bad, but do you think there are any stores that aren't going to survive COVID?"

She was honest with me, "Oh my God…yeah. There are quite a few that aren't going to make it."

I asked if she would keep her ear to the ground for me, and she agreed. In my brain, I knew that when stores would begin to bankrupt and drop out of their retail spaces, landlords would become eager and start dropping the price of rent. If I timed it right, I could basically lease ocean-front property inexpensively.

Very soon thereafter, my friend called and told me about a storefront that had opened up. I grabbed Deron—who knew next to nothing about Rehoboth Beach. I told him to trust me enough to at least go look at the place…and he agreed.

Throughout the entire drive up there, he and I came up with a million reasons why this was a horrible, horrible idea. How there was no way anyone in their right mind would open a third location in a tourist destination during a global pandemic. How we couldn't stretch ourselves so thin while we were in the middle of an ownership transition. And how the burgeoning supply chain issues were making it more and more difficult to secure raw ingredients for our product.

Nobody would do something this stupid.

Nobody.

Anyway, we got there and signed the lease.

Before you pass judgment, let me defend myself by saying that Deron and I created a fail-safe during our drive. We decided—with iron-clad certainty—that we would *not* sign a lease unless the rent was below a certain amount.

When we talked to the landlord, he pitched us a rent amount that was way below THAT number. In other words, Deron and I came up with a number that was low, and the landlord came in under *that*.

It was glorious.

And damn scary.

But I poked my head out the door and saw that ocean, a mere one hundred and fifty yards away. We practically just *stole* a place on The Avenue, the main drag through Rehoboth Beach.

Deron summed it up perfectly: "I can't find a reason not to do this."

We signed the lease in December 2020. The lease specified that we had to be open for business by March 2021. The pandemic was still crippling the construction industry (and every other industry, short of powerful, multi-national conglomerate businesses) …so we had a problem. There was nobody to hire to help us build our space.

Deron and I rolled up our sleeves and did it again. Like Myrtle Beach, once the original owner vacated, we had about two months to get everything done. A credit to my family in Delaware, they are amazing builders. They showed up like a hammer-swinging army and got the shit done. We also had the help of our buddy Johnny from Jersey who was wiring the lighting till the second we opened the door.

A third grand opening later, and Deron and I now run three locations and have built a nice operation. Throughout the pandemic, the only businesses that grew exponentially in wealth were Walmart, Amazon, Netflix, Social Media Platforms…and Shining Sol.

You can read all about it when you attend business school at Wharton.

Or something like that.

* * *

There's actually another reason I started Shining Sol. This reason I dont talk about much. But…. here goes.

Bret is at the apex of his world, which has many obvious perks. But it also means he pays for everything—including the jet fuel for his plane. Without exaggeration, sometimes that is as much as $15,000 a flight.

With that in mind, I firmly believe that most friends split costs when they are hanging out. If I'm going to a concert with Chuck (for example), I offer gas money; or we take turns paying.

And often I will buy lunch or dinner or whatever but…. I can't live up to what it cost just to be Bret Michaels.

That doesn't bother me...I get it.

So here was my thought: *Maybe one day, I'll sell enough candles that I can buy the jet fuel on a trip*.

Not that Bret ever needs it...I've seen his bank accounts. He probably won't take it when the day comes.

But it would mean something to me.

CHAPTER 10:
PICTURES ON THE WALL

This is going to be a short chapter—but an important one for me. The first nine chapters of this book were all about the bricks that came together to build the solid wall of my career. This chapter will be more about the pictures I hung on that wall after it was built.

I do not brag about myself—frankly, I am prone to do the exact opposite. But when I take the time to go through a book like this in my head, I can't help but think about how fantastic the journey has been. I have gotten to do some of the most amazing things anyone should be legally allowed to do (and maybe a few that stretched that definition a bit...). Bear with me as I remove my hat and pay homage to the wonderful ways the music industry—and Bret Michaels specifically—has treated me to a fantastic career.

* * *

Following *Rock of Love*, I entered my fourth year as the guitar player and musical director for Bret's band. I was comfortable in my role, as was Bret with me. He was a household name, and he was as big as Poison ever was. For example, during the summer of 2008, Bret released a compilation album of his biggest solo hits (and three new songs), called *Rock My World.* That same summer, Poison released two compilation albums of their own—*Live, Raw & Uncut* (which also included a live concert DVD), and *Seven Days Live.* Bret's album sold more copies and peaked at a higher chart position than either of those Poison records.

Every single night was sold out. We took his private plane everywhere. We played insane gigs that nobody gets to play.

Bret was taking the world by storm...AND STILL IS!

And he really became a world-wide phenomenon. Obviously,

he was the star that everyone wanted, but I got to tag along and experience a front-row-seat view of the grandeur that his life had become. I'll talk more about our international tours in a bit, but following *Rock of Love*, Bret leaned hard into his television career.

In 2009, he was the inspiration and star of another VH-1 series, *Rock of Love Bus*. From there, 2010 found him as the centerpiece of a third reality series, *Bret Michaels: Life as I Know It*. I already wrote about those two shows at the end of Chapter Eight. Once again, he and I wrote theme songs to each show, and had a second and third round of videos shooting up the VH-1 Countdown.

Quick point of fact, *Life as I Know It* featured our theme song, "Riding Against the Wind." That song is my favorite he and I have ever written. I'm only in the music video for about two seconds total (don't blink!), but I consider it an honor. The video is centered around Bret's family—and they are WAY more photogenic than me!

Also in 2010, Bret was selected to be a contestant on Season 9 of *The Apprentice* (also referred to as Season 3 of *The Celebrity Apprentice*). I got to be on set with Bret throughout most of the filming—and it was so much fun to experience. The producers of the show really cast Bret in a positive light, bringing even more star power to his brand. And—spoiler alert! —Bret won that season, edging out Holly Robinson Peete in the series finale.

Following his victory on *The Apprentice*, Bret was asked to be a part of another type of reality show. In August 2010, he was tapped to co-host the 2010 Miss Universe Pageant, alongside TV correspondent, Natalie Morales. We flew to Las Vegas for that gala. I don't need to tell you how amazing that night was.

Bret's appeal and status as a household name could not have been higher.

In between all those reality shows, I got to produce a song that Bret did for the television series, *The Penguins of Madagascar*. I don't need to tell you how enormous it was to work for DreamWorks Animation and Nickelodeon. Not to mention, the *Madagascar* film series was a huge hit—so the spin-off television show (which produced 149 episodes) was equally as huge.

All throughout Bret's meteoric rise to fame, I was pulled along by the current. I became the Richie Sambora to Bret's Jon Bon Jovi. I was the Joe Perry to Bret's Steven Tyler. I quietly did whatever I could to support him.

And suddenly, Pete Evick started getting asked to do things like radio interviews, podcast interviews, magazine interviews…and to refer to himself in the third person. In fact, *Guitar World* magazine did an interview and feature article about me. I had been a voracious reader of *Guitar World* for over a decade prior to that moment—so when I got the call, it checked off yet another box of "MTV Famous" success. Since then, I have been featured in *Guitar World* magazine several times…and it never gets old to me. I owe that all to my now good buddy Rich Bienstock who has been incredibly supportive of me over the years.

Not to mention, all my heroes became my peers. Bret headlined a major shed tour (20,000+ -seat amphitheaters) and several huge bands from the genre opened for us. I will address this concept more thoroughly in the next chapter—and will tell you about how Dee Snider hired EVICK—but it was another surreal development in my ridiculously fabulous career.

While I'm on the topic of life goals and the shed tour, BMB played at Jiffy Lube Live (formerly known as the Nissan Pavilion), a 32,000-seat amphitheater in Bristow, Virginia. That shed opened when I was 23 years old (1995) and was literally ten minutes from my home. I can't tell you how many shows I watched from those seats. And now I was playing guitar on that stage.

I still shake my head over that shit.

**I never watch YouTube videos of us, but there is a clip of me playing the EVERY ROSE solo taken from the top of the venue looking down on all 32,000 people that I might watch occasionally ;-)

But wait! There's more!

In no particular order, I toured with Bret through Australia in support of Mötley Crüe. We also headlined tours through South America, Canada, and were honored to play for our troops over in Iraq.

I still can't believe that one. I played for the troops in *Iraq*. I performed in Saddam Hussein's palace, with a giant American flag hanging behind me. Who could have predicted that for a rocker kid from Manassas?

Bret was killing it on the road. It was like the name "Poison" ceased to exist. Obviously, I'm overstating that point. But Bret Michaels was the current poster boy for success and celebrity *juice.*

Everything Bret touched turned to gold. In 2015, he decided he wanted to veer away from rock and roll for a minute. He wanted to do another country song, which he did. He never wanted boundaries. He had been in contact with 2014 Grammy Award winner ("Best Country Album" Producer; *Same Trailer Different Park*, Kasey Musgraves) and 2015 Academy of Country Music Award winner ("Songwriter of the Year"), Luke Laird. Interestingly, Luke was also a Pennsylvania native.

Luke, Bret, and I sat down and wrote a song called "Girls on Bars." True to form, that song instantly became the most viewed debut video of all time on CMT (Country Music Television). Check it out on YouTube. I guarantee you're going to love it.

Bret Michaels had now conquered the country music world *again*—just like he did with "All I Ever Needed," back before I was in the band. And I am damn proud to have been a small part of it.

Also in 2015, yet ANOTHER lifelong dream was fulfilled. Bret was to perform on a bill in Puerto Rico with Night Ranger. Headlining that evening was (are you sitting down for this?) Sammy Hagar.

Heard of him? The Red Rocker? That guy from Van Halen? *That* guy?

Anyway, not only did I get to meet Sammy Hagar, but I got to chat with him. AND THEN (yes, there's more…), I got to share a stage and play with him…although that was a few years later.

Long story short (ha! you know better by now), a wealthy CEO hired Bret to play a private corporate event. He loved Bret and didn't bat an eye at the fee to have Bret perform. The event went off without a hitch, and I became good friends with the guy (no, I will not name him).

Fast forward to the following year.

The same guy held the same corporate private party, except this year he hired Sammy Hagar to perform. However—and this is how you know you've done well for yourself and your company—he hired Bret and I to fly in and play four songs with Sammy.

Four songs.

I got to be on stage and play with Sammy Hagar and Bret at the same time. After the gig, Sammy sent Bret a text about me. I am going to tell you what it said in the next chapter, but I asked Bret to screenshot that text and send it to me. I literally have proof that Sammy Hagar thinks I'm okay.

Sammy, the guy who sang for my favorite band of all time, texted Bret, the greatest front man of an entire genre, about *me*.

And I got to meet up with him again briefly in 2018, when Bret was invited to be a guest on an episode from Season 3 of Sammy's television show, *Rock and Roll Road Trip with Sammy Hagar*.

We had a funny moment during the taping of that episode. I was hanging out with Sammy. A thought occurred to me—and I said it out loud.

"Sammy…I just want to tell you. I remember exactly where I was the very first time I ever heard 'Why Can't This be Love.' I was in sixth grade, and I was by my locker. A friend of mine had it taped off the radio. He brought it and he played it for me."

I collected myself for the emotional punch line.

"And Sammy…the second I heard that song, my life changed forever."

Sammy paused for a moment and scratched his chin. When he looked up, he smirked and delivered the line of the century.

"Hmm. Mine did too!"

We both cracked up. It was so amazing.

MTV famous? I feel like I'm well past that, my friend. And all because Bret Michaels gave me a chance.

* * *

There have been so many other things I have gotten the opportunity to do. So many pictures hanging on this wall. If I try to see them all at once, I can't see any of them. It's only as I sit here and slowly unfurl my memories for this book that some of these pictures begin to stand out against the rest.

I have been the musical director for a show done by Steve Augeri—a guy who sang for Journey. Can you get any bigger than Journey was through the 80s? I have also been musical director for Mark McGrath (of Sugar Ray). Mark was, is, and always will be one of the absolute coolest guys on the planet.

The Hard Rock Hotel Riviera Maya (their all-inclusive resort in Cancun, Mexico) created a "Bret Michaels Suite" in 2017. They didn't just ask for a bunch of his memorabilia to position around the restaurant and down the hallways of the resort. Instead, they consolidated it all into one mega-themed suite. A lot of the outfits he's worn on stage over the years are in there. The motorcycle he rode in the "Fallen Angel" video is in there. It's a wild ride (pardon the pun) through his rock star history.

Anyway, because of that relationship with the Hard Rock, the company booked Bret to play several festivals all over Mexico. I remember having one of those existential moments as I was playing in front of thousands of people right in front of the ocean and thinking, *How the fuck did I get here???*

We've had a few experiences playing in front of giant crowds at sporting events. We played a halftime show on the field during an Arizona Cardinals game at (what is now) State Farm Field. We've played the concert that closes out the home season for the Tampa Bay Rays at Tropicana Field several times. We've played shows before tons of NASCAR events—including major races like Darlington and Dover.

Not to mention, Bret has done concerts all over the world to raise money for charitable causes. He is passionate about supporting the JDRF (Juvenile Diabetes Research Foundation) and raising awareness of the disease itself. He has also done shows on behalf of the U.S. Military and the Wounded Warriors Foundation.

He's seriously one of the most generous guys I know. And he opened the door and let me join him on this incredible journey. I'm not saying I owe my life to him. But I do owe the life I've lived to him.

* * *

That pretty much brings us up to today. This book is being written during the late summer, 2022. I'm sure that many, many more things will happen to me as I move ahead into my fifties and sixties. Maybe a third book somewhere down the road? I have no intention of slowing down—I am a rock and roll warrior after all.

The final part of this book will be devoted to odds and ends that didn't seem to fit cleanly in the timeline. These are anecdotes, musings, and philosophical tidbits that I think are still important to tell—and seemed to arrange themselves and fit together nicely into four discreet chapters.

The first of these four chapters was difficult to write, but necessary. I know I talked about how wonderful my life has been (despite the depressive hiccup when I got divorced and no longer lived with my sons full-time), but there have been moments of despair and loneliness that literally *every* single touring musician has felt.

I'll write about a few of those moments, and then close with random stories of rock and roll success—stories that were *lived* by me, and stories of things that Bret *taught* to me.

Let's move into Part III.

PART 3:

MY LIFE...HIGHS AND LOWS

CHAPTER 11:
LONELINESS

Hunter S. Thompson once wrote, "We are all alone; born alone, die alone, and…we shall all someday look back on our lives and see that, in spite of our company, we were alone the whole way."

I don't know if Mr. Thompson ever spent time on the road as a touring musician, but I know this for certain: he nailed it.

Playing music for a living is a cool career to have—most of the time. Being on stage and commanding the undivided attention of thousands of people is the most incredible feeling in the world. Feeling camaraderie among fellow musicians is, as I have written earlier, an experience akin to being around family.

And therein lies the ultimate paradox. The band becomes your family. The tour manager is your parent. The musicians are your siblings. The crew guys are your cousins. But in real life, you leave your family behind. There is *so much* you miss out on because you are called to the road.

I have heard stories (and have lived stories) of things like missing weddings, funerals, and/or the birth of their children because they were off playing or recording. It is a choice—but it really isn't. If you suddenly leave a tour because you get a phone call that your wife has gone into labor, the show is dead in the water. Nobody in the band or crew gets paid. The promoter is pissed because he has to refund ticket money. The venue is pissed because they just lost out on parking or concessions or their cut of the gate. The fans are disappointed because they didn't get to see the show.

There are literally thousands of people who depend upon every member of the band to show up and do their job. Replacement musicians are available—sort of. None can replace the front man. None can get to the venue on short notice. None truly know how to play your songs cold, such that they can step in without ample preparation.

Thousands of people, man. All depending on you.

So, the show must go on. No matter what is happening in an artist's life, he or she has to suck it up and forge ahead. We tell our spouses and children that we will see them as soon as we can. We send regrets and gift cards instead of attending the milestones and celebrations of the people we love.

We all learn to cope. We immerse ourselves in the show. Some grab booze or drugs to help them cope. Some use sex as a salve to ease the pain of disconnection and existential angst. We get by.

But there are moments, man…times when it doesn't matter what or who is happening around you. You feel like you are floating on an ice shelf, a million miles away from the rest of the world. These are the moments when your existential angst turns into existential loneliness. Moments we feel so empty and alone that it almost crushes us like a beer can at the bottom of the ocean.

These are the times when we almost don't want to be. I have had four such moments in my career.

* * *

Nothing to Lose

The moment that stands out the clearest in my memory happened early in 2010. I've got another one coming from later that same year, but this one happened soon after the song "Nothing to Lose" was released as a single. It was off an album Bret and I had done together called *Custom Built*.

Incidentally, this song was unique in that Miley Cyrus sang it with Bret. She was doing a cover of "Every Rose Has Its Thorn" for her *Can't Be Tamed* album and wanted to work directly with Bret on a project of his. Bret was delighted, of course…Miley was a huge star, and this song was a hit.

As a bit of context to the moment I am about to chronicle, it was during this period that the friendship between Bret and I was really taking form. We had grown close over the course of the couple years leading up to 2010. Conversely, Bret's band (which was still my band, EVICK) and I were growing further and further apart.

Those guys had been my close friends once upon a time—so it was distressing to feel the separation taking place.

To give you a taste of just how big of a schism was taking place, we toured on two buses. Bret and I were on one bus, and the rest of the band was on the other. The idea was born of pragmatism. Bret and I did a lot of writing and recording during this era. He wanted to have the time and space to create with me when the mood struck him.

For more context, I will add that I was recently divorced at this time and was not currently in a committed romantic relationship of any depth. The tour and the road were my mistresses.

Anyway, the single came out in March. The morning it was released to radio stations, we were in Dubuque, Iowa. Despite the friends I had in the area, Dubuque did not cure my loneliness.

I was up early because I was excited to keep tabs on how the song was doing. While the sun rose and Bret slept back in his room, I received notice that our song was the Number 1 song added to radio that week.

Bon Jovi and Nickelback had also released songs that day—and ours outpaced theirs. It was exhilarating. In my brain, this was one of those singularly most defining moments of my life. Once again, I felt an immense sense of "I've arrived" satisfaction. I was involved with something that was trending better than Bon Jovi or Nickelback.

How cool is that?

Not to mention, the album itself was selling like crazy. I think we debuted at #17 on the U.S. *Billboard* 200 album chart (it peaked as high as #14) and was #1 on the *Billboard* Top Hard Rock Album chart.

It was a Top 20 record, right? It was everything, man. When I heard that news, all the sacrifice and all the pain was worth it. Every dream I held since I was five years old was coming true. It was such a thrill to consider that something I had a hand in creating was as popular with fans as it was. Heck, between the divorce and the growing divide between my friends and me, this good news was like a life raft floating past a drowning man.

When Bret emerged from his back room, I informed him of

the news.

Bear in mind, Bret comes from the 80s—when a top 20 album meant it was going Platinum. You couldn't crack the top 20 back in those days without moving over a million units.

Not anymore, my friend. In the digital age, album sales are a mere shadow of what they used to be. That doesn't mean that the fans weren't getting the new music; they were just getting it for free. File-sharing began in the late 90s, and artists took a punch right to the nose because fans chose to pirate music rather than purchase it. Then streaming services and YouTube popped up and grew in popularity, thereby killing off any remaining incentive to purchase music.

Some fans still like to support the artists and buy a physical CD or an album…but they are fewer and farther between than ever before. Maybe they like the album art and the liner notes. They might like the feeling of putting a record on the turntable or inserting a CD. Or they may have a stereo system or a good car audio system—music played through tweeters and subs has a different feel than music pushed through Bluetooth earbuds.

I'm not here to give you a lecture about the shifting landscape of music economics. I'm here to tell you about a dark, dark time in my life.

Maybe that's why I went down the rabbit hole of economics. This shit is painful to remember. Way more painful than I expected, to be honest.

Anyway, Bret strolled into the galley, and I jumped up to tell him the news. As I told him we were the top radio add for the week, I'm sure I was as delirious as a kid barreling through his parents' bedroom door on Christmas morning (*Wake up! Wake up! SANTA WAS HERE!!!*).

He asked, "How were the sales?"

By this particular moment in time, I hadn't looked into sales numbers specifically. More fans liked our record than Bon Jovi's or Nickelback's records. *That's* what was important to me.

I looked up the number and gave it to Bret. I could see he wasn't nearly as excited as me—but how could he be? He wrote "Every Rose Has Its Thorn." With one song, he had changed the landscape of hard rock, and overnight, every band *had* to have a song just like it. While this was a victory to him…it wasn't THAT.

He gave a little smile and nod and walked back into his room. To Bret Michaels, this day was just like any other day. He wasn't disappointed—not at all. Nor was he cold toward me in any way. He just took in the numbers and went about his day.

Bret was happy and proud of the success. But I imagine it's like being a pro football player who had won Super Bowls—and then years later they changed the field to 50 yards instead of 100 yards. You are still the best at what you do, but the win at 50 yards just doesn't feel the same as 100 yards. And yes, even though I'm not a sports guy, I know they have never shortened the field. Just trying to paint a picture here.

I wish I could adequately put my subsequent feelings into words. I honestly felt like we had just released the next "Stairway to Heaven." I wanted our song to change history…but there was no way for it to match that expectation. Given the tide of the industry, nobody will ever have another "Stairway to Heaven."

Maybe I needed it to be that huge because of everything else I was dealing with in my life. When Bret didn't have a "Stairway to Heaven" reaction, I began to spiral downward. It was like someone sliced a hole in my gut and all the happiness and hope and elation spilled out and washed away. The space it had occupied was now filled with loneliness.

Joy is a living organism—growing bigger and stronger as it is passed around. Each *person* grows bigger and stronger as they pass it around. And when joy spreads, it changes the mood of everyone it touches.

What good is joy if there is nobody with whom to share it? When you receive good news, I will bet there is at least one person you can't wait to call and tell. That's how it works.

At least, that's how it was supposed to work for me on that morning in Dubuque.

Bret didn't go out of his way to shit all over my parade. He was as cordial and conversational as he ever was. Instead, he merely did not *share* my exact amount of joy. He walked away, leaving me with nobody else to tell.

Sure, I could have told my friends in the band. But we were already teetering on the brink of dissolution. Not to mention, they didn't have the same involvement with the song or with the album as I did. Whatever the case, I was already raw and sad…it wasn't worth the risk to tell the band. They might have stolen whatever little dignity that I had left.

I couldn't tell my wife. I didn't have a wife. I *used* to have a wife. That was already painful enough on its own.

I could have told my family, I suppose. They loved me. They knew it was my passion. But they couldn't relate to the grind or the sacrifice. In the end, they would have done their best to share my joy…but that would have been even more painful to me.

I fell back into my chair…defeated.

I gazed out the window. We were in a parking lot. In Iowa. It was overcast and bleak outside.

And I was overcast and bleak inside.

Never in my life had I felt so utterly alone.

The greatest achievement of my life was gone. It didn't matter to anybody but me.

In that moment, I was overtaken by the emptiness. I literally started crying. All the grief I had bottled up from my divorce came pouring through. All the sadness and separation I felt from my children came pouring through. All the disappointment I felt over the parting seas of my friendships came pouring through.

It was like a lifetime of pain came pouring out of me as I wept, all by myself, on a bus parked in Dubuque, Iowa.

In a span of five minutes, I went from being the happiest guy in the world to being the *only* guy in the world.

I would have rather been dead.

Sturgis

While mulling over this chapter, I came to an interesting insight. When you work as a touring musician, your life feels very "spread out." For example, when I am on the road, my family is back home. The guys I grew up with are back home. I am on a bus or on a stage or in a studio, and they are buzzing around the hive, living their daily lives without me.

When I am at home, my best friend (Bret) is on the other coast. He lives on the west coast, and I live on the east coast. Not to mention, the fans are sprinkled all throughout the rest of the country…as are the other musicians with whom I have become friends.

In a more immediate sense, even being on stage is an odd juxtaposition to reality. We are in a place surrounded by thousands of people who *love us*—and yet, there is a barrier between us and them. An imaginary "fourth wall" exists, separating the performers from the audience.

As Bob Seger sang, "Out there in the spotlight, you're a million miles away."

I have grown accustomed to always feeling disconnected from someone. It's like a teeter totter—if I am closer to Bret, I am further from my family. If I am closer to my family, I am further from Bret. It's one end or the other; never both. I am always vulnerable to being on the wrong end of that teeter totter when something happens on the other end.

And that's exactly what happened on our way to Sturgis.

An enormous motorcycle rally is held in Sturgis every August, aptly named the Sturgis Motorcycle Rally. Attendance averages around 500,000 people, who ride their bikes into town for a 10-day event filled with vendors, music, and camaraderie.

The population of Sturgis (the rest of the year) is around 7,000 people. You can do the math from there. It's insane—and insanely fun.

Bret was headlining a show at the rally that year, as we had done several times and still do, so we loaded onto the bus and took off across the vast openness of rural Minnesota and South Dakota. Seriously—it's like driving across the moon, provided the moon was completely flat and even *less* populated than it already is.

And that's where I was when it happened. Smack dab in the middle of an abandoned moonscape. It's amazing that I was able to get cell service, but my phone rang. The caller was from Delaware… and the news was grim.

My dad was gonna die.

I hung up, dazed. My mind tried going in two directions at once. On the one hand, I was shoved headlong into the grieving process. It was a process I never wanted to begin, but there I was, letting the truth soak into my brain while it pushed back with, "No! This can't be happening!"

The other part of me—the more pragmatic side—was working on a plan. A death in the family doesn't just bring out emotion; it brings out friends and family. Neighbors bring a covered dish. Family travels to assemble and celebrate the life of the deceased. Bread is broken, stories are shared…memories are made.

Unless you're on a bus, driving across the moon.

I don't know if any of you have ever driven I-90 through South Dakota, but believe me when I say that you can't get anywhere quick. Major airports do not exist. Major cities do not exist. In fact, little towns are spread out like stars in a galaxy.

When we got to Sturgis, I played the show. What else was I going to do? There was no way I could get home. I would have much rather jumped on a red eye to Florida (where my dad lived the later years of his life) and sped back to be with my family…but I was stuck.

Stuck on the moon.

I don't remember much about the show itself, other than Bret giving a heartfelt tribute to my dad. My mind was elsewhere, as you can imagine.

Some of the action was captured by Jesse James Dupree (lead singer of the band Jackyl) for his TV show, *Full Throttle Saloon*, on TruTV. By the time our bus pulled up, Jesse had caught wind of my father passing—so when I stepped off the bus, the camera was there. I was taken off guard…but I understood. Remember all the things I said about Season 3 of *Rock of Love*? I understood reality TV.

I love Jesse. He comes off as rough around the edges, but he's one of the sweetest dudes on the planet. In fact, that particular episode is even dedicated to my father in the end credits. But for all that, I watch the episode and think things like, *Wow... I don't even remember that.*

It wasn't until the following evening that I was able to cobble together a way to get home. I was sad…and a little bit angry. The road is such a fickle mistress. She can feed and bathe you in comfort —but betray you in the blink of an eye.

I will add that Bret offered to get me home on his jet, but the jet was in Arizona. By the time he rounded up the pilots and then they flew in and rested (you have to rest a certain number of hours by law), I could have gotten to the commercial airport and spent a lot less money.

You never feel quite as alone or isolated as you do when you can't get back to your people. In the song Wasted Time, Bret wrote a line that goes, "The same road that carries me, is now the road that buries me."

I was with him when he wrote that line—and it gave me chills. He wrote that line just prior to his brain hemorrhage; almost like he had a prophetic vision. The road giveth and the road taketh away.

It's hard to explain to people who have never lived this way. I do love it—I would never say anything to the contrary. But there is a darkness to it. All of us experience it eventually.

The same road that carries me, is now the road that buries me.

And on that day, in a bus on the moon, the road took me away from my father's final moments on Earth. My whole family was there. I wasn't. He'll always be my dad…but I wasn't there when he passed away.

I'd like to add that in the hospital, although he was truly gone, they kept him on life support long enough so that I could get there when they pulled the plug. But it was very clear there was no line to resuscitation; no miracle was gonna happen. Machines just kept his heart pumping till I got there.

9-11

I know the timeline is a bit jacked up here, but I am going to move backwards to tell you of another moment that made me feel alone on the road. I'm sure you all remember where you were on 9-11. It remains one of the few codifying moments in our societal memory. The space shuttle *Challenger* blowing up and the O.J. Simpson Bronco chase are two other biggies.

I wasn't yet in Bret's band in 2001 but found myself flying

on 9-11. It was hard enough leaving that morning because my wife was pregnant with our son. I was so excited about being a dad…I didn't want to miss a thing.

But there I was, pulling up to Dulles at ungodly-o'clock in the morning. I boarded my Delta Airlines flight without incident. Atlanta was the destination. I was on my way down to play with a band called Radio Daze that I had become good friends with and admired very much. They were a full-time cover band who worked a lot—and while I never wanted to leave EVICK, I was considering my options and trying to figure out what was gonna be best for my bank account (since I was about to be a dad).

The plane took off, hit cruising altitude, and glided southward. All was well.

We were probably somewhere over North Carolina when the first tower got hit. This was back before they had WiFi on airplanes and people could follow the news on their phones. As a result, nobody around me had any clue about what was happening to the world below them.

We touched down at Hartsfield Airport (Atlanta) before the second tower was hit—so we weren't diverted to Canada. I'm not being hyperbolic for effect—that was the deal on that day. Once the second tower went down, all US airports and all US airspace were basically shut down. Mine might have been among the last planes allowed to land on US soil on 9-11.

As we disembarked, a mob of camera crews and reporters swarmed around us. They asked what we thought and what we knew—we were coming from Washington, DC, after all.

It was disorienting because I still had no grasp of the reality around me. My brain didn't take seconds to catch up—it took minutes. Scraps of information had to be absorbed and synthesized. I had to push past the defensive reaction of, "No…this can't be happening."

It was a nightmare.

The airport itself was an odd mixture of frenzied panic and silent shock.

As for me, I extricated myself from the mob and ran to call my wife. No bueno.

I don't know if you recall, but the phone lines to DC and New York had basically collapsed as the towers were collapsing. With everyone on earth trying to get in touch with their loved ones, the circuitry was quickly overwhelmed and shut down.

Cell phone towers…land lines…I stood no chance of finding out if my family was alive or dead. Information was scarce. Let me rephrase that—*reliable* information was scarce. The media was pumping out information as fast as they could get it, but not even they knew exactly what was happening. Not to mention, everyone in the airport—hungry for any shred of information—was playing the telephone game. Stories grew and bent over time and with sloppy repetition.

I tried my wife again.

Nothing.

I systematically went down my contact list. Back then, my entire life was centered in Virginia (read: Washington DC) and New York. Nobody in those regions was able to place or receive phone calls. Email and the internet were around back then, but they were nowhere near as ubiquitous as they are today. Plus, connectivity was achieved via dial-up telephone modem—so now we're back to square one.

Every number in my list came up snake eyes. Then I got down to the name and number of a guy I knew. He worked in Los Angeles.

I dialed his number. I was so desperate to talk to *somebody*. I just wanted to hear the voice of someone who was outside of the damned Atlanta airport. When he answered…my God…I was so grateful.

Our brief chat re-energized me. It was time to grab a rental car and head for home.

I think you see where this is going.

It would have probably been easier to steal the Hope Diamond than to get a rental car on 9-11. Defeated, I headed for the home of Todd Bradley, the leader of the band I was checking out. Bear in mind, outside of Todd, I didn't really know the guys in this band. So that night, I was surrounded by strangers while my family was completely disconnected from me and living near a city that was probably the first target for an enemy nuclear strike.

I was all by myself. No wife…no unborn son…no friends. Once again, the music business had taken me away and left me stranded. Marooned on an island of loneliness.

I felt like I was a loser. I felt like everything was terrible. My family needed me…but I wasn't there. I was in Atlanta with my guitar, trying to be a rock star.

The choices I've made have hurt the people I love.

Bret's Health Scare

In the first section of this chapter, I told you there would be another instance of crushing loneliness from 2010. This is it. It happened soon after the release of "Nothing to Lose," meaning the divorce was still fresh and I was still feeling separation from my group of friends in the band.

I will add that in the midst of my rocky personal life at home, Bret and I had truly become the best of friends. We were rocking the world and having the time of our lives.

Well, we were having the time of *my* life. Bret has done so many things, I'm not sure these years are the top of his list. But we had a great time—he couldn't deny that if you asked him. His solo career was going great…and I was there every step of the way.

In a nutshell, he was there when I needed him most.

Early one morning in April of 2010, I was in my home. I had spent a couple days puttering around and trying to get my Virginia life back in order. I was in a good mood, packing my bags. I was scheduled to get on a plane and fly to Bret's house with our drummer Chuck, who to this day is about equal in Best Friendism—but with more years than Bret. We were due to write some more music and hopefully lay down a few tracks for a new record.

We got to the airport to catch a 7am flight; all good. It was 5:30am my time—and 2:30am in Arizona, where Bret lived.

My phone rang. It was Kristi Gibson, Bret's long-time girlfriend and the mother of his two daughters. She told me Bret was rushed to the hospital with a hemorrhage near the base of his brain.

All I could think to ask was, "Well…is he going to live?"

Her words made my soul turn cold.

"I don't know."

You don't want to fuckin' hear that, man. You don't want to hear it. *I* didn't want to hear it. I didn't know what to do with that information. I felt helpless.

"What should I do?" I croaked into the phone.

"Get on the plane," she replied, "Whatever happens, you should be here."

I've never spoken to Kristi about that phone call. But I will say, it was obvious she had pulled herself together for the sake of their daughters. THAT CAN NOT BE AN EASY THING TO DO. But I will forever be appreciative for the call and her calmness while talking to me.

It's a five-hour flight from Washington, DC, to Phoenix, Arizona. In case you haven't figured it out by now, my brain is wired in such a way that it does NOT like having too much time to think. And as I discovered, five hours is way too much time to think.

I completely immersed myself in a sucking vacuum of loneliness and depression. All I could ruminate on was how my marriage was over and how my friends had disavowed me and whether or not one of my best friends in the world—hell, my *last* friend (other than Chuck, who I still felt distant from at the time even though he was on the plane with me) in the world—would be dead when I landed in Arizona.

That may sound selfish in the face of Bret struggling through a life-threatening condition, but loneliness and depression are selfish by definition. That sounded harsh…let's just say that loneliness and depression are afflictions that cause you to look inward and focus on the hopelessness of your situation.

It was terrible.

And like on 9-11, my brain turned on me. I felt like a piece of crap for being all the way on the other side of the country when my friend needed me. I felt like a deserter.

It's ridiculous, I know. I couldn't have stopped that brain hemorrhage even if I was standing next to him when it was about to happen. Same with my father's death. I had no way of knowing when he was going to die—and what if I *had* known? Was there anything I could have physically done to stop the Grim Reaper from taking him away?

Of course not.

Unfortunately, those are all *thoughts*—and they don't match the power of my feelings.

In every one of these scenarios, I kept returning to the thought, *Most people live their lives near the people they love.* I didn't. I was a thousand miles away from my pregnant wife on 9-11. Later, I would be in South Dakota when my dad died (he was still alive at this time). And I was an entire continent away when my friend was lying on a hospital bed, walking the fine line between life and death.

How could I do this to them?

I must be a horrible person to choose music and fleeting stardom over relationships and real intimacy.

Obviously, and thank God, everything with Bret turned out okay. In another frightening twist, Bret was diagnosed with a hole in his heart a few weeks after the brain hemorrhage. That guy has the will of Hercules when it comes to fighting for his life. The doctors put him back together, sent him on his way, and he was right back out there killing it.

* * *

I didn't write this chapter to make anyone feel sorry for me. I work through it and forge ahead the best I can. It gets bad at times. My fear of leaving my family behind had morphed into a fear of flying in general. Recently, when the Ukrainian War broke out, my anxiety spiked into full blown panic. I now feel a paralyzing fear when I think about going to the airport. I can't stop thinking about DC being targeted by a Russian nuclear strike.

What if Putin hits the U.S. while I am on an airplane? And then my family is dead, but I am still alive?

I love my music, don't get me wrong. But now I just want to grab my kids and hug them and squeeze them against me and never let them go. Seriously—it's getting worse instead of better for me. I guess I cope by soldiering on. I always do manage to get on that plane and get done whatever needs to get done.

It ain't fun being trapped in my head sometimes, man.

But again, that wasn't the point of writing this chapter.

Rather, I wrote this chapter to give everyone a little insight into what life is really like on the road. Obviously, my crazy brain will make some molehills into mountains, but every touring musician feels the pangs of loneliness and questions his or her life decisions once in a while.

Rock stars can seem like gods when they strut across their version of Mount Olympus—a stage and jumbo-tron before a stadium filled with screaming fans. But they are not. They are all human; real men and women who just so happen to make their living —or sometimes get STUPID rich— as rock stars.

CHAPTER 12:
NOTES FOR MUSICAL PEOPLE

I will share two over-arching messages to anyone trying to make a living playing music. I will also provide some context and a few stories to illustrate my experiences in learning the lessons leading to me understanding the two messages.

* * *

Be kind

This message seems so foundational and simple, it almost begs to be left out of the book. However, sometimes the simplest messages are the most important ones to emphasize—and also the first that may be forgotten along the way.

The music industry is quite competitive in many ways. At the top of the pyramid, there isn't a lot of room. Look at the music videos on YouTube, for example. Hundreds of thousands of singers and bands have videos posted for the world to see. A good number of them might hit 1,000 views on one of their videos.

Very few of those might hit over 100,000 views.

Way fewer hit over a million views.

And a *tiny* handful of artists have videos that have registered over a billion views.

There is a race to the top—and a race that, for some, includes throwing some elbows along the way. Whatever it takes to get noticed ahead of the other guy.

However—and this is a major point—in my experience, the music business *feels* more competitive than it really is. If you put the work in and do your homework and hustle to promote yourself and get in front of decision-makers, you will find your way. Not necessarily on MTV, but you can earn a nice living playing music.

Yes, I realize MTV no longer plays music videos. Let's not get lost in the details here.

What I am trying to say is that if you treat music as being collaborative rather than competitive, you will expand your network and give yourself a better chance of succeeding long-term. If you are likable, helpful, and available, people will more likely want you around.

Venue operators want bands that will pack the place, sure. But all things being equal, they will give the nod to a band they know they can trust to be courteous and responsible to the fans, the staff, and the facilities. More gigs means more money means better longevity and can mean a nice career. Not to mention, your reputation gets out. The world of musicians is a small one. Getting hired into bigger bands helps your career.

I remember visiting a friend who lived out in the country. We were in his front yard tinkering with fixing his fence when one of his neighbors drove by. He waved, I stared.

I asked if he knew that neighbor, and he said, "Not very well."

When I asked why he waved so friendly, he said something that has always stuck with me.

"Always wave to your neighbors out here, Pete. You never know when you're going to need them."

I guarantee you'll be remembered.

Let me share four quick stories with you. These stories all involve guys who made it to the "MTV level" in music. But when I crossed their paths, I was a nobody and they were a somebody. Yet, they were so unbelievably nice—so kind and generous—that I will forever sing their praises.

Andy Timmons & Bruno Ravel

Bruno Ravel was the founder and bassist for the popular late 80s band, Danger Danger. Andy Timmons was not a founding member, but played guitar for the band. I don't know either of them as well as I know Steve West (Drummer) or Ted Poley (Singer), but both of them made an impression on me because of their kindness.

Incidentally, Ted Poley has an indoor pool.

(sorry—inside joke)

In 1989, Danger Danger had two hit songs off their self-titled debut album ("Naughty Naughty" and "Bang Bang"). The songs were in heavy rotation on MTV and had unlimited potential. Their follow-up album, *Screw It!* spun off two singles and continued their presence on MTV. They were eventually asked to open for Kiss, who was touring behind their *Hot in the Shade* album and getting ready to release *Revenge*.

Danger Danger was on their way to becoming a big deal… and I was a big fan.

During the Kiss tour, Danger Danger had a night off and booked themselves to play a club near Washington DC. A lot of bands will do that when they tour as an opener. They like to stay busy to remain sharp, to have the opportunity to headline, and (of course) to make more money.

It was the rock club in the area, and they were the headliner. As luck (and hard work) would have it, EVICK was booked as the opener. I was thrilled. Not one to pass up an opportunity to meet guys I looked up to, I arrived early and did a little hanging out with the band.

Dude…Andy Timmons was so damn nice. I don't know if he completely understood how big of a deal it was for me to meet him, but I don't think it would have mattered anyway. He's that nice of a guy. Before the show, Andy let me hang out on the bus.

And let me say, most bands are somewhat protective of their tour bus. Yeah, you hear stories of wild parties and sexcapades happening in the "back of the bus," but it is also their home away from home. They need to cordon off a little space to relax and unwind away from the public eye.

I told you that to say this. I was still young and new enough that I had never been on a tour bus. I had seen them, of course, but would never have been brazen enough to ask any of the other musicians to step aboard and look around.

But that's exactly what happened with Andy. We got to talking and he invited me onto Danger Danger's bus to see one of his guitars. To a young Pete Evick, it was like getting invited into the personal residence part of The White House.

In my defense, I'm just like every person you pay money to see on stage. Every one of them was a fan before they were successful.

Soon thereafter, I was playing my guitar backstage with Andy. He was showing me how to play some of the more complicated riffs in their library, and I was eating it up. At some point, Bruno sat down with us and had a nice conversation with me. We talked about the business, about music, about whatever.

I remember asking him (half kidding) at one point, "Hey buddy…why are you being so cool to me? Like, nobody is ever that cool to the little local openers."

He smiled and said, "Be nice on the way up because you're going to see them on the way down."

Let's cut away to a similar scene, years later.

There we were again: EVICK was opening for Danger Danger at Jaxx (same club I wrote about in an earlier chapter).

Anyway, Bruno is a bassist by trade. At some point before the gig, Bruno realized that he was having trouble with his bass amp. Not to be dissuaded, he approached me about it.

He let me know about the amp trouble, and I immediately offered for him to use our bass amp. To me, it was a no-brainer. I don't remember even having to think about the offer—I just made it without hesitation.

To Bruno, it *was* a big deal. Most touring musicians are total geeks when it comes to equipment, and we treat our gear like members of our family.

He plugged into our amp and got himself straight and settled. Then he sought me out to say two little words.

"Told ya."

We hadn't spent one second talking about the past. He had a problem, and I had a solution—end of story. But he remembered telling me that he was nice on the way up because he'd see me on the way down…and he was right. Not to say he was on the way down, but it was during that era where guitar driven melodic rock wasn't exactly *en vogue*.

I had to stop and laugh. It was one of those moments that everything in the background fades away and life becomes clear.

I don't see or talk to Bruno very often these days. But if I happen to have a conversation with Steve West, who I do run into from time to time, he'll always say, "Hey man, Bruno says hi…he sends his love."

Kindness goes a long way in this dark, shitty, evil-run business. Be kind. Put out good energy and the universe will return good energy.

Bill Leverty

Fans of the genre surely know the band Firehouse. From their double-platinum debut album to their top ten hits, to their ballads—they made great music in late 80s, early 90s. All their hits were written or co-written by Bill and Firehouse's front man, CJ Snare. As a creative duo, they were awesome.

From my perspective, Bill is a homeboy OG. We're both from Virginia, so grew up in basically the same music scene. He currently resides in Richmond and I'm in the DC area, but we have stayed in touch over the years.

But, like the Bruno Ravel/Andy Timmons story, EVICK opened for Firehouse at the same rock club (Jaxx) where we opened for Danger Danger. Crazy, hey?

And, like the Bruno Ravel story, Bill had trouble with his gear. His foot switch was fucked up. Clearly frustrated, he had his tech Jon Stensland, approach me.

I'm the same guy I've always been. I let him use my gear without thinking twice. He was so cool and so grateful and so thankful; we struck up a bit of a friendship. We've been buddies ever since.

When I got into Bret's band, Firehouse played with us more times than I can count.

Anyway, and I hate to jinx him like this, but TWICE the airlines lost Bill's guitars on his way to play shows with us. And again, with our relative roles reversed, he approached me, "Oh man…can I play your guitar?"

Let me tell you, that's a *weird* thing for a guitar player to ask or hear. I've talked about how the bus is sacred space and how our gear is like family—but my *guitar*. A guitar player's guitar is about the most personal thing we own. It would be like asking to wear someone else's shoes on stage. You'd be like, "*What?!?*"

Bill knew how big of an ask this was, but he had no choice. Both times, I said yes without missing a beat.

Since that day, our friendship grew and grew. We kept in touch more often. And I will say this: if I walked away from the music industry today, Bill and I would still be friends. It's probably the same for anyone—that you have friends at work who are just your "work friends" and friends outside of work who are your "real friends." Music is no different. We are all friendly to most of the guys on the road and catch up when we get a chance to sit around and party with. But when it comes to friendship—to actually calling someone to see how they're doing—those people are far rarer.

Bill is one of those guys for me. We talk all the time about whatever nonsense we've got going on. Not to mention, we're both uber nerds when it comes to gear. We will geek out on gear chat for long lengths of time. He loves to produce records and I do too. He's world-class…and I have learned a lot from him.

And it all started with simple acts of kindness.

Define "success"carefully

The drive I mentioned in the previous section—that burning desire to do whatever it takes and never leave a crumb on the table—can completely consume and burn out a musician if he or she isn't careful. The way my brain works, I don't think I could have rested if I had never reached the level I am at today. For better or for worse, that seed planted by MTV had grown into a mighty oak tree of vacuous desire for me. I didn't just want to reach MTV level—I *needed* to reach MTV level.

Along the way, I didn't realize how damaging this desire had been for me.

I missed out on a lot. Being on the road cost me time at home. It stressed my marriage (which ended) and took me away from opportunities with my kids. It amped up my anxiety and has (no doubt) eroded my physical health.

All this came into sharp focus when a buddy rang me up a few years ago. He invited me to a bar-b-cue at his house, and thought he could lure me in by using the following line:

"Don't worry about it…nobody will treat you like a rock star. Nobody will know who you are."

And I remember thinking, *Well…that sucks*. I had worked my whole life to become a rock star, why the heck would I shy away from having people recognize that?

I have been recognized out of context many times over the past twenty years. Playing in Bret's band has certainly been the catalyst that makes it possible. It's humbling and pretty awesome, if I do say so myself.

There have been some doozy stories. Like, I was swimming in my neighborhood pool one day. It was the middle of the day in the middle of the week. Having bad anxiety means that I try to venture out in public when there is the lowest chance of interacting with other people. So in order to go to the pool, I have to do it at 11 in the morning on a Tuesday.

Anyway, I was swimming along and came up for air in the corner of the pool. As I wiped the water from my eyes, I saw a pair of feet inches from my face. I looked up, and there was a woman looking down at me.

"You're Pete from Bret Michaels's band, aren't you?" Her name is Amy Sikes, and since that day she and her husband have been great friends to me.

I thought it was pretty cool. But this was in my own hometown and around my own people, so it made a certain amount of sense. However, then there are the moments that happened completely out of any context whatsoever.

Like, I remember vacationing years ago in the outer banks of North Carolina. If you've never been there, it's the greatest place in the U.S., other than maybe Arizona. When you're there, you feel relaxed because that area is a throwback to a simpler time. It's like people live an "old" way of life…where the things that matter the most are their beaches, their fish, and the sea.

Anyway, I was walking out of a Food Lion grocery store with my kids, and a woman chased me down in the parking lot. She said,

"Hey, hey hey…you're on *Rock of Love* with Bret Michaels, aren't you?"

That one was actually a very cool moment for me because my kids were there. My younger son was too young to know what I did for a living, but my older son was at an age where he knew but it was hard for him to really understand what I did. To him, people like Miley Cyrus lived in Los Angeles. We lived in Manassas…and I was no Miley Cyrus. **I use that as an example because Gavin was very aware of who she was via the Disney channel.

In fact (indulge me one more story), his teacher called me one day because she was concerned about my son. It seemed he told the class that his dad was in a band with Bret Michaels and toured the world. In a nutshell, she figured he was lying to cover up for God-knows-what issue he was having at home.

I corrected her, "No, no…he's telling the truth."

I suppose it's difficult for anyone in the area I live in to wrap their head around what I do, since it is primarily a government and IT-driven area. And I love to get those little reminders of my success.

But then it dawned on me. Did that make me a narcissistic ego-manic? Did my singular focus on becoming "MTV successful" mean that I had narrowed my priorities until they encompassed nothing except myself and my desire?

That didn't sound like the me I used to know.

On the other hand, I felt completely justified wanting to be recognized. I had sacrificed too much to not want this. I had given blood, sweat, and tears. I had poured every dime I had ever made (and a lot of other people's dimes) into my career. I had slept on dirt floors and allowed myself to be treated like shit for most of my musical life—I DESERVE THIS!

I want the whole fuckin' world to know who I am!

Oh my God…I *am* a narcissistic egomaniac.

Never being satisfied in your career translates to never being satisfied with who you are as a person. And when you are not satisfied with who you are as a person, it is difficult to let other people close to you—because you feel you have very little to offer until you reach whatever place you feel defines "success."

The phone call from Gavin's school made me sit back and

rethink how I felt about myself and my life. I realized that if I had never met Bret Michaels, I had *still* reached a plateau many musicians would have loved to achieve. I *did* have a record deal. I *was* playing to big crowds. I wrote and recorded really good music (well, I LIKED IT).

And bottom line, I was making a nice living in the music industry.

A lot of folks—who are probably way better human beings than me—make a good living playing music. They are men and women you have never heard of. Their bands have names you might only run across in your "recommended friends" section of Facebook. But they get out there, night after night, and love what they do. At the end of the show, they go home to their families and feel good knowing they are taking care of what needs to be done for the people around them.

Not to mention, there are people who work in other corners of the industry. These are the people who work in production or management or graphic design. They might love their careers and wake up excited to go to work every day.

They are satisfied with themselves and their lives.

Wanting to be "MTV famous" is like aiming at a pinhole in the giant universe of possibilities.

Would all those other folks love to be Ace Frehley or C.C. Deville or Eddie Van Halen? Or for the support staff, would they love to work with clients or artists who operate at that level? Probably…of course they would. But they don't *have* to be. They play the hand they're dealt and are proud of it.

I'm not saying that you shouldn't think of yourself or your career as a work in progress. We are all capable of changing for the better. Rather, I am saying that we should also enjoy who we are and where we're at.

Take a minute and smell the roses, you know?

MTV seems to have corrupted that hidden file on my hard drive. And I've had opportunities to be happy and enjoy my success a few times along the way. I feel grief nowadays, when I look back at the moments I squandered because they didn't make me MTV famous. I call these moments "Arenas or Failure." Because for the longest time, if it wasn't playing an arena, I considered myself a failure.

My message to all of you: every job in the music industry is important and can bring you a sense of fulfillment if you allow yourself to appreciate what you've got and what you're doing.

Odd Jobs

For a very short time, I worked in a record store as a kid. To my impressionable MTV brain, that wasn't a part of the music industry. That was a job I took to make some pocket money and get the inside track on new releases and cut-outs.

On the surface, that's true. You don't even have to like music to work in a record store. I personally don't know why you would if you didn't like music, but it's just pushing buttons and stocking shelves. If someone comes to you with a more complex compare/contrast question, you can always refer that customer to one of the hardcore music fans…like me.

And that was the point. I was in the music industry because I was immersing myself in the other end of the musical pool. Deep cuts, up-and-coming bands, and B-sides were now at my fingertips. I could spin them over the overhead speakers, or I could bury myself in the liner notes. My encyclopedia of music knowledge expanded beyond whatever singles we heard on the radio.

Oh—and we were the tail-end of the machine that makes sure the artists get paid. Mucho important back then…despite being almost nonexistent today.

Then I went to Music City, a musical instrument store. I wrote a lot about the owner and manager of this store in my first book. These guys were father figures and teachers to me. They gave me insight that I carry with me today. Then I went to Melodee Music in sterling Virginia, another musical instrument store Again a whole new set of lessons and a whole new group of people that became family to this day.

From there, I started to teach guitar lessons. I really enjoyed teaching guitar. Eventually, I expanded to teach piano and vocals as well. Not only a great way to pay the bills, but teaching is also a great way to foster a deeper appreciation of music in the students.

For some of the students, I (as their teacher) might be the person who makes or breaks their love of music. Great teachers motivate and inspire while they teach.

If that doesn't define an important job in the music industry, I don't know what does. A lot of folks make their living as instructors. More power to them.

Alas, my brain couldn't feel satisfaction with that role. I always battled a nagging string of intrusive negative thoughts.

What am I doing? I'm wasting my time.

I should be working on my stage show.

I need to be writing a hit song.

I led myself to believe I was in no way working toward being successful. But now I look at it this way: A music teacher can make $75 (USD) per 30-minute lesson. At $150 per hour, even working a mere 20 hours per week (or a little less), that comes to well over $100,000 per year.

Not too shabby…unless you can only define success as being "MTV Success." I was constantly disenchanted; even when I did something ground-breaking and (frankly) revolutionary.

The Tip of the Spear

When I was 25 years old, I was offered a job by a company called Z Tango. That company, and my position in particular, changed the telecommunications industry. Don't get too impressed—I didn't sit in on the invention of streaming or the engineering of 5G. Instead, I was asked to do something nobody in the United States had ever done before—but many people have done since.

I was the first person in the United States to be hired by a telecom company to develop ringtones for cell phones. Up to that point, phones just rang with a monotonous beep-beep-beep (you'd recognize the patter if you heard it). One of the people at that company decided that ringtones should be made more interesting and personal. So, they hired me.

Full disclosure, I did not want the job. I still harbored the "Arenas or failure" mindset and felt this would be treading water instead of swimming forward in my career.

Or maybe more accurately, this would be *drowning* rather than swimming forward in my career.

But I had to do it. I had to take the job. I had a baby on the way and a mortgage at the time. I needed a steady income. The company offered me $56,000 plus benefits (health insurance, vacation days, etc.).

Most of the days blurred into each other, but I distinctly remember building a ringtone based on the song "Last Resort" by Papa Roach. The guitar riff on that song is iconic. Give it a quick listen on YouTube. Within the first thirty seconds, you'll be like, "Oh yeah! *That* song!"

That ringtone did give me a bit of a professional thrill because it ended up in a commercial for AT&T. In my brain, that was like a hit song. Even though I didn't write the original riff, I did build the ringtone from the ground up.

In hindsight, I get it. I was a pioneer. I was one of the first people to marry the music industry with the telecommunications sector. Similar efforts were taking place in European countries, but in the U.S., *I was the guy*.

I made ringtones for AT&T (as mentioned) and Verizon. My tones were also purchased by a Canadian telecom company called Rogers Communications, Inc. The company I worked for was growing by leaps and bounds and I was there on the ground floor. It was eventually purchased by RealNetworks, a company that was on the vanguard of streaming technology. Originally named Progressive Networks, they made several versions of RealPlayer, a software package you almost certainly had on your computer back in the early to mid-2000s.

Throughout my tenure with Z Tango, I was working hard in the telecom industry. I should have been on top of the world, right? I mean, Bill Gates and Mark Zuckerberg seem to have done okay for themselves in the world of evolving technology.

But I slogged through that job, depressed. I wasn't "in the music business." It was one of the darkest runs I have ever had in my life. I couldn't stand myself, I couldn't stand my life, and I felt like I had betrayed everything and everyone who had ever believed in me. If the CEO, Vern Poyner, and the rest of the original crew weren't such cool people, I would have probably killed myself. It was exciting to have friends outside the music industry, and they were all great people, most of whom I still talk to today.

It got to where I thought my mom was haunting me because I was a failure. She had passed away just prior to my taking this job. She spent my entire life sacrificing anything to give me the opportunity to make it in the music business. She believed in me above and beyond any belief I have ever felt from another human being.

She is the one who told me to never give myself a fallback plan. If I wanted to make it in the music business, I should structure my life so that I had no choice *but* to make it. As a result, I felt that I was a complete disappointment to her. In fact, I was so embarrassed about that telecom job, that I would never even bring it up to the people around me when I would go play bars or clubs, which I was still doing several nights a week. I would tell them I didn't have any other job. Because that's what my mom told me to do—to never settle for anything less.

To that extent, I had failed miserably. I had taken a job that stole my focus and energy from the one thing I had to be: MTV Famous. I felt like I was nowhere near the industry…and floating further with each passing day.

But that's the ironic thing—I *was* making it in the music industry. I just wasn't in the MTV Famous part of it. Once again, I envy the folks who can take pride and satisfaction while working in other facets of the industry. I wish I had been wired that way. My life and my family might have turned out differently.

Not that I dislike my life or my family—that is absolutely not true. But I could have caused a lot less stress and pain to the people I love had I been a guy who wasn't corrupted by the insidious demand of becoming MTV famous.

I wasted all that time and all that emotional energy. Now that I've played arenas and made it to the level I had wanted, I look back and feel awful that I put myself and my family through the roller coaster of my despair and self-loathing. Let me be clear, I never feel bad for following my dream. I feel bad about my bad attitude when I thought it was never going to happen.

* * *

There are so many opportunities to make a good living in the music industry—and ways that have nothing to do with ever playing a note or writing a piece of music. Sales, marketing, production… how many people are listed and/or thanked in an album's liner notes? How many are listed at the end credits of a movie, as the soundtrack tunes are scrolled? How many work to build or sell the musical instruments themselves? How many work at the venues and clubs and the music stores around the world?

Hundreds of thousands, that's how many.

Every single one of them has an opportunity to feel good about their contribution to keeping the music industry alive. Even working as a professional musician, you can play enough to keep the bills paid and the money coming in. There are literally *thousands* of people doing that successfully right now.

I'm proud of who I am and what I've done. It took me way too long to "get it."

CHAPTER 13:
SUCCESS REFLECTED FROM SUCCESSFUL PEOPLE

As was mentioned WAY earlier in this book, I was born in the poorest part of Manassas, Virginia. Most of the kids in my neighborhood went to a nearby school. However, the cul-de-sac I lived on was inexplicably zoned for a school across town—a school that was populated by kids from the other part of town. It was the side of the town where the grass was always lush and green.

During my younger years, I was aware of this disparity. I never had the coolest shoes or clothes the other kids had. I would constantly fight—many times literally—to keep up with the Joneses.

To this day, I *hate* the concept of keeping up with the Joneses. Thank God for the guitar. It became the great equalizer. All the well-off kids would come to my house to watch me play guitar. They wanted to hang out; or if they played an instrument, they wanted to jam. I never felt as though I was better than anyone. Rather, I was doing something they thought was cool.

With music as my ally, I never had a problem with self-esteem. I wouldn't hesitate to ask out the prettiest girl in school. Chicks dig a rock and roll rebel, man.

But the other pendulum my school years put into motion was more subtle. It is one that still occasionally makes me feel like I am somehow "less than" the people around me. Don't get me wrong—when it comes to playing guitar, I am still a pretty confident cat. I'm not the most competitive guy in the world, but when I walk off stage, nothing gives me more satisfaction than knowing somebody is looking at me and thinking, "Holy shit—I didn't know he could play like that!"

In those moments, my sense of success comes from what gets reflected to me from the people around me.

So, I know my way around the fret board. But when I am around musicians who I perceive as having "made it," I suddenly feel like a Mustang in a line of Bentleys. Somebody installed a little voice in my head that is constantly whispering, "You're not one of them…they know something you don't know…you're an outsider…they'll never tell you what they know…"

Getting asked to join Bret's band did wonders for my self-image. I knew I was good enough to be in the same room with these guys, but never felt like I was as good as them.

And add that to the fact that I spend too many hours of my life agonizing over how to manage my crippling anxiety. The anxiety doesn't keep me from living my life (obviously), but it ebbs to a nearly debilitating level at times. I wake up almost every morning feeling like I'm having a heart attack.

Seriously.

Panic attacks are a bitch, man. My mind wakes up, and the switchboard between my ears lights up with an immediate barrage of everything I need to get done that day, the knowledge that there is no way I will ever get everything done that day, and the panic of trying to reconcile those two thoughts.

With all the nervousness and self-doubt swirling in the background, it is with great humility that I can point to a handful of moments—and I mean they are literally moments—when that little voice was quieted. Let's be clear: during these moments, that little voice wasn't just quieted…it was wrapped in barbed wire and tossed over the side of a boat.

Telling the stories surrounding these moments makes me extremely happy. They are the moments that made me feel as if I had finally made it; when I felt like I was a part of the "in crowd" with my rock and roll heroes.

This chapter is going to make it seem as if I'm name-dropping—but that's the point. These stories all involve people I have admired for almost my entire life. And now they are returning a little of that love…reflecting it like a self-esteem-building funhouse mirror.

Ain't nothing better.

* * *

Bret Michaels

Yes, the first story involves Bret Michaels.

We were in the studio and laying down some tracks for a record we were making. I can't remember what exactly I was trying to do, but I had my mind set on writing a lick that would sound like something Eddie Van Halen would play.

Bret watched patiently while I struggled and tried to emulate Eddie and channel the single greatest guitar player of all time, space, and dimension.

The session dragged on and on. I kept trying to create the damn lick and kept explaining to Bret what I was trying to do. I can't imagine how annoying I must have been because I would *not* shut up about it.

In case you haven't figured it out yet, EVH is my favorite guitar player.

Finally, Bret had had enough. He sat forward in his chair and said, "Hey—if I wanted Eddie Van Halen to play on this record, I'd hire Eddie Van Halen. I want *you* to sound like *you*."

He wasn't kidding. Bret had known Eddie and certainly had the money to hire anyone he wanted. That's what made this moment so jaw-dropping for me. He wanted ME, and my style on his song.

If I could bottle and preserve an instant of my musical life, it would be this one. It will never leave my brain. Bret Michaels, one of my rock and roll heroes, was choosing me over Eddie Van Halen, a man whose guitar walks on water. Again, I know it wasn't like me and Eddie were standing there, and he pointed at me instead of Eddie. But… when your heart needs a little boost, your brain can twist things just enough to help your ego!

In that split second, there was no denying that I had made it. I was kissed into The Club and was now a patched-in member of the rock and roll club.

Alas, that feeling never lasts long. I don't know why I keep needing reminders, but I do. My confidence fades and I return to the rank of "outsider."

The next story comes about several years later.

Sammy Hagar

I alluded to this story back in chapter ten. If you recall, I said that Sammy Hagar sent Bret a text message about me. Seeing as how this is the chapter about other people's words pumping my self-esteem, the exact transcript of that text message seemed to fit better right here.

I'll re-set the table for you. On this night, we were at a Sammy Hagar show in Las Vegas. The wealthy corporate executive hired us to play a few songs with Sammy.

So, we did. Bret and I joined The Red Rocker for a few songs. I got to play Sammy's guitar. The crowd of partying corporate types went into an absolute frenzy. What a scene—these men and women are probably "button-down conservative" regarding demeanor…and yet here they were, raising hell and having a fucking fantastic time. It is mind-boggling how much sheer talent those two guys have when it comes to being the perfect front men.

We did our thing and left, which was the plan. In fact, that night could have faded into being just one of thousands of live shows I have played. It was cool to play with Hagar…but that night stands out from the rest because of one brief text message.

Later that night, Sammy sent Bret a text that read, "You tell Pete that anytime, anywhere he is welcome on stage with me."

Can you imagine?

Sammy Hagar thinks I'm good enough!

In fact, Sammy Hagar *and* Bret Michaels think I'm good enough.

Dee Snider

Here is the full story behind the other cool moment I portended in chapter ten: the one with Dee Snider. The punch line to this story involves another text message from another rock and roll legend. My self-esteem soared once again.

Twisted Sister was the first concert I ever saw in my life. I probably looked like a zygote in the crowd; a fourteen-year-old, smooth-faced cherub belting out the lyrics, flashing devil's horns with my fingers, and losing my ever-loving mind. Believe it or not, there was a time in my life when Twisted Sister was as big as Van Halen to me. Never bigger…but just as important and influential to my upbringing as an aspiring axe man.

I told you that so you can appreciate how big of a deal it was when Dee Snider (front man for Twisted Sister) hired me to be the musical director (MD) for an event he was hosting, and for me to bring my band up to be HIS band.

*This opportunity would have never happened without my close friend and rock and roll brother, Danny Stanton.

Dee was hosting his annual Dee Snider's Ride, a motorcycle extravaganza where riders take to the streets and raise money for charity. Dee is an avid biker and has raised an amazing amount of money since the ride first began in 2004. As a part of the event, he has live music. Riders arrive at the destination and eat and drink and dance the day and night away.

I thought we were fantastic that day. Even cooler, Dee came on stage and fronted the band for a set of Twisted Sister songs. How cool is that? I was on stage with the first singer I had ever seen with my own two eyes in an arena playing loud rock and roll.

I was on stage with Dee Snider, but that wasn't even the best part. The best part was a text conversation he and I had the following day. I'll never forget what he wrote:

"Bottom line, you kicked ass. You rocked it."

I remember that being another one of those simple moments that made me feel like I was truly a professional now. I was being respected amongst the very people that had influenced me to take this journey.

Eric Brittingham

Most of the 80s rock scene was defined by the Sunset Strip bands flooding onto the stages at the Whiskey a Go Go, The Viper Room, The Roxy Theater, and The Rainbow Bar and Grill.

But while all that was going down, another legion of rock bands were coming out of the east coast. Bands like Kix, Extreme, and Firehouse dotted the rock landscape.

Arguably the biggest band to come out of the east coast during this era was Bon Jovi. Jon had an enormous influence during the 80s, and ushered in two bands that went on to have GREAT careers, Skid Row…and Cinderella.

Eric Brittingham was (and still is) Cinderella's bass player. He has also played on many other projects that have taken him all over the world. In a somewhat ironic twist, he filled in (briefly) for Bobby Dall during Poison's 2009 tour.

Anyway, the front man for Cinderella, Tom Keifer, has one of the most recognizable voices in the genre. Love it or hate it, you have to respect his raspy timbre and the amazing vocal range. I personally love it.

I had known Eric for a long time. When our current bass player in the Bret Michaels Band was leaving the band due to a family medical situation, we brought in Eric. He and I got along great and became fast friends.

So much so, that he and I ended up forming a band called This, That, and The Other. Nothing serious…we played a few dates (when Bret was with Poison or filming TV shows) and had a lot of fun. We hung out a good bit during that time, and occasionally would talk about how difficult it was for vocalists to sing Cinderella songs.

Tom Keifer's voice is NOT easy to reproduce.

Not one to back down from a challenge, I figured we could do three Cinderella songs in our This That… set. As a reminder, I am the lead vocalist.

We rehearsed the songs and performed them live—with Eric's blessing. Just the fact that Eric felt I was good enough to sing those songs was a tremendous honor for me.

That band, by the way, also played in a benefit thrown by an incredible friend of mine, Bruce Sisk. It was hosted by Eddie Trunk. Eddie is one of the most knowledgeable and influential rock journalists in America. He knows everyone and everything in the industry and hosts a major show airing on two SiriusXM channels.

After we did our set at the benefit, I came off stage and was approached by Eddie. We had known each other for well over a decade.

He met my eyes and said, "Pete, you've still got your voice, man. Your chops are still great. And you're such a *good* front man."

I was taken aback. This was the ultimate high praise form a guy who will shoot straight and tell it like it is. I didn't know what to say, but that didn't stop me.

"Thanks, man! I have spent the last fifteen years playing next to the best front man in the business. If I *wasn't* a good front man by now, there would be something seriously fuckin' wrong."

Between Eric and Eddie, my spirits were soaring. Here was more evidence that I had transcended that kid playing chords over and over in his bedroom during middle school. It has been hard to completely internalize, but I cling to these moments and these stories when I am filled with self-doubt.

Before I leave this Cinderella segment completely, I have to give a shout out to Jeff LaBar, their lead guitarist. Sadly, Jeff passed away in July of 2021. He was the definition of rock and roll.

Jeff was a supporter of mine. I remember being the "new kid in town" and playing the Wild Horse Saloon in Nashville. I could look down at any time and see Jeff in the crowd, screaming my name, cheering me on (as usual) and having a great time. I'm sure he did that for everyone…he loved music. But it meant the world to me that night.

And to tie this all together, he and Eric took a liking to me when I first joined Bret's band. They were always extremely kind to me. Most professional musicians are nice…but remain somewhat distant. But then there are the noteworthy few that rise above the rest in their kindness and generosity. Jeff and Eric belong to that group. I will always owe them a debt of gratitude.

The final example I will write about moves us forward in the musical timeline but has been just as impactful to me.

Mark McGrath

Obviously, one of the biggest bands to come out of the late 90s and early 2000s was Sugar Ray. Their 1999 album, *14:59*, went triple platinum and spun off two *Billboard* Hot 100 top 10 hits, "Every Morning" and "Someday". To say I was a fan would be an understatement.

Bret had always had this amazing concept for (what is now

known) as the Party Gras Festival. In fact, we are going out in the Live Nation sheds with it in 2023 and the buzz is huge. Bret's vision is unique: Instead of having opening acts, keep one continuous set of hit music going while interchanging singers.

We have done this twice in the past with Mark McGrath. So as Bret's music director, I also become Mark's music director for his portion of the show.

Mark does several events annually where he is hired to sit in with other bands and play his songs. On the first day we did this, Mark arrived, and we went into the dressing room—where we began to rehearse the songs with him.

We counted in the first song, and Mark's eyes lit up.

"Holy shit! You guys…you really know this stuff. You really did the work and can play these songs."

I don't know if he had been through bad experiences in the past with this kind of thing. None of that mattered. His excitement over how prepared we were and how well we performed his songs spoke to how professionally he viewed the band. It was another moment where I felt like I did something right.

I came very close to feeling like I deserved his praise.

Mark McGrath, man…what a super cool dude.

* * *

It might seem that I wrote this chapter to toot my own horn. But I assure you, I am not that guy. I don't want you to like me because of who I know or who knows me. I would much rather earn your respect through my music or my personality.

The reason I wrote this chapter was more to help you realize that you can help yourself when you are feeling down or feeling insecure. Instead of focusing on what you might have done wrong or on the things you are not good at (or comfortable doing), focus instead on the times when you have received praise by somebody who really means it. Or perhaps focus on the praise you have received from somebody you really respect. A person who tells the truth and takes a shine to you.

Those moments are back there. You may forget them because they are buried under a pile of negativity or self-doubt. You may over-emphasize a criticism you received and completely pass over the praise. Like, in a room of 100 people—99 of whom really like you—do you hyper-focus on the ONE person who thinks you're a hack?

I totally get it…I'm that way too. Which is why I lean so heavily on the stories I just wrote. Sometimes I need to literally force myself to recall the Sammy Hagars and Dee Sniders and Eric Brittinghams and Mark McGraths in my life. And Bret Michaels, who is the sole reason any of this happened. Without them, I don't know if I would ever be able to get out of my own way.

Find those people in your life and hang with them. There's enough negativity out there if you want to find it—search instead for the positives. Keep people in your life who are good for *you*.

CHAPTER 14: COMMANDMENTS FROM ROCK AND ROLL MOUNT SINAI

I am going to finish the book by writing about the walk-and-talk I had with Bret in Nashville. I opened the book with an excerpt from the story, and I will close the loop here. Mostly, the chat was about what it takes to make it in the music industry. Before I get to my talk with Bret, let me first tell you about two examples of the earliest "advice" that resonated with me and my desire to play music as a fulfilling career.

* * *

Bob Seger

I was a younger-ish Pete Evick (who didn't yet refer to himself in the third person) when I saw Bob Seger sit down for an interview on television. I don't recall the show or the year, but one thing he said made so much sense to me, it changed how I focused my drive to become a professional musician.

During the broadcast, the interviewer asked Bob a question that was probably a little bit insulting. He mentioned that Bob didn't "look" like any of his rock star contemporaries—he wasn't a sex symbol. Therefore, to what do you credit your massive success?

Bob took it in stride and replied, "I showed up."

I know it sounds overly simplistic, but everything changed for me in that moment.

When you are a big fish in a little pond—like, if you're the top band coming out of Manassas, Virginia—you get wrapped up in the heat of being number 1. You begin to grow spoiled, demanding only to play a certain club on a certain night in a certain time slot.

You are a local celebrity, getting recognized by someone every time you walk into 7-11 to grab a Slurpee.

Lost in that shuffle of self-aggrandizing baloney is the desire to get out of your comfort zone. But that was a problem—and that's what Bob Seger taught me.

Following that interview, I called every agent I knew and told them to book me into anything they could. I didn't care if it was a Laundromat at noon on a Monday—if they had a stage and an open slot, I wanted to be there.

Bob Seger taught me to get out and play. Show up—anywhere and everywhere. Grow your audience and get repetitions working your craft. Get paid what you are worth, but get out there and get after it.

I don't know if that's what Bob intended when he said, "I showed up," but that's what I heard. And because of his advice, I entered a space that not many artists go into. I was signed to a record deal because of the original music I was able to produce, but I was also gigging heavy as a cover artist. I placed a foot firmly in both worlds.

As I mentioned in an earlier chapter, I remember disagreeing with the label about that—they wanted me to pare back and focus my time and energy on clubs that boasted all original music. But I wanted to play as much as possible, which meant doing a lot of cover gigs.

In fact, I'll remind you again of a club I mentioned earlier, in Panama City Beach, Florida, Club La Vela. Back in the day, they did the unthinkable: They paid acts to play seven nights per week. And as you can guess, I hustled down to FLA and played seven nights per week.

It worked for me. Just show up, man.

John Mellencamp

In 1998, John Mellencamp was on an episode of the VH1 series, *Behind the Music*. I watched his episode like I watched every episode of that program: Glued to the TV, concentrating on any morsel of advice or guidance I could glean.

At one point, John was reflecting on his struggles to make it big in the early 80s. In fact, he framed it more as confusion than a struggle. He talked about how it vexed him (at the time) that he was not as big as the Beatles. He knew he had good songs; he knew he looked good…he had everything the Beatles had. So why wasn't he making it big?

As I watched, I was thinking, *Man…I will never be the Beatles*.

And at that moment, John Mellencamp said, "And then it hit me…I ain't the Beatles."

My brain turned upside down.

Suddenly, it all fell into place. I wasn't Kiss; I wasn't Van Halen. And I am never going to be.

I knew I had to get away from the notion that I had to be like somebody else. My takeaway from the VH1 show was that everyone who makes it big has to be *different*. Whether an individual artist or a full band, they have to somehow separate themselves from the pack and prove to the fans why they are worthy of maintaining a huge audience. If you're a band that is just like Van Halen, why would fans continue coming to your shows or buying your records when they can just as easily stick with Van Halen?

You might get some fans at first—especially if you're good at being like Van Halen—but the bands and artists with real staying power are those who are different from everyone else. Elvis Presley…The Beatles…Michael Jackson…Madonna…Van Halen… and (of course) Poison…they dug in and stayed the course, despite the entire world trying to force them into a more comfortable box. They were genuine, to the end.

Did I have the star power to do that? I didn't know. But I was going to figure it out. I didn't look terrible and had a record full of good songs. I had to discover what else I needed.

It'll take more than good songs and talent. John figured out what else it took because he made it to "Arena-level" big. A car needs more than a slick paint job and a bitchin' stereo to function as a car.

John Mellencamp went on to talk about how he learned to stop faking it. He wasn't getting anywhere trying to imitate other artists. He needed to drop that façade and be an original.

That has been my mantra ever since. I can't be in a grunge band because that's just not who I am. I've had opportunities, all of which I have politely declined. Nothing against that style of music… it just isn't going to come across as authentic if I play it. I've got to be true to who I am as a person and as a musician.

Love it or leave it, you've got "Pete Evick Authenticity" every time you meet me or see me perform.

Bret Michaels: Family, Focus, Follow-Up

"Listen, if we're really going to be a band, let's you and I go over some things…"

That statement began my conversation I had with Bret back in Nashville. It's the one I wrote about in the prologue. That two-hour conversation was a big deal to me because it led to three bolts of insight. It reconfigured how I thought about family, focus, and follow-up.

Family

As it pertains to "family," I would have never dreamt Bret would want me to be in a bona fide band with him. I figured the gig with Bret would last for a year—MAYBE two years—and then it would be over, and I would be back to hustling with EVICK.

On the one hand, being a member of a band would provide a stable income. I own a house and cover the expenses of being a single dad. I never miss a payment when it comes to bills or child support. And as you can imagine, being a working musician means that I think of the concept "steady and predictable income" as describing the situation of other people.

Financial considerations aside, and far more importantly, there was also an emotional component for me. Being in "a band" meant being a part of a *family*. Loyalty is an important part of my personality—in fact, it might be the guiding principle that underscores most every decision I make. Loyalty toward my children, toward my family, toward my friends…I am the guy you can count on to have your back. Likewise, I am the guy you can call when things are good or bad—the guy who will fight your battle if you don't want to.

And now, Bret was inviting me into his inner circle…his "Circle of Trust," as Robert DeNiro coined in *Meet the Parents*. I was honored. But before I could take a minute and digest everything that was happening, he had many more things to tell me.

Focus

His voice shook me out of my reverie, as he shifted into the main topic of his agenda. He wanted to coach me up with regard to *focus*.

"I notice that you always know a lot about the other bands on the bill."

He was spot on, of course. Bret doesn't miss a thing.

I felt like an outsider when I first started to tour with Bret. To me, I was getting to hang out with my heroes when we were sharing the bill with the bands I loved and getting into the behind-the-scenes stuff with dudes I considered to be real rock stars.

But to Bret, that was all a distraction.

"You always know what songs made Warrant's set list or what Cyndi Lauper is going to wear on stage. I understand that we are all friends and love each other's music—but you need to let that stuff go and only worry about *your* band."

In a nutshell, Bret was telling me to stop filling my brain with fanfare nonsense. In fact, he said that the guys I was spending time learning about were absolutely NOT spending their time learning about me. They were focused on *them*…and I needed to focus on us.

Or occasionally I would say something like, "Did you hear about the back line malfunction KISS had during their show last night?"

Bret would just nod and say something to the effect of, "Yup…but their malfunction happened in front of 50,000 people—who all bought tickets to their show. I'd rather have a malfunction in front of 50,000 people than do the best set in the world in front of 500."

That is probably the most amazing truth ever spoken.

In other words, keep it simple. Focus on your band or your company or your product. Make sure you direct all your time and effort toward helping yourself and your team Stay away from the quicksand traps of gossip, idolatry, or the soul-sucking swamp of internet reviews.

I can't tell you how many hours I have wasted scrolling down, down…down. Burning away my life trying to figure out what everyone *else* is doing. That kind of mindlessness will cause your brain to atrophy.

His words switched on a light bulb in my head. He wasn't being mean—he was being a good leader and mentor. When Bret gives you feedback, he does it in a way that is meant to be constructive rather than destructive. To this day, I almost always leave a conversation with Bret feeling good about myself and better prepared for the future.

This time was no different. To be honest, once my eyes were opened, it was very easy to flip that switch internally. In an instant, I became better at being a professional.

I had spent my entire career thinking I *was* focused—because I always gave 100% of what I had to offer. But he was absolutely right. Too much of my hard drive was clogged with superfluous garbage that stole from my ability to pour all my heart and soul into my band. I was giving 100% of what I had—except some of that energy was flowing into unproductive channels.

As Yoda said in *The Empire Strikes Back*, "All his life he looked away…to the future, to the horizon. Never his mind on where he was…What he was doing."

In other words, don't spend your energy lamenting the past or worrying about the future. Help yourself by being laser-focused on the here and now. My kids probably cringe when they hear me say "laser focused." I've tried to teach this lesson so much.

Work smarter, not harder—right?

Bret is the personification of this advice. He is a caricature of focus and follow-through. And in that moment, it all made sense. *That* is what it takes to make it in this business. Heck, that's what it takes to make it in *any* business.

Attention to detail is critical. Every signpost has to point toward the direction of success. It gets down to the granular level, man. For example, Bret reminded me that whenever I step off the bus or step out of my hotel room, I must be "on." Not fake—that would never work for guys like Bret and myself. Rather, I needed to always be the best version of myself. There could be a fan waiting outside the bus or hotel…and this person might have stood there all day, waiting to meet the person they *hope* I am.

You never know who will be standing there.

I might be under the weather or I might have just had an argument with my girlfriend or I might be coming off a horrible night's sleep on a lumpy hotel mattress—but I represent the band and the band represents success. Always, and in every moment,

I had never looked at it this way. But for a guy like Bret, it has become a lifestyle.

Let me say that differently.

For a guy like Bret, it has *always been* his lifestyle. A lot of guys can sing and play guitar—but very few have the self-discipline and focused drive that he has. Some of it comes naturally to him; some of it has been cultivated throughout a lifetime of being a rock star.

I needed to hear that message. It helped me understand why I had worked so damn hard…yet continued to toil away along a frontage road instead of on the highway of big-time success.

I took in his words and digested them like a fine wine. They filled me with a smooth warmth and made me a little bit high. Focus on *my* band. Be the *best* version of me all the time. Concepts began to fall into place like tumblers in a lock.

Let me give you a longer but very specific example of the focus and attention to detail it takes to be on top.

* * *

When I got my first record deal in late 1997, it was with my band, Some Odd Reason. A label called Sol 3 Records signed us, and they really went out of their way to give us the tools we needed to succeed.

As mentioned in previous chapters, we were able to get a heavy hitter, Richard Gottehrer, to produce our first album, *To*

Whom It May Concern. Richard's credits are as long as your arm.

We also had Nelson Ayers and Michael Goldberg engineering and mixing the album. Michael was relatively new on the scene, but Nelson had worked with Faster Pussycat, Britny Fox, Skid Row, and Soundgarden (plus a host of other acts) by the time he worked with us.

The album came out in April 1998, and I think it's perfect to this day.

We struck out on tour to support the album, and things seemed like they were going well. We booked into 300-500 seat venues and were selling them out at 60-70% capacity. Seemed like a good plan…we had our sights set on building momentum and growing our fan base past our local market.

One day, my (now ex) father-in-law came to me with some advice. Bear in mind, I was NOT one to take music industry advice from anyone who doesn't own a guitar. I was a petulant young lad at the time.

Anyway, he came to me and said, "Listen, Pete…the band is great, the songs are great, I love what you're doing. But eventually, you have to pack the house."

I'll never forget him saying that to me.

Likewise, I will never forget my internal reaction: *What the fuck do you know?!?*

Of course I need to pack the house! I would have *loved* to get 500 people into the venues. Not to mention, I was doing everything in my power to pack those damn houses. I put flyers on car windows and light posts. I did interviews and promotions every chance I could. I gave 100% toward being a non-stop guerrilla marketing machine.

Fast forward to my early days with Bret.

I don't think he ever said this out loud, but I noticed right away that he did everything in his power to pack the houses. Except there was a big difference in his approach: He would play in venues he knew would be sell-out business.

In other words, the goal was always to take his solo band into sheds and arenas. Building a brand is like playing a video game: you have to conquer one level before you can advance to the next.

So, he started from scratch—as if Poison hadn't even existed. He played clubs (large clubs that were certainly *venues* and not bars). These were venues he could easily fill. Then he moved to theaters. As fans left the shows, they would generate a buzz about how packed the place was and how fun the show was and how they couldn't wait for Bret to come through town again.

My stubbornness (my ego?) led me to burn countless hours and untold amounts of energy in the wrong direction. Had we started small and built our fan base, we would have had a better chance to succeed. There were plenty of 50-to-150-seater all original music venues at the time, but I wanted to go straight to headlining the bigger venues in which I had spent so much time opening for my heroes.

Let me point out that this is an apples-to-oranges comparison. I'm not for one second comparing any of my bands and the venues we played to Bret's start of his solo career. I'm talking about playing 50-seaters instead of 500-seaters. His "small" venues were 1,500 seaters or more. Again, just trying to paint the picture of inspiration here.

Follow-up

Along those lines, Bret taught me about his relentless attention to detail and *follow-up*. To pack the house, fans don't just fall out of the sky and into their seats.

I had known that, of course. Otherwise, I wouldn't have tirelessly placed flyers around town. But I was missing the bigger picture. You must attack from all sides.

When Bret was doing (and coming off of) his massive television show, *Rock of Love*, his subsequent tour wasn't a slam dunk accidentally. He was a known quantity around the country because of his band, Poison, but now he was also the star of a record-breaking prime-time program on VH1.

Promoters these days can get lazy. They might figure they can take out a Facebook ad and 10,000 people would flock to the venue to see Bret in person.

But that's not how it works. People have a lot of options and a limited budget to go out to shows. There is intense competition for those fans.

So, Bret made sure that every base was covered and that a multi-pronged marketing campaign was launched ahead of the tour. And I've said it before: he is tireless when it comes to making sure everything is done right.

Like, when you purchase radio ads, you sort of take a leap of faith that your ads will really play. Unless you have a mole in the town you are about to play, you really have no way of knowing if your 35 spots actually made it onto the air. Bret taught me to do everything in my power to ensure the ads were produced properly, purchased properly, and placed properly.

It's a task that sounds Herculean because it is—but that's what separates the successful from the not successful. And that cemented the message Bret conveyed to me.

Since that day, I have been borderline psychotic with my insistence on follow-up. At least, that's how people make me feel.

It's funny—people really don't like it when you hold them accountable to do their job. Like, I will call a promoter and ask for receipts that show he or she has actually placed the ads or the radio spots they promised. I'm not trying to be a dick…I'm trying to follow-up and make sure there is no stone unturned.

Over the years, some people have gotten frustrated with me. As if it is a tremendous inconvenience for them to demonstrate they've done what they are supposed to do. But I stick to my guns. I follow up and follow through like a maniac. It may not be efficient, but it is effective.

Bret is the bull in a proverbial china shop…and so am I. It is the reality of owning a brand or a business: nobody is looking out for you like you look out for yourself. You have to give it 100%. And you manage the disappointment when other people do NOT give 100%.

That is a perfect segue into the final message I took from that walk-and-talk with Bret. And if I'm being completely honest with myself, this one was even more important to who I have become as a friend, a dad, an employer, and a band mate. In fact, this lesson might be the singular most critical insight I have ever reached as an adult.

* * *

You don't just make it to the top—you have to separate yourself in order to *stay* at the top. When you look at Bret Michaels, it's easy to fall into the trap of thinking that everything came easy for him. Good-looking guy, talented performer, catchy song writer, consummate front man…he's the total package for whom life accommodates. But that's not the case at all. Bret works his ass off every moment he's awake.

I told you that because I have always been that same kind of guy, I work my ass off every moment I'm awake. But when I compare myself to Bret, I am humbled. It's like I'm giving 100%, but he's giving 150%.

I'm no math whiz, but even *I* know that isn't possible.

Or is it?

Sadly, no.

And that is where the lesson lies for me. This was a big one: Not everybody's 100% is the same.

Dude…I so wish I had figured that out decades ago. I remember putting bands together when I was a teenager. I would lose my mind and kick guys out of the band because I couldn't figure out why they weren't willing to do as much as me. In my twisted brain, the difference in our output represented a difference in commitment. Ergo, if I was doing more than they were, I was more committed to our success than them.

Or to put it in the negative, their lower output meant they *weren't* committed to the band. I didn't want to work with guys who didn't share my passion, so they were removed and replaced with a new guy.

I'm a little bit embarrassed when I think back upon some of my ideas and behaviors. I must have been seen as quite the asshole to an outside observer. But here's the thing that was so confusing: when I would talk with the guys who I viewed as having a lesser drive than me, they would always tell me they were giving it all they had. At the time I didn't believe them—they must have been leaving something on the table. Otherwise, they would be whirling dervishes like I was. I kept getting angrier and angrier and angrier.

As I analyze the situation today, with my 49-year-old brain instead of my seventeen-year-old brain, I recognize that their perceptions might have been true. It is totally possible they were giving me everything they had—except their 100% didn't match my 100%. Everyone is different, man. I had to evolve to the point of being able to accept that.

Looking at Bret, I could easily feel inadequate because he gets out there and kills it in a way I could never match. And it's not like I'm holding anything back—I'm giving it everything I've got.

My 100% doesn't match Bret's 100%.

And the thing that's so amazing to me is, he doesn't judge me for that. I never feel that I have let him down or that he questions my total commitment to everything we do as a band. Sure, I constantly *worry* that I am letting him down or disappointing him, but that's just me. My anxiety can look at any silver cloud and find a grey lining.

I'll take a moment to add that this revelation doesn't just affect my life in the music industry. Understanding that everyone can have a different 100% has made me a better manager and business partner.

When I look at my evolution with Shining Sol, my candle company, I see myself developing into a much more effective leader. It's not about chastising people for not doing things as well or as thoroughly or as quickly as I think they should happen—rather, it's about motivating people to be their best through supporting and encouraging their best performance.

It might be an old cliché that I brought up a few minutes ago, but the following idea is apt for this lesson: Not even the best employee cares about the company as much as the boss. The sooner a business owner can accept that notion, the better off everyone is going to be. It will drive the owner insane if he or she continues to beat their head against a wall to get everyone to hustle like they hustle. Instead, they must recognize people for who they are—folks with families and stresses and lives outside of the business. Your employees might give it all they've got when they are at work, but work is merely a *part* of their life…not something that consumes their life.

As the owner, I am consumed with Shining Sol. I want it to

be the best candle company in the world. I'll tell you this: it is my *favorite* candle company in the world. If you are producing a product or service that isn't your favorite—then why are you even doing it in the first place? Your product has got to make you happy, man. Mine does. I might be weird in the way I think about it, but here it is: With every project I take on, I always approach it in a way that would make my kids proud. And that means I give it my all and try to communicate in a way that inspires others, people feel accepted in the way they give their 100%.

* * *

The conversation me and Bret had was the pivotal moment of my career. It was like an entire education was directly downloaded into my brain. Not only did he put the information out there, but I absorbed and retained it. From that day forward I continued to study the information; I turned it over and over, reading every nuance and examining every speck.

It completely overhauled my way of thinking.

Oddly, it all seemed so easy—and yet it all seemed so new. However, I didn't question what he said because it made *sense*. When we returned to the bus, I felt elated.

I don't know that I have ever used the word "elated" before. But it certainly fits. I felt like I was set free.

EPILOGUE

Some of the stories you just read have been told and retold a thousand times. Some have been spun a few times over shots with close friends. And then there were a handful that I have never told to anyone before. Those stories have remained dormant in a cluttered recess of my mind. Faded photos buried behind others on that brick wall I spoke about in chapter ten. Once I sat down and began to reflect upon my career in its entirety, it was like I shook the memory tree and fruit started to fall all around me.

It's been pretty nuts (pardon the pun).

Obviously, walking with Bret around that hotel in Nashville was a moment of paramount importance to me. It is one of those memories that I can recall so vividly, that when I completely immerse myself into the scene, I can literally feel the cool temperature of the night air on my arms.

The memory is so powerful and so visceral, that it is like I am there again. Like Doc Brown got himself another DeLorean and took me back to 2004. There are only a handful of memories that pack that level of punch.

A second one involves the opening note of Van Halen's song, "Jump." That low rumble of the synth!

Anyway, to this day, anytime I hear that opening, it transports me back to February 25, 1984. I was in my bedroom at home, and I heard Casey Kasem's voice on my stereo.

"This week, we have a new Number 1 song. It's by four guys from Pasadena, California. It knocked Michael Jackson from the top spot, and it's called Jump."

Then the note played…that low C pulsing through my subwoofers.

As I sit here writing this, I am right back in that bedroom. The walls were baby blue. I had KISS posters plastered over almost every square inch of wall space. And the temperature on one arm was warmer than the temperature on the other. The sun was spilling through my window and landing directly upon my left arm. My right arm, by virtue of being shielded by my body, was in the shade.

Not kidding…my left arm feels warm right now.

Certain songs transcend time and place for me. Emotion pulls me under like a riptide; it's like I'm hearing the song for the first time…again. Jump is one of those songs, as mentioned. Another is "Right Now," by Van Halen (1992). I still remember the first time I ever heard that song. I was in my recording studio and slid their new CD (*For Unlawful Carnal Knowledge*) into the CD player.

The album opens with Eddie running an electric drill over the pickups of his guitar to begin the song "Poundcake." Iconic, man.

Way down the song list, sitting humbly at #9, is "Right Now."

By the time this song came on, I was neck deep, tinkering with this and that in the studio. I don't know that I was even tuned into the music, to be honest. I loved Van Halen, and often played their albums in the background.

"The Dream is Over," track 8, ended and there was the standard pause between tracks. And then…the piano part started. I wish I could have you close your eyes and hear that riff through the magic of media—but books don't work that way yet. For now, just stream it on your phone. The opening riff is one of the most inspiring pieces of music ever written. I get goose bumps every time it plays, even 30 years after it was released.

Back in my studio that day, I looked up from what I was doing and felt the goose bumps for the first time. Even before Sammy's voice joined the song and sang the first word, my brain knew this was going to be the greatest song ever written. I sound like a hyperbolic teenager, I know. But I don't think I'm over-stating my point.

Even in 2022, the year I am writing this book, I use that song for inspiration. When I play an EVICK gig, I play "Right Now" as the opener. Every time I christen a new Shining Sol store, "Right Now" is playing through the overhead speakers the second we open the doors for the first time.

Songs can put you on a path, man. Someday I will write a book of all the songs that have changed my life, and the stories that accompany them. Don't wanna wait until tomorrow. Why put it off another day? That was exactly the message Bret taught me in Nashville when he dusted me off and turned me into a professional rock and roller. In short, I have been able to support and feed my children because Bret gave me a chance to play my guitar.

He did that for me. But all the songs and all the memories aside, becoming MTV famous wasn't really what made a man out of me. *That* evolution happened when I first held my children in my arms. Looking into their little faces, I knew they needed me to be there. They needed me to do whatever it took to make sure they could play and thrive and watch the world and listen to the music.

They needed me to be their dad.

I thought I wanted to be MTV famous. But all along, it turns out I just wanted to be a dad. My two kids…they have been my reason.

AUTHOR'S NOTE

As I wrap up this book, I realize I didn't even scratch the surface. I obviously have enough memories to write five more books. I can't control my anxiety at this moment, anticipating the phone calls, texts, or emails saying, "I CAN'T BELIEVE YOU LEFT THIS OR THAT OUT."

For example, there was a club called Mainstreet in Stafford that I could write an entire book about. The friends I made and memories I have in that place…amazing, Now I want to write a book called *The Clubs that Made Me* to follow up *The Moments that Make Us*.

My brain is on fire as I type, thinking about all the people and stories in my high school years that I didn't touch on. Jenny Eggert, Brandi Miller, William Sheetz, Jeremy Griffith, Jamie Hurdle, Bruce Nicholson…. The list of friends goes on and on.

The stories in Some Odd Reason and EVICK—I didn't even give you guys a glance of what really happened in all those years. I could go on and on. And I haven't even touched on my current life with Tina or the introduction to Boba in my life. I didn't write about my current musical endeavors with Young and Chad, or the amazing friendships I've struck with Rick and Tracy. The list just goes on and on. So many people and places that make me who I am.